COMMUNICATION, SOCIAL COGNITION, and AFFECT

COMMUNICATION

A series of volumes edited by
Dolf Zillmann and Jennings Bryant

COMMUNICATION, SOCIAL COGNITION, and AFFECT

edited by

Lewis Donohew
Howard E. Sypher
University of Kentucky

E. Tory Higgins
New York University

LEA LAWRENCE ERLBAUM ASSOCIATES, PUBLISHERS
1988   Hillsdale, New Jersey   Hove and London

Lawrence Erlbaum Associates, Inc., Publishers
365 Broadway
Hillsdale, New Jersey 07642

Library of Congress Cataloging-in-Publication Data

Communication, social cognition, and affect.

(Communication)
Based on a meeting held at the University of Kentucky's
Carnahan Conference Center in late April, 1986.
Includes indexes.
1. Communication—Psychological aspects—Congresses.
2. Social perception—Congresses.   3. Affect
(Psychology)—Congresses.   I. Donohew, Lewis.
II. Sypher, Howard E.   III. Higgins, E. Tory (Edward
Tory), 1946–   .   IV. Series: Communication
(Hillsdale, N.J.) [DNLM: 1. Affect—congresses.
2. Cognition—congresses.   3. Communication—congresses.
4. Psychology, Social—congresses.   BF 637.C45 C734 1986]
BF637.C45C6485   1988   302.2   87-13512

ISBN 0-89859-975-X   *58, 246*

Printed in the United States of America
10   9   8   7   6   5   4   3   2   1

CONTENTS

10. "THE NATURE OF NEWS" REVISITED: THE ROLES OF
     AFFECT, SCHEMAS, AND COGNITION
     Lewis Donohew, Seth Finn, and William G. Christ

11. COMMUNICATION, SOCIAL COGNITION, AND AFFECT: A
     PSYCHOPHYSIOLOGICAL APPROACH
     John T. Cacioppo, Richard E. Petty,
     and Louis G. Tassinary

CONTRIBUTORS

JOHN A. BARGH • Department of Psychology, New York University, 6 Washington Place, 7th Floor, New York, NY 10003

CHARLES R. BERGER • Communication Studies, Northwestern University, 1815 Chicago Avenue, Evanston, IL 60201

JOHN T. CACIOPPO • Department of Psychology, University of Iowa, Iowa City, IA 52242

WILLIAM G. CHRIST • Department of Communication, Trinity University, 715 Stadium Drive, San Antonio, TX 78284

WALTER H. CROCKETT • Department of Psychology, University of Kansas, Lawrence, KS 66045

LEWIS DONOHEW • Department of Communication, University of Kentucky, Lexington, KY 40506

SETH FINN • Department of Radio, TV, & Motion Pictures, University of North Carolina, Swain 044A, Chapel Hill, NC 27514

E. TORY HIGGINS • Department of Psychology, New York University, 6 Washington Place, 7th Floor, New York, NY 10003

JEFF KASMER • Department of Psychology, University of Missouri, Columbia, MO 65211

C. DOUGLAS MCCANN • Department of Psychology, York University, 4700 Keele Street, N. York, Ontario, Canada M3P130

RICHARD E. PETTY • Department of Psychology, Ohio State University, 404 C West 17th Avenue, Columbus, OH 43210

BEVERLY DAVENPORT SYPHER • Department of Communication, University of Kentucky, Lexington, KY 40506

HOWARD E. SYPHER • Department of Communication, University of Kentucky, Lexington, KY 40506

LOUIS G. TASSINARY • Department of Psychology, University of Iowa, Iowa City, IA 52242

DOLF ZILLMANN • Institute for Communication Research, Indiana University, 419 N. Indiana Avenue, Bloomington, IN 47405

MARVIN ZUCKERMAN • Department of Psychology, University of Delaware, Newark, DE 19716

At an early stage in the development of this volume, the editors prepared a list of topics to be covered and possible contributors on those subjects. This was our optimal list of topics and chapter authors—many of the best-known names in our fields. Although many other worthy contributors could have been included, these were our first choices and we hoped some of them would be excited enough by our prospectus for the proposed volume to want to participate. The response matched our most optimistic hopes. Everyone accepted.

In late April 1986 the authors met at the University of Kentucky's Carnahan Conference Center. They presented first drafts of their chapters, exchanged ideas, and came to know each other considerably better. Out of these interactions has come a book that we feel has broad interest across several areas of psychology and communication.

The purpose of this book is, first of all, to explore the interrelations among communication, social cognition, and affect. We believe the contributors of this volume significantly add to our knowledge of this interdisciplinary domain. While answering a number of questions, the authors also pose other questions for future examination.

Each of the editors comes to this venture from a different background. Lewis Donohew is a former working journalist and one of his graduate degrees is in political science. However, his graduate work in mass communication and psychology at Iowa turned him toward what has become a sustained interest in psychophysiological approaches to communication. Howard Sypher's undergraduate degree also is in political science and his interest in the relationship between cognition and communication developed at the University of Michigan. Tory Higgins has an equally interdisciplinary background. He did his undergraduate work at McGill in anthropology, followed by graduate work at the London School of Economics, then a Ph.D. in social psychology at Columbia. He has blended an original interest in developmental and anthropological approaches to communication with cognitive psychology in focusing on interpersonal goals and communication. Although each of the authors' backgrounds is different, all share the belief that the area of research explored in this work is best illuminated by interdisciplinary efforts. Obviously, not every perspective could be accommodated in this volume. The editors sought to limit this effort to psychological perspectives while allowing for theoretical diversity.

Why, then, a volume focusing on communication, social cognition and affect at this time? There are several reasons:

1. *The area is receiving a great deal of attention.* Even a cursory examination of the latest issues of *Journal of Personality and Social Psychology, Journal of Personality, Human Communication Research, Social Cognition,* for example, shows that a tremendous number of scholars in communication and psychology have focused their attention on this area. There has been a rash of books and papers examining several aspects of social cognition, affect, and communication. But for the most part, psychologists and communication theorists have ignored parallel work being done in each other's bailiwick. We see this project as a continuation of recent research reported at two 1984 conferences, the Gannett-sponsored symposium at the University of Tennessee, which focused on arousal, affect, and mass media, and the Conference on Cognition and Interpersonal Behavior held at the University of Kansas, which had a social cognitive flavor.

2. *The topic is confusing.* Unfortunately, most of the researchers in this area use different definitions and different methods of determining what they mean by affect, communication, and cognition, and different standards for evaluating how these interact to change attitudes and behavior. One of our main purposes in editing this volume was to get a number of outstanding scholars in this field to contribute pieces that focused more on their similarities than their differences. The differences still come through but hopefully the reader can see the similarities.

3. *The analysis of social cognition and affect can illuminate the study of interpersonal and mass communication behavior.* One of the important results of this kind of research is that we are beginning to see linkages made between cognitive processes and behavior. For a number of years these linkages were not being explored and we believe that efforts in this direction can provide important theoretical as well as very practical contributions to our understanding of human behavior. In communication, we see this influence in increased work on attention, message comprehension, the role of activation and arousal, the impact of schemas, and so on. Obviously, we do not have all of the answers but we have begun to address important questions.

4. *The area of work is maturing into more interdisciplinary modes of research and theory.* Although the research in this volume is of necessity somewhat focused, there is considerable theoretical and methodological diversity. However, an examination of other recent research in anthropology, social, developmental, clinical, cognitive, and personality psychology, education, and interpersonal and mass communication—to name a few—will reveal an incredible variety of methodologies being utilized to explore what appears to be similar issues. Examinations that are outside traditional disciplinary boundaries often lead to significant advances and allow one to see connections that need to be made explicit.

ACKNOWLEDGMENTS

It is always difficult to repay intellectual debts and still stay within page limits. Yet we must briefly mention a few who contributed to this volume.

The editors would first like to thank their colleagues in the Department of Communication at the University of Kentucky (and especially Jim Applegate) for their support in making the conference and this volume possible. We also appreciate the input of Dolf Zillmann, Lawrence Erlbaum Associates' series co-editor and a contributor to this text, for his valuable advice.

John Haas managed logistics for the mini-conference almost flawlessly. We say "almost" because his scheduling of Marvin Zuckerman's airline ticket under the first name "Myron" left us vulnerable to Professor Zuckerman's retaliatory wit.

We also thank the discussants, who had much to say and were given too little time to say it in—Jim Applegate again, Bob Bostrom, Jack Haskins, Phil Palmgreen, Chris O'Sullivan, and Jim Weaver.

Howard Sypher would like to thank Daniel and Barbara O'Keefe for giving him insights that he is only now beginning to take advantage of. Thanks also go to Jesse Delia for obvious reasons, and the following individuals for their contributions, direct and indirect, B.B., R.B., D.S., R.S., R.C., C.D., R.N., L.D., J.A., and W.G.—you know who you are. Finally, he wishes to acknowledge the most important contributor to his career, his colleague and spouse, Beverly Davenport Sypher. Our spirited debates on concepts and methods and her incisive critiques of my individual and our joint research efforts have led to much better products including our most recent and best collaborative effort, Ford.

Lewis Donohew wishes to express special and long overdue thanks to the surviving member of his father's generation, his Aunt Nellie, whose early encouragement has had more effect than she ever imagined. He also expresses gratitude to his wife, Susan, whose careful review of grant proposals and insistence on rewrites led to the research funding from which indirect costs were obtained to make the conference—and ultimately this volume—possible.

1 An Overview of the Roles of Social Cognition and Affect in Communication

Howard E. Sypher
Lewis Donohew
University of Kentucky

E. Tory Higgins
New York University

Implicit in many contemporary theories of human communication is an assumption that individuals seek out and process appropriate information in order to logically and with full self-awareness arrive at "rational" decisions. To be sure, there are individual differences in cognitive abilities, with some of these persons employing more complex processing schemes than others, or being otherwise better equipped to proceed to cope with each day's tribulations and amusements. In this book, however, the authors severely challenge the assumption, so pervasive in the literature of research on both interpersonal and mass communcation as well as in the person-perception literature of the 1970s, that ordinary human beings employ logical thought processes and arrive at decisions in self-aware ways.

Research in the most recent of the areas covered here—social cognition—was begun in the early 1970s, about the time that consistency models ceased to dominate work in psychology and communication. In most social–cognitive models that developed, emotion, affect, or motivation was seen as secondary in importance to cognition—a position that is beginning to come into question (see Higgins & Bargh, in press; Lazarus, 1982; Zajonc, 1980, 1984).

In this general framework, humans are seen as "naive scientists," who work to uncover the causes of their own and others' behavior. As this rational model of human functioning has developed, errors are most often viewed as being due to nonrational motivations. From this perspective, the usual attribution process is seen as a quasi-scientific cognitive analysis of causes, with occasional interference due to some motivation-based departure.

Unfortunately, people often are not so rational and tend to be somewhat more limited in their information-processing capacity than the "naive scientist" metaphor might suggest. The chapters in this volume report research results and theoretical advances that provde further questions concerning our cognitive capabilities. A great deal of previous research has shown that our cognitive information-processing system is limited in some respects and under certain conditions we tend to take mental shortcuts or use heuristics. These heuristics or cognitive simplifying devices allow us to make quicker judgments or reduce complex internal data-processing demands. Indeed, work on heuristics has developed into a separate area of research in its own right (see, for example, Kahneman, Slovic, & Tversky, 1982).

In addition to using heuristics, our cognitive processing often is overridden or interrupted by affect. Some might even argue that affect or arousal of some sort initiates cognitive activity and not the other way around. However, it seems equally reasonable that emotions can alter one's goals and hence one's processing priorities, perhaps setting the agenda for cognitive activity (see McCann & Higgins, this volume).

We believe, as do many others, that some sort of combination of emotion-arousal and cognition largely controls communicative behavior. Some have advocated parallel rather than interactive influences, but the final decision on these issues still rests with the jury.

We do know, however, that from a physiological perspective, the human system has needs for stimulation of the brain and energy for the body. More than one third of the brain's volume involves pleasure centers seeking continuous stimulation (Campbell, 1973; Olds & Forbes, 1981). Although this need for arousal varies across individuals (Zuckerman, 1978, 1983, this volume), arousal is nonetheless fundamental to human behavior.

Although for some fields, emotion remained an integral part of theorizing and research efforts, this was by no means universally true. Now, after a number of years of inattention, affect or emotion once again has become a part of inter-disciplinary discourse among social and behavioral scientists.

A number of communication researchers, for example, have long been concerned with affect or emotion and its use in public discourse (pathos), television, newspapers films, humor, persuasive message effects, and so on (Donohew, Finn, & Christ, this volume; Zillmann, this volume). However, although communication researchers have not completely forgotten about affect, a great many have tended to implicitly de-emphasize emotion in efforts to explore the utility of information-processing models for communication.

The picture that emerges from this book is of human beings possessing the capability to behave in a cognitively "controlled" manner when it is demanded by the circumstances—such as in the presence of threat or unfamiliarity, but who, under less demanding circumstances, do not draw so heavily upon the precious resource of attention and all its alerting and energizing capabilities (see Bargh, this volume). Instead, affect, much of the time, appears to play a considerably greater role in the guidance of the system. By *affect*, we mean the whole wide range of emotions, remembered feelings, moods, and physiological reactions that the concept embraces.

Thus, there is considerable interest in the role that affect plays in our conversations and in other aspects of our day-to-day lives, including exposure to the mass media. For example, while engaging in the pursuit of arousal, the newspaper reader or television watcher is likely to be responding to subtle influences on the attention process of which he or she is not aware. These sources of influence may have little or nothing to do with the subject matter, but rather may include such elements as design of the message itself (Donohew, 1984; Donohew, Palmgreen, & Duncan, 1980; Donohew, Finn, & Christ, this volume; Finn, 1983).

Recent research on automaticity in social information processing (e.g., Berger & Roloff, 1980; Higgins & Bargh, in press) had underlined the importance of arousal-inducing elements in attracting and holding an audience. The research has indicated that human beings make full use of their conscious thought processes far less than is assumed in most contemporary theories. Instead, when entering situations similar to ones they have previously encountered and to which they have "overlearned" a set of responses—such as reading a newspaper— they tend to reduce their level of attention and shift to a state often referred to as *automatic pilot, automaticity,* or *mindlessness*. This state has been found to occur in communication situations such as reading and even talking with others as well as in other familiar circumstances, including our morning drive to work. Findings from this research have considerable implications for the study of communication (see Bargh, this volume).

For example, this research would suggest that in the area of mass communication the way news stories are written may at times be more important than the subject matter or the content itself in attracting and holding readers and viewers. In situations where individuals are operating at low levels of self-awareness— that is, on automatic pilot—it appears likely that there is more reliance on arousal and less on what we commonly think of as cognition in guiding the system through routine decisions. Such decisions might include whether or not to read or watch a story and whether or not to continue exposure to it—or, for that matter, to another person. On the basis of previous research, it appears likely that we operate at these reduced levels more often than commonly realized.

Some clarification is needed here, however. In engaging in behavior that can be accomplished without concentrating attention on it, an individual still is drawing on knowledge structures often referred to as *schemata* (see, for example, Bargh, this volume; Crockett, this volume; H. Sypher & Applegate, 1984).

Clearly, from our view, both cognition and affect or arousal are involved in human communication, beginning with the capture of attention and continuing throughout the communication process. The influence of each on the other, however, is not a matter of consensus and many questions remain unanswered. For example, when does one precede the other? What effect does each have on the other? Are there, as some believe, separate systems? And, as previously noted, additional questions might be asked about the role of automaticity and automatic processing that may raise doubts about the relative effects of each. Finally, we should ask ourselves what are the implications of this research for interpersonal and mass communication behavior? Obviously, these are only a few of the questions one could ask about communication and affect.

This volume brings together researchers employing a variety of approaches to the study of affect, cognition, and communication. Although their theoretical stances (and in some cases their levels of analysis) differ, they all emphasize the intraorganismic function of emotion, seeing emotion as often disruptive and, on occasion, motivating. The volume does not include sociobiological or antropological functions and for the most part our contributors do not address the antecedents, expression of or control of emotion in any detail. These areas of research are certainly important but are covered elsewhere (e.g., Scherer & Ekman, 1984). We, of necessity, have sought to restrict the focus of the text while allowing for theoretical diversity in the individual contributions. One group of essays emphasizes the physiological or psychological and cognitive explanations. This group is represented in the work of Dolf Zillmann, Marvin Zuckerman, John Cacioppo, Richard Petty, Lewis Donohew, Seth Finn, William Christ, and others. Another group has focused its attention on social–cognitive explanations. This group is represented by the work of Charles Berger, Tory Higgins, Walter Crockett, Doug McCann, John Bargh, Howard and Beverly Sypher, and their colleagues.

The contributors to this volume offer critical (and at times speculative) assessments and reports on original research on questions evolving from consideration of affect, social cognition, and communication, including many of the issues just raised.

In the next chapter, Bargh questions not only assumptions that people are entirely conscious and rational (as does Crockett in a later chapter) but also the assumptions of others that processes carried out at a low level of awareness are therefore automatic. Bargh makes the point that many behaviors carried out at a low level of awareness are nonetheless intended. He discusses the role of automatic processes as they apply to perceptual activity influencing reception of interpersonal information. He observes that, in the act of media consumption, "(t)he type of information one attends to, how much attention one pays to it, how one encodes and interprets it, and consequently how one remembers it are all greatly influenced by one's processing goals while encountering the information." Bargh also makes the important point that automatic processing is not always "bad." If the automatic responses correspond to reality, then relatively effortless processing can be adaptive and functional. Moreover, conscious, controlled processing can override automatic processing in order to adapt to changing environmental contingencies. When this does not happen, however, people may respond irrationally.

Crockett (chapter 3) provides a general review in which he delineates the notion of schema and its relationship to social communication and affect. Crockett employs a variety of examples to illustrate schemas and their utilization in information processing, communication, and action plans. Finally, Crockett explores the interaction of schemas, affect, and arousal. He concludes with a discussion of affect and category-based judgments and a theoretical account of the connection between schemas and affect.

McCann and Higgins (chapter 4) argue that an understanding of the relation between affect and cognition is important if we are to understand the impact of communication and social interaction on the participants' attitudes toward and feelings about others. They propose that individuals' chronic personal motivations and momentary social-interaction goals influence their interpretations of social events, which in turn produce emotional reactions specific to the interpretations. The implications of this ''motivation–interpretation–affect'' relation are discussed concerning both self-persuasion from dyadic communication and emotional vulnerability in interpersonal relationships.

Sypher and Sypher (chapter 5) outline work on the impact of mild cognitive affect and cognitive differentiation on communicative performance. More specifically, Sypher and Sypher suggest that mild positive affect influences cognitive structure and persuasive message generation in several ways. Following a brief discussion of affect and interpersonal communication, this chapter reports a study examining the relationship between affect and persuasive message generation. The results of this investigation suggest that we have more differentiated cognitive structures for liked others (as opposed to disliked others) and that we generate more arguments for convincing known-liked others (as opposed to known-disliked others) but do not find this same difference when the receiver is an unknown other. The study also suggests that frequency of interaction may not play as significant a role in this process as previously suspected. Other results in the study are less clear and further research efforts are called for.

Borrowing from the artificial intelligence literature, Berger (chapter 6) links plans and action production to work in social cognition and communication. Berger contends that procedural knowledge as a whole has not received the kind of attention it deserves especially given the obvious importance plans have as linking knowledge and action. Berger reports previous research in which individuals involved in initial interactions were provided with incompatible goals. In this work, incompatible individual goals significantly impacted on verbal and nonverbal communication. Berger also provides the reader with a discussion of plan formulation, the role of goals and metagoals before speculating on the relationship of planning and affect. Finally, Berger reports original research aimed at illustrating the potential of his planning approach to the study of action in a dating situation.

Petty, Cacioppo, and Kasmer (chapter 7) review their Elaboration Likelihood Model for understanding the basic processes underlying the effectiveness of persuasive communications. They discuss how the same message source variables (e.g., attractiveness, expertise) can influence persuasion through a variety of different routes as a function of the likelihood that recipients of the message will cognitively elaborate upon the information contained in the message. They then extend this logic to the central issue of how affect influences persuasion, and suggest that affect can also influence persuasion by different routes depending on the extent to which message information is elaborated.

Authors of the final four chapters in the book concentrate more on affect, and appear to share a number of general assumptions about stimulus selection. In describing processing of stimuli competing for what Zuckerman refers to as "the most viral aspect of consciousness"—attention—they tend to place a greater emphasis on physiological responses to aversive stimuli or those generating pleasurable states.

In chapter 8, Zillmann, who has conducted extensive research on physiological responses to mass communication, offers a theory of stimulus arrangement, or mood management. The theory is an extension of Zillmann and Bryant's (1985) theory of affect-dependent stimulus arrangement. Its fundamental proposition is that individuals arrange and rearrange their entertainment environments—music, comedy, drama, sports, and the like—so as best to minimize aversive states and maximize pleasurable states. In other words, Zillmann proposes that individuals consume media entertainment purposively to modify moods. However, like Donohew, Finn, and Christ, he notes that individuals also may not be aware of their motivation. He also notes, in agreement with other investigators in this section of the book, that stimulus arrangements may require considerable activity or be entirely passive.

In chapter 9, Zuckerman, whose research on human sensation seeking has broad implications for communication studies, most clearly enunciates the role of individual differences in the types of stimulation sought. He notes that high sensation seekers seem to sample widely from their environment and "clearly prefer stimuli which are novel, complex, ambiguous, and which elicit strong emotional reactions." He speculates that low sensation seekers, who tend to avoid high intensities of stimulation, "may have a type of nervous system that rejects such stimulation or inhibits cortical reactivity to high intensity stimuli." He describes studies offering support for sensation seeking from both behavioral and biochemical perspectives.

Donohew, Finn, and Christ (chapter 10) draw upon optimal level of arousal and cognitive models of information exposure and processing to describe the mechanisms of news exposure and processing. These mechanisms appear to differ from those of entertainment in the level of tolerance for stimuli that are discrepant with the reader's or viewer's beliefs, values, or attitudes. Despite the fact that such stimuli might be considered noxious, consumers often continue their exposure and processing because of other motivations stored in their cognitive systems. Nonetheless, level of activation in part generated by the way messages are constructed and presented is presumed to exert subtle influences on consumer selection and use of news items, extending well beyond the nature of the content itself. The authors present and compare predictions generated from two models of information exposure, both of which draw on assumptions of need for arousal.

Cacioppo, Petty, and Tassinary (chapter 11) offer a psychophysiological perspective on the study of communication, social cognition, and affect. They note that one promise offered by the procedures employed by psychophysiologists is for construct validation because these techniques provide nonverbal, objective, and relatively bias-free indices of human reaction. The authors emphasize, however, that physiological indices are not linked invariantly to psychological processes and this relationship should be approached with greater care than has been the instance in some past research. On the basis of a review of theoretical analyses of efferent activity during problem solving, imagery, and emotion they report shared assumptions regarding specificity and adaptive utility of shared responses and offer principles on which future research might be based. One promising area of research involves the face. Although one area of research on the face, of course, involves nonverbal communication, the authors note that not all intra- or interpersonal processes are accompanied by visually or socially perceptible and interpretable facial expressions. A psychophysiological technique that allows the measurement of both covert and overt facial efference is electromyography (EMG). This procedure measures electrical potential at the skin created when a muscle action potential (MAP) passes along a nerve fiber. The authors report on a broad range of research using facial EMG recordings that "has revealed several interesting somatic consequences of communication, social cognition, and affect."

SUMMARY

The chapters in this volume address a number of different aspects of affect, cognition, and communication. Although there is some disagreement, here and elsewhere, on the extent to which cognition or affect is emphasized, we should not forget that they are interrelated phenomena separated only for purposes of conceptual analysis. They are evaluated independently only when we seek to understand their part in the communication process. In everyday life, people think, act, and communicate emotionally, arguing with their friends, lecturing their children, attending church, or shivering with fear in horror movies. In other words, affect and cognition are so intertwined as to be virtually impossible to separate. Authors of the essays in this volume seek to describe the crucial role of this relationship in understanding the communication process.

REFERENCES

Berger, C. R., & Roloff, M. (1980). Social cognition, self awareness and interpersonal communication. In B. Dervin & M. Voigt (Eds.), *Progress in communication sciences* (Vol. 2, pp. 46–64). Norwood, NJ: Ablex.

Campbell, H. J. (1973). *The pleasure areas: a new theory of behavior.* New York: Delacorte Press.

Donohew, L. (1984). Some implications of automaticity and arousal for the mass media. *Science and Public Policy, 11,* 388–390.

Donohew, L., Palmgreen, P., & Duncan, J. (1980). An activation model of information exposure. *Communication Monographs, 47,* 295–303.

Finn, S. (1983). *An information theory approach to reader enjoyment of print journalism* (Doctoral dissertation, Stanford University, 1982). Dissertation Abstracts International, *43,* 2481A–2482A.

Higgins, E. T., & Bargh, J. A. (in press). Social cognition and social perception. *Annual Review of Psychology, 38.*

Kahneman, D., Slovic, P., & Tversky, A. (1982). *Judgment under uncertainty: Heuristics and biases.* Cambridge: Cambridge University Press.

Lazarus, R. (1982). Thoughts on the relations between emotion and cognition. *American Psychologist, 37,* 1019–1024.

Olds, M. E., & Forbes, J. (1981). The central basis of motivation: Intracranial self-stimulation studies. *Annual Review of Psychology, 32,* 523–574.

Scherer, K. R., & Ekman, P. (1984). *Approaches to emotion.* Hillsdale, NJ: Lawrence Erlbaum Associates.

Sypher, H., & Applegate, J. (1984). Organizing communication behavior: The role of schemas and constructs. In R. N. Bostrom (Ed.), *Communication yearbook 8* (pp. 310–329). Beverly Hills, CA: Sage.

Zajonc, R. (1980). Feeling and thinking: Preferences need no inferences. *American Psychologist, 35,* 151–175.

Zajonc, R. (1984). On the primacy of affect. *American Psychologist, 37,* 117–123.

Zillmann, D., & Bryant, J. (1985). Affect, mood, and emotion as determinants of selective exposure. In D. Zillmann & J. Bryant (Eds.), *Selective exposure to communication* (pp. 157–190). Hillsdale, NJ: Lawrence Erlbaum Associates.

Zuckerman, M. (1978). *Sensation seeking: Beyond the optimal level of arousal.* Hillsdale, NJ: Lawrence Erlbaum Associates.

Zuckerman, M. (1983). *Biological bases of sensation seeking, impulsivity, and anxiety.* Hillsdale, NJ: Lawrence Erlbaum Associates.

2 Automatic Information Processing: Implications for Communication and Affect

John A. Bargh
New York University

One of the most enduring existential questions facing human beings is that of free will—how much control, if any, we have over how we think, feel, and behave. Perhaps it could be said that during the short history of psychology as a science, the issue of whether free will exists and (if it does) how much of a role it plays has been responsible for more major paradigm shifts (see Kuhn, 1962) than any other. Freud was one of the first (and the most influential) who initially challenged the entrenched assumption that unless one was mentally ill, one was in complete control of one's thoughts, desires, and actions (see Bowers, 1985; Erdelyi, 1985). Within experimental psychology, growing dissatisfaction with the unreliability of conscious introspection as a data-gathering technique resulted in the violent rejection of not only the awareness aspect of consciousness, but the intentional aspect as well (see Watson, 1919). Thus was born the model that would dominate psychology for the next 50 years, in which people were seen to be controlled by their stimulus environments and driven by their physiological need states. Consciousness was relegated to the status of an epiphenomenon, and free will was but an illusion (e.g., Skinner, 1971).

Consequently, the study of consciousness and all of its correlates was unofficially if not officially banned as "unscientific" until the cognitive revolution of the 1960s. By that time, stimulus–response psychology had run into methodological difficulties of its own, limiting its explanatory power to the extent that disguised appeals to the constructs of intention, awareness, and choice were necessary (see, e.g., Lachman, Lachman, & Butterfield, 1979). The manifesto of the cognitive revolution, Neisser's (1967) *Cognitive Psychology*, contained a

9

lengthy treatment of such "executive" or intentional processes, and of the role of focal attention and awareness in processing environmental information.

As Crockett (this volume) points out, there has been a tendency to quite inaccurately characterize the cognitive perspective in psychology as viewing people as entirely conscious and rational. This erroneous characterization is deserved up to a point, however, as an early and important working model within cognitive psychology, of people-as-computers, did assume that people were logical and rational information processors (see the critique by Dreyfus, 1972). It was quickly discovered, however, that if anything, people were better described as *faulty* computers—their natural cognitive functioning produced all kinds of biases and distortions formerly thought to be motivational in nature (e.g., Carroll & Payne, 1976; Hamilton, 1979; Kahneman & Tversky, 1973; Nisbett & Ross, 1980). Cognitive psychology was disabused of the assumption of human rationality quite early in the cognitive revolution.

Nor was it ever assumed that one was aware of all cognitive processing. From a functional perspective, it would make little sense for one to be aware of all cognition, to be aware of each step along the way from sensation to perception to memory storage and retrieval and combination of information in judgments, and so on; we would be more "lost in thought" than Tolman's rat was ever accused of being! A general principle is that people are aware of the output of their cognitive processes, but not of the processes themselves (e.g., Nisbett & Wilson, 1977).

As a consequence of this general lack of awareness of cognitive processes, one cannot use awareness of a process alone to distinguish between a process that one controls and a process that one does not control. For example, a person may be driving along a highway and suddenly "wake up" to realize he or she has no memory of driving the last 50 miles. Clearly, most of the driver's actions in keeping the car on the road at the right speed and avoiding other cars were accomplished with little attentional control. But at another level, it is certainly the case that he or she was *intending* to drive the car. To take another example, typing for an experienced typist may be an uncontrolled act in the sense that he or she does not control the process of translating the written copy into movements of the fingers on the keyboard, but the typist did intend to type the material in the first place. Speech production also may be considered an effortless and uncontrolled phenomenon, but we do control the act of speaking itself.

Thus, control over a cognitive process or a behavior may be conceived of at several different levels (Logan & Cowan, 1984). As the previous examples illustrate, one can intend and control a process that then may proceed outside of awareness. The important distinction between processes that are controlled and those that are *automatic* or uncontrolled should not be made on the basis of one's degree of awareness of that process, therefore, but on the basis of whether one intended that process to occur. For something to be *automatic* in the common sense of the term is, after all, for it to always occur; for a cognitive process to be automatic, then, it should not depend on what a person's desires or intentions are at that moment.

Automatic processes are those that are unintentional, uncontrollable, and use only minimal amounts of one's limited cognitive processing capacity (e.g., Posner & Snyder, 1975; Shiffrin & Schneider, 1977). They develop from frequent and consistent experience with a specific class of environmental information (Schneider & Fisk, 1982): a certain person or a recurring situation, for example. They are distinguished from controlled processes, which are intentional, flexible, and are much more demanding of processing capacity (e.g., Posner, 1978; Schneider & Shiffrin, 1977). Most information processing entails a combination of both automatic and controlled processes (Logan, 1980; Shiffrin & Schneider, 1977).

Thus, if we label some aspect of thought or action as *automatic,* we implicitly state our conviction that the person is not intending or in control of that thought or action. And, getting back to the issue of free will for a moment, making the implicit assumption that a person's thought or action is not being controlled by him or her leads to the inescapable conclusion that the thought or action is being controlled by something else—namely, the environment of people, their behavior, the roles they fill, and the situations they create.

THE EXTENT OF AUTOMATIC INFLUENCES

What is the extent of the environment's direct control over thought, feelings, and behavior? Automatic, unintentional influences on cognitive processing occur predominately if not exclusively at the perceptual end of thought. This is for both logical and mechanistic reasons. The purpose of conscious awareness is to deal with what is going on in the world, not with the process of *how* we know it (see the excellent arguments by Bateson, 1972, on this point). Thus, it is logically necessary for the preliminary analysis of the environment to be carried out prior to the products of those analyses being furnished to consciousness. Neisser (1967) referred to these as *preattentive* processes, which segment the environment into figural units that then serve as the raw material of conscious processes. The idea of preconscious processing dates back much further, however, and was studied most intensively by Gestalt psychologists interested in what they termed the *microgenesis* of perception — the stages involved in the creation of what appear to us to be the "given" of perception (e.g., Werner, 1956). These studies revealed that a great deal of cognitive work precedes our awareness of an environmental object or event; it is created for us by a series of processes so fast as to seem phenomenally immediate.

The mechanical reason is that cognitive pathways between stimulus receptors and the more abstract memory representations such as categories (e.g., chairs, honest behaviors, graduate students), procedural knowledge (i.e., how to go about attaining a frequently held goal; Smith, 1984), and action plans (Miller, Galanter, & Pribram, 1960; Shallice, 1972) become automated only to the extent that they are *frequently* and *consistently* employed (Schneider & Fisk, 1982; Schneider & Shiffrin, 1977). The greater the number of links in the chain between the environment (sensation) and the given level of mental representation, therefore, the less likely it will be for there to exist an automatic pathway between them.

Moreover, the higher levels of abstraction are under greater strategic control, and so they will be matched less consistently with a given stimulus event. Take (once again) the case of driving. You are coming around a blind curve in the road when you suddenly encounter a red stoplight. You immediately kick your right foot onto the brake pedal (unless you live in New York City or Boston, of course, in which case you well might accelerate through the intersection instead). The next day, you happen to be walking up to the same intersection, and you notice the traffic light is red. Do you automatically kick out your right foot toward an imaginary brake pedal, possibly bruising an innocent bystander? No, fortunately, and this is because you do not always follow the sight of the color red (or even the sight of a red stoplight) with the same behavioral response each time.

Similarly, one does not always process information about oneself or other people in the same way every time (Srull & Wyer, 1986; Zukier, 1986). There are occasions when we are with other people and are trying to understand what type of people they are—that is, form impressions of them—and so we think about their words and deeds in terms of personality traits. At other times we may have other processing goals concerning a person's behavior, such as deciding whether to ask him or her for a date, and then picking the right moment to do so (see Berger, this volume). On those occasions, we are not actively encoding the person's behavior in terms of a trait-based impression, but in terms of that person's opinion of us. One does not form an impression of another person unless one has the explicit goal of doing so (Bargh & Thein, 1985). Thus, because social behavior is not always or even usually processed with the purpose of using it to make judgments about the person in question (see Wyer & Srull, 1986), automatic pathways should not exist between the pickup of social information and social judgments such as impressions and attributions (see Bargh, 1984; Higgins & Bargh, 1987).

Unlike behavioral responses and the more abstract forms of thought such as judgment and planning, perception *is* characterized by frequency and consistency of processing. There is much less strategic control over perception than over judgments or behavior. For example, one cannot choose to see the sky as red instead of blue just because one wants to, no matter how hard one tries. In summary, sensation and perception are driven mainly by the environment, whereas judgment and behavior are driven mainly by goals and intentions.

AUTOMATIC PROCESSING AND INTERPERSONAL COMMUNICATION

This section deals with the *reception* aspect of communication of information concerning oneself or another person, as the concept of automatic processing relates to it. (For a treatment of social–cognitive factors influencing the *transmission* of interpersonal information, see McCann & Higgins, 1985 and this volume.) The term *social information* is used here in a general sense, to refer to all socially relevant features of a person's behavior, verbal or nonverbal, and the context in which they occur. The basic thesis is that this reception set can be tuned both by aspects of the current situational context and by long-term experience. Furthermore, this reception set is shown to exert a selective and interpretive bias toward certain forms of social information over others.

Temporary Social Construct Accessibility Effects

Because automatic processes apply mainly to perceptual activity, they influence the reception of interpersonal information principally through their effects on social perception. Research on social-construct accessibility has direct bearing on the issue of how much of social perception is automated. Social constructs or categories represent classes of social behavior, such as kind, dependent, or ruthless. Because of the typically ambiguous nature of social information (e.g., Bruner, 1958), it can usually be construed in several different ways. For example, even such a seemingly clear-cut "kind" behavior as someone doing a favor for another person can be viewed alternately as "manipulative"—the person may want some kind of favor in return. The consequences for one's subsequent opinion of the favor-doer are very different depending on how the act was categorized. Outside of the domain of abilities, such as intelligence or athleticism, it is actually quite difficult to come up with examples of social behavior that cannot be interpreted in multiple ways.

Bruner (1957) pointed out that given such ambiguity, social perception is determined to a great extent by which of the mental categories relevant to a given behavior are most *accessible,* or easily activated. What determines the relative accessibility of the relevant categories, according to Bruner, is the person's *current* expectancies, goals, needs, and recent experience. All of these forces have the result of making one category temporarily more active than other categories, and so requiring less in the way of direct stimulation from the environment to become fully active (Higgins, Bargh, & Lombardi, 1985; Higgins & King, 1981). Thus, if you recently had been reading a biography of Mother Teresa, you would be more likely to encode the act of doing a favor as kind, whereas if you had been studying Machiavelli's *The Prince* (perhaps to pick up a few pointers for the next faculty meeting), you would be more likely to take the act as being manipulative.

Several studies have found such temporary accessibility effects on impression formation. In experiments using the unrelated-studies paradigm, subjects are exposed to adjectives related to a certain trait (Bargh, Bond, Lombardi, & Tota, 1986; Bargh & Pietromonaco, 1982; Higgins et al., 1985; Higgins, Rholes, & Jones, 1977) or behaviors related to a given trait (Srull & Wyer, 1979, 1980) in a first task that they are led to believe is completely unrelated to the second, impression-formation task. In all of these experiments, subjects who are exposed to trait-related information in the first task are more likely to interpret the subsequently presented target behaviors in line with the given trait, and to form impressions of the target person as possessing that trait. Thus, use of the category in the first task made it more accessible and likely to be used to interpret the ambiguously trait-relevant behaviors in the second task.

Automatic Categorization of Social Behaviors.

The Srull and Wyer (1979, 1980) findings provide evidence that categorization of social behaviors in terms of trait concepts is an automatic process. Srull and Wyer (1979, 1980) presented subjects with either hostile- or kindness-related behaviors in a first, "sentence comprehension" experiment. Subjects were presented with four words in scrambled order, and were to construct a grammatically correct three-word sentence out of them (e.g., "hit kick dog the"). Processing these behavioral descriptions resulted in the activation of the overarching trait category (e.g., hostile), even though the task did not require subjects to categorize the behavior (and so subjects did not intend to do so). Thus, the behavior categorization occurred automatically, without the intention of the subject. Similar findings of automatic categorization of behaviors in terms of traits when subjects have quite different processing goals at the time they encounter the behaviors have been reported by Winter and Uleman (1984; Winter, Uleman, & Cunniff, 1985; see Higgins & Bargh, 1987).

Experiments in our laboratory (Bargh, Bond, Lombardi, & Tota, 1986; Bargh & Pietromonaco, 1982) have supported the automatic categorization hypothesis as well, by demonstrating that trait-related stimuli presented subliminally, outside of the subject's conscious awareness, still result in the activation of the trait category and the consequent temporary accessibility effect on the subsequent impression formation task. In these studies, the trait adjectives are presented very briefly (60 ms each) outside of the subject's foveal visual field, and are immediately masked to prevent any awareness of the word contents. In fact, subjects are not aware even that words have been presented at all; their task is to press a button as soon as they see a "flash" on the screen. Yet they rate the target person they read about next as possessing more of that trait than subjects who are not exposed to the trait terms, and this result has been replicated for three quite different kinds of behavior (kindness, hostility, and shyness). Again, the trait category was activated automatically by the detection of trait-relevant information, as the subjects in these studies did not intend to categorize the priming stimuli and in fact were not even aware of their existence.

Automatic Input, Controlled Output

It is very important to note that it is not the impression judgments themselves that are made automatically by subjects in the Srull and Wyer experiments and our own experiments. What is occurring automatically is the categorization of the behavior or adjective, *and not the target person,* in terms of the trait category. The automatic activation of the trait category, which occurs without the subject's control or intention and at times without even his or her awareness, makes that trait construct temporarily more accessible. Only when the subject has the *conscious and intentional goal* of forming an impression of a target person will these temporarily accessible categories then bias the interpretation of ambiguous but potentially relevant information in their direction. The automatic categorization that occurs in the perception of trait-related material "sets up" the subsequent controlled impression formation process to be slanted toward those traits. However, if the subsequent information is not relevant to the activated trait construct, no such bias will occur. In other words, the automatic effect is in the form of an interpretive bias, but if nothing happens to which the activated category can be applied, no such bias can result (Higgins et al., 1977).

Long-Term Accessibility Influences:
Individual Differences in Automatic Processing

What I have outlined thus far are general automatic influences on social perception that would be expected to occur for almost everyone who has a given trait concept available for use in understanding social behavior. But trait categories can become *chronically* accessible as well as temporarily accessible. Higgins and King (1981) proposed that social constructs can become so frequently used to interpret environmental information that they become more likely than other relevant constructs to be used in general—that is, even when they have not been activated recently by the environment or by controlled thought processes. In an experimental test of this hypothesis, Higgins, King, and Mavin (1982) selected subjects who possessed a chronically accessible construct for given trait domains (e.g., friendly) on the basis of the fact that those traits came first to mind for them when describing other people. Subjects later read a series of behaviors performed by a target person, and it was found that memory for behaviors related to the subject's chronically accessible constructs was better than memory for inaccessible-construct related behavioral information. This finding was obtained even though the free-response questionnaire used to select subjects was administered 2 months or more before the experimental session in which subjects read about and remembered the target's behaviors, and the experimenters made no attempt to prime or preactivate the subject's trait constructs.

Bargh (1984) argued that because chronic construct accessibility was presumed to develop as a result of the same factors that are thought to underlie automatic process development—namely, frequency and consistency of use— chronic constructs should show evidence of automatic processing capabilities. Several subsequent experiments in our laboratory have supported this hypothesis, demonstrating that chronically accessible constructs meet all three theoretical criteria for automatic processing.

One of these criteria is that automatic processing is much more efficient in its use of the limited cognitive processing capacity (e.g., Miller, 1956; Posner, 1978) than is controlled processing. Thus, it should be much less affected by a shortage of processing resources. When attentional resources are in short supply, as they are under conditions of information overload, having a relevant chronically accessible construct with which to process the target information should make one more likely to pick up and be influenced by the information than if one did not have such a construct. An experiment by Bargh and Thein (1985) tested this hypothesis. The target person that subjects read about either performed twice as many honest as dishonest behaviors, or twice as many dishonest as honest behaviors. Subjects were asked to read the behaviors that this target person engaged in with the purpose of forming an impression of him.

The critical manipulation was how long each of the behaviors was presented. Some subjects read each behavior at their own pace, thus having plenty of time to consider the behavior, using a controlled and intentional process, in terms of that behavior's implications for the target's personality. The other subjects saw each behavior for only 2 seconds each, just enough time to be able to read it once before the next one was presented. These latter subjects thus had no time to actively consider the implications of each behavior while it was being presented. Subjects who had a chronically accessible construct for honesty clearly differentiated between the mainly honest and mainly dishonest targets in their impressions, whereas subjects without the accessible construct could not. Apparently, the chronically accessible construct required minimal processing capacity to deal with the construct-relevant information. In fact, on all dependent variables (free recall, cued recall, impressions), subjects with the accessible construct showed the same patterns as did subjects in a nonoverload control condition, in which there was plenty of time to consider the target's behaviors.

In the Bargh, Bond, Lombardi, and Tota (1986) study, previously discussed, an additional factor in the design was whether the subject had a chronically accessible or an inaccessible construct relevant for the target behaviors. It was found that subjects with such a construct rated the target person more extremely along that trait dimension, even in the condition in which no trait-relevant information was presented beforehand. Thus, as in the Higgins et al. (1982) study, no prior activation or priming was necessary for the chronically accessible social construct to influence the interpretation of the ambiguously relevant behavioral information. It is therefore an automatic influence as subjects were not aware of their interpretive bias and did not intend or control it.

A recent study by Bargh and Pratto (1986) has found that even when subjects try to ignore a source of information relevant to a chronically accessible construct, they cannot. This experiment employed the Stroop color-naming paradigm, in which words are presented in various colors and the subject's task is to name the color of the word as quickly as possible. The word itself is to be ignored as a potential distraction from the subject's focal task. To the extent that the word is processed anyway, it constitutes a competing response to the color name itself that must be inhibited if the subject is to make the correct response (e.g., Logan, 1980). This inhibition, however, comes at a cost of processing resources, and the consequence is that subjects take longer to name the color of that word. In our stimulus word list, we included adjectives related to each of four different personality dimensions (intelligence, sociability, rudeness, and conceit). We then compared the color-naming latencies for words corresponding to the subject's chronically accessible constructs to the latencies for words corresponding to the subject's inaccessible constructs. As would be expected from the hypothesis that chronically accessible constructs are activated automatically by relevant information, the time to name the color of the "chronic" adjectives was significantly greater than for "nonchronic" adjectives, across each of the four trait dimensions.

Taken together, these studies show chronically accessible constructs to satisfy the three criteria of an automatic process: They do not require the subject's intention or goals to become active upon the presence of relevant information (Bargh, Bond, Lombardi, & Tota, 1986; Higgins et al., 1982), their activation cannot be controlled by the subject even if he or she wanted to do so (Bargh & Pratto, 1986), and they make minimal demands on processing capacity (Bargh & Thein, 1985). Thus, whereas all social behavioral information that is clearly relevant to a particular trait construct automatically activates that construct (Bargh, Bond, Lombardi, & Tota, 1986; Bargh & Pietromonaco, 1982; Srull & Wyer, 1979, 1980; Winter & Uleman, 1984), information relevant to a chronically accessible trait construct results in still greater automatic sensitivities and biases. Everyone possesses these sensitivities to certain domains of social behavior, and biases to interpret one's own behavior and that of others in terms of those constructs. There are wide individual differences as to which personality dimensions a person is biased toward in this way, however, and not much overlap between any two individuals selected at random (Higgins et al., 1982). Thus, two people may pick up very different kinds of information about a third person, and interpret the same information in very different ways.

The automaticity and uncontrollability of these perceptual representations make them a quite formidable force in determining the input on the basis of which we make our judgments and decisions concerning people. Because they operate outside of our control and potentially outside of our awareness altogether, we cannot adjust for them through some intentional and controlled process. We cannot say, for example, "Oh, maybe Carol didn't mean it that way," and decide that we can still be friends with her, because as with the color of the sky, we do not question the validity of automatically produced perceptions.

AUTOMATIC VERSUS GOAL-DIRECTED PROCESSING IN MASS COMMUNICATION

Because the processing of mass-communicated information is almost always a matter of choice (Zillmann, this volume), automatic and unintentional information processing does not play much of a role outside of the perceptual biases previously discussed. We choose to watch television rather than not watch it at all, and choose one program over another, in order to satisfy our goal of achieving a certain desired level of arousal (Zillmann, this volume). We choose to read the newspaper or to watch the television news program, for any one of a variety of goals—to gain information about the world (e.g., Epstein, 1977; Zukier, 1986), to reduce our anxiety in times of world or national crisis (see following), or to be entertained (Donohew, Finn, & Christ, this volume). Whereas information processing may proceed somewhat "mindlessly" (Langer, 1978) once the initial step to watch or read has been taken (Donohew et al., this volume), the outcome of such processing can be very different depending on the overarching goal that is driving the act of media consumption. The type of information one attends to, how much attention one pays to it, how one encodes and interprets it, and consequently how one remembers it are all greatly influenced by one's processing goals while encountering the information (e.g., Cohen, 1981; Srull & Wyer, 1986).

Voluntary and Involuntary Attention

A distinction made nearly a century ago by William James (1890), between *voluntary* and *involuntary* attention, is potentially quite useful in understanding the preferences people have in their media consumption—for example, why most people prefer watching television news over reading a newspaper. For James, voluntary attention was characterized by its effortful and intentional nature. It is what we mean when we say we have to "concentrate," when we must ignore all other distractions and focus on the task at hand. Involuntary attention, on the other hand, requires little effort to be maintained. James (1890) distinguished further between *immediate* or innate and *derived* or learned sources of involuntary attention.

In the case of television, there are intrinsic features that easily capture our attention and hold it there because they correspond to immediate sources of involuntary, effortless attention. Much of the visual aspects of television correspond to stimulus features that we naturally and involuntarily attend to: motion, color, contrast, contour, intensity, and change (James, 1890; Neisser, 1967). There is an innate bias to attend to changing features of the environment, which is easily explainable in terms of its adaptive value (Neisser, 1967), and a preference for visual information over that delivered by the other senses (e.g., Kaplan, 1976). For example, upon smelling smoke, one might investigate further as to whether something was burning, but upon the sight of fire one does not usually feel the need for further investigation before acting on the information! People are also much more influenced by concrete than by abstract verbal information, because the former is more easily visually imaged (e.g., Nisbett & Ross, 1980). Because television deals directly in concrete visual images, its ability to grab and hold attention is not difficult to understand.

Entertainment Versus Information-Seeking Goals

Donohew et al. (this volume) discuss the power of certain aspects of newspaper stories that naturally capture one's attention. Screaming headlines in enormous letters (intensity), followed by a (concrete) case or example in the lead paragraph, and then a (familiar) narrative-like structure for the story itself (corresponding to a derived, learned form of involuntary attention; see Bower, Black, & Turner, 1979; Zukier, 1986), all reduce the amount of effort needed by the reader to process the information. This is a critical determinant of whether the story will hold the person's attention when he or she is reading it with the goal of resting the overworked voluntary attention mechanism.

On the other hand, such attention-grabbing devices are not so necessary if the person is reading the article with the goal of information-seeking. During and in the days following the United States bombing of Libya and following the nuclear accident at Chernobyl, the ABC television news program ''Nightline'' had higher ratings than its time-slot competition, NBC's ''Tonight Show,'' which typically has the highest ratings (Corry, 1986). Thus, people well may watch the news on television with the intent of being entertained, and this may even be the usual reason they watch it, but it is not the *only* reason they might be watching. Entertainment value may predict a viewer's choice among different news programs, but it does not explain why a news program would receive higher ratings than one of the most successful entertainment programs in television history. Something else is going on during such times of crisis and uncertainty, and Zillmann's (this volume) framework provides a good way to understand viewer preference in both instances. One need only assume that such fearful news as the initial reports of the Libyan bombing and of the Chernobyl disaster creates anxiety and uncertainty that is unpleasant and that the viewer seeks to reduce through the acquisition of additional information (Sorrentino & Short, 1986; Zukier, 1986).

As these examples illustrate, consumption of mass media is a controlled and not an automatic process because it is intentional and goal directed; that is, it involves choice. Different patterns of viewing or reading would be expected given different processing goals. If the goal is to rest the voluntary attention mechanism through some sort of cognitively effortless activity, viewing or reading choices will tend to maximize the use of involuntary attention and minimize the use of voluntary attention. Involuntary attention can be driven either by innately interesting stimuli or through stimuli that are interesting due to the viewer's past experiences. Examples of the latter are programs or stories that match one or more of the media consumer's interests, or which are relevant to other important goals the consumer might have (see Csikszentmihalyi, 1975). To the extent the program or article requires too much in the way of voluntary attention, continued viewing or reading would not serve to achieve the overarching goal, and either a new program or story would be found that did achieve that goal, or the entire activity would be abandoned. (See Berger, this volume, and Miller et al., 1960, for more on the strategic and flexible quality of plan- or goal-directed behavior.)

Entirely different viewing patterns would occur, of course, if the goal was information acquisition, for here the goal is not to minimize the use of voluntary attention but to maximally focus attention on the material in order to learn more about the world in general (Epstein, 1977), oneself (e.g., Markus & Smith, 1981) or events that have important consequences for oneself (e.g., Chaiken, 1980, 1987), or to reduce uncertainty or anxiety about the short or long-term future (see Sorrentino & Short, 1986). Depending on which of these goals is in operation at any given time—and there are certainly many more possible processing goals than I have elaborated here (see, e.g., Srull & Wyer, 1986)—different patterns of mass-communication processing will result.

AUTOMATIC PROCESSING AND AFFECT

Affect does not have a single cause; it can result from a variety of automatic as well as controlled cognitive processes (see Hoffman, 1986; Zajonc, 1980). Figure 2.1 presents a model of three possible sources of automatically produced affect, elaborated in this section. Affect can be an innate response determined by the stimulus features themselves (Path A; Zajonc, 1980), such as the 1-day-old infant's cry in response to another infant's crying (Sagi & Hoffman, 1976), or the emotional meanings that are universally extracted from facial expressions (Ekman & Friesen, 1975). In addition, evaluation can be an automatic response attached to primitive stages of cognitive analysis such as feature detection and pattern recognition (Path B; e.g., Leventhal, 1980), or a natural and unintended

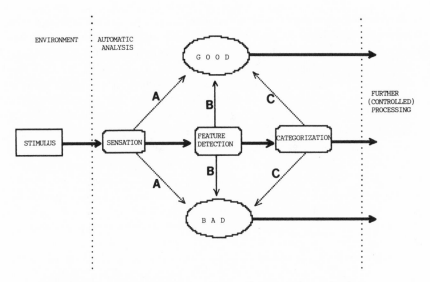

FIGURE 2.1. Three potential sources of automatic evaluative responses.

consequence of the act of categorization (Path C; Fiske & Pavelchak, 1986). (In fact, there is now evidence that affect may automatically arise from the quality of the *relation between* two different categorical representations; see Higgins, Bond, Klein, & Strauman, 1986.) In this chapter I do not address the proposal that affect can be a direct reaction to a sensation, requiring no cognitive transformation of the sensory data whatsoever (Path A in Fig. 2.1); the interested reader is referred to recent statements of such a model by Zajonc (1980, 1984; Zajonc & Markus, 1984; Zajonc, Pietromonaco, & Bargh, 1982).

Automatic "Good/Bad" Classification

Fazio, Sanbonmatsu, Powell, and Kardes (1986) have obtained evidence that suggests social stimuli are automatically evaluated as "good" or "bad"—that is, preattentively and without the person's ability to control this evaluative process. Such an automatic dichotomous classification of incoming stimuli as either evaluatively good or bad is represented by Path B in Fig. 2.1. In their Experiments 1 and 2, a noun, "attitude object" (e.g., *party, crime, snow*) was presented 300 ms before a target adjective. The subject's task was to respond whether the target adjective was positive or negative, as quickly as he or she could. When the attitude object prime was of the same valence as the target, the subject's task was facilitated, but when the attitude object and the adjective had the opposite valence, interference with the task occurred. Because the time between the presentation of the attitude object noun and the target adjective of 300 ms is not

21

enough time for the subject to have developed a conscious expectancy concerning the valence of the target adjective (Neely, 1977; Posner & Snyder, 1975), the activation must have been automatic and not the result of a controlled process, as Fazio et al. (1986) concluded.

Importantly, the automatic evaluation activation effect occurred only for those attitude object stimuli for which the subject possessed a strongly-held opinion (strength being defined by Fazio et al. in terms of the speed with which subjects could respond "good" or "bad"), and not for other attitude objects. Because it is not clear from the description of the procedure for these experiments whether the attitude objects for which most subjects had strong attitudes (e.g., *death, hell*) were different from those for which most subjects had weak attitudes (e.g., *recession, snakes*), one cannot draw unambiguous conclusions from these findings. It could be that the differences between the strong and the weak attitude conditions were due to differences in the stimuli themselves, independently of the strength of the subject's attitude towards those stimuli.

The results of a third experiment conducted by Fazio et al. (1986) shed light on the forces responsible for the automatic evaluation effect. In that study, identical attitude object stimuli were employed in both the "strong" and the "weak" attitude conditions, which were created experimentally through an accessibility manipulation. The attitude objects were selected on the basis of their unanimity of evaluation as either good or bad and the weakness of most subjects' attitudes towards them (as assessed by response latencies) in the first two experiments. The automatic evaluation effect was obtained in *both* the strong and weak attitude conditions, but it was reliably greater in the strong attitude condition.

Attitude strength therefore does not appear to be a prerequisite for the automatic evaluation effect. All of the attitude objects in Fazio et al.'s (1986) Experiment 3 were selected on the basis of the relatively weak attitudes subjects held toward them. Even when this initially weak attitude was not strengthened further by the accessibility manipulation, the automatic evaluation effect occurred. Why did it obtain for the weakly held attitudes in Experiment 3 when it did not obtain in the other two experiments? The difference was that only in Experiment 3 were the attitude objects preselected in terms of the consistency with which subjects evaluated them as good or bad. Recall that consistency of processing is presumed to be necessary for the development of any automatic process except those that are innate (e.g., Neisser, 1967; Shiffrin & Dumais, 1981).

Thus, the automatic evaluation effect appears to hold for social stimuli that have been "consistently mapped" (Schneider & Shiffrin, 1977) as either good or bad, regardless of the accessibility of their corresponding attitude or even if no attitude exists at all. Because the effect was not obtained by Fazio et al. when the stimuli were not selected for their consistency of evaluation by subjects (Experiments 1 and 2), the automatic evaluation does not seem to depend on characteristics of the stimulus alone. Instead, it depends on whether the stimulus had been consistently evaluated the same way (as good or as bad) by the subject in the past.

In an attempt to explore in more detail the precise nature of automatic evaluative processing, Bargh, Litt, and Pratto (1986) asked subjects to make different kinds of judgments concerning trait adjectives presented below the subject's conscious recognition threshold (which ranged from 40 to 90 ms for immediately pattern-masked stimuli). On a given trial, the subject decided whether or not a word had been presented at all (*presence* judgments), which of 2 alternatives was a synonym of the presented word (*semantic* judgments), or whether the presented word was positive or negative (*evaluative* judgments).

The stimulus adjectives were taken from those developed by Anderson (1968) for use in impression formation research. Four groups of adjectives were selected on the basis of Anderson's (1968) likability rating norms: extremely positive (e.g., *loyal, cheerful*), moderately positive (e.g., *lucky, innocent*), extremely negative (e.g., *evil, phony*), and moderately negative (e.g., *passive, forgetful*). We varied the extremity and the valence of the adjectives in this way in order to test whether the automatic evaluative processing effect was sensitive to the intensity or the positivity of the stimulus, or was instead only a crude, dichotomous good/bad classification. (No attempt was made in the Fazio et al., 1986, Experiments 1 & 2 to distinguish among the attitude objects or the target adjectives in terms of the extremity of their evaluation, and so one cannot tell whether their results were due to the activation of a global good or bad evaluation representation in memory, or to a more sophisticated extraction of the affective intensity of the stimuli.)

Subjects made each of the three types of judgments (presence, semantic, and evaluative) at each of four presentation durations: 5, 15, 25, and 35 ms below their recognition threshold for the presence of the stimulus words. For the presence judgments, a word was actually presented on half of the trials, and no word was presented on the remaining trials. The semantic judgments consisted of a choice between two alternatives as to which word had the same meaning as the flashed word. The alternatives were a synonym of the flashed word and another word that was unrelated in meaning to the flashed word, but which was of similar valence and extremity. In this way, subjects could not use the affective quality of the flashed word as a basis for making the semantic judgment. Finally, the evaluative decision was of whether the flashed word was positive or negative in valence. Only one of these questions was asked per word-flash trial, and subjects were informed as to which question would be asked before the trial started.

We were interested in seeing at how far below threshold subjects could still make any of the three types of judgments at better than a chance level (50%). The results of the experiment are presented in Fig. 2.2. Subjects were able to report on the presence of a stimulus event at a better than chance level even when the adjective had been presented (and immediately masked) 35 ms below their recognition threshold. But for none of the four presentation durations were subjects able to answer the semantic questions better than chance. In this apparent absence of any access to the semantic meaning of the adjectives, subjects were still able to answer the evaluative questions at a better than chance rate until the

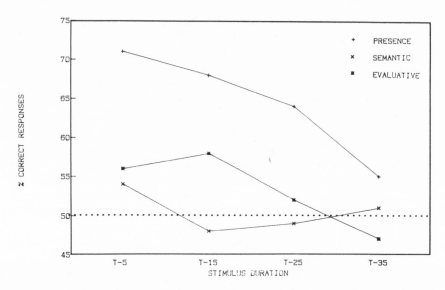

FIGURE 2.2. Percent correct responses to the presence, semantic, and evaluative judgments as a function of presentation duration of stimulus (in milliseconds below recognition threshold). Dotted line represents chance responding. (Data from Bargh, Litt, & Pratto, 1986.)

presentation duration dropped to 25 ms below threshold. Path analyses revealed that the ability to correctly answer the evaluative question was unrelated to the ability to get the semantic question right. Interestingly, correct evaluative responding was found to depend on correct detection of the stimulus event; there were reliable paths between correct presence judgments and correct evaluative judgments at both the T(hreshold)–5 and T–15 presentation durations.

We did not obtain differences in the pattern of results shown in Fig. 2.2 as a function of the extremity or the valence of the adjectives — the results were the same no matter whether the adjectives were positive or negative, extreme or moderate. Thus the preattentive evaluative processing documented by the Bargh, Litt, and Pratto (1986) study, as well as that evidenced in the Fazio et al. (1986) experiments, would seem to be rather simple-minded, in the form of a binary good/bad classification instead of a more sophisticated analysis in terms of intensity. This finding is consistent with Neisser's (1967) argument that preattentive processes provide only a crude analysis of the environment, leaving more detailed processing work to focal attention. It would seem that the preattentive evaluation process is no exception to this rule.

The Bargh, Litt, and Pratto (1986) and Fazio et al. (1986) results are not accountable by the operation of an affective processing system that is completely independent of and prior to any cognitive transformations (Zajonc, 1980, 1984). A prerequisite for the effects shown in these studies is the development of an automatic pathway between stimulus features and the "good" or "bad" evaluation, based on consistency of mapping a set of features onto one or the other evaluation. Inconsistently evaluated stimuli would not be expected to show the automatic evaluation effect. Thus, a model in which affective processing may occur following primitive (cognitive) feature analysis, and before such higher levels of cognitive processing as semantic feature analysis and stimulus recognition (e.g., Gordon & Holyoak, 1983; Leventhal, 1980) is supported by our data.

Automatic Activation of Category-Based Affect

Whereas an accessible attitude towards the attitude object stimulus apparently was not *necessary* for the evaluation-priming effect in the Fazio et al. (1986) Experiment 3, it did result in a reliably *stronger* effect. Although it is only speculation at the moment, I believe that the additional strength of the affect priming in the strong-attitude condition came from a second source: the activation of the categorical representation of the attitude object, in which is stored an evaluative component (Path C in Fig. 2.1). In other words, whereas all consistently evaluated stimuli automatically activate their evaluation in the course of the early, pre-semantic stages of processing (Path B), only those attitude object stimuli for which the subject possesses an accessible attitude are able to proceed further and activate their categorical representation. If there is an evaluative component stored within this category, a second source of activation will spread to the good or bad representation (Path C) and increase its activation.

Note that this is the same conclusion made above concerning the existence and the extent of automatic activation of social constructs. The subliminal priming studies showed that all subjects were capable of automatically processing the trait adjectives, regardless of the long-term accessibility of their mental construct for which those trait stimuli were relevant (Bargh, Bond, Lombardi, & Tota, 1986; Bargh & Pietromonaco, 1982). Other studies, however, found the extent of such automatic construct activation to differ as a function of chronic construct accessibility (Bargh & Pratto, 1986; Bargh & Thein, 1985). And in the Bargh, Bond, Lombardi, and Tota (1986) study in which the simultaneous impact of subliminally presented adjectives and long-term category accessibility was investigated, the two sources of activation were found to combine additively, in just the manner I am proposing here that the two sources of automatic affect combined in the Fazio et al. (1986) Experiment 3.

Fiske (1982; Fiske & Pavelchak, 1986) has proposed that affective or evaluative responses are stored within social categories. If so, the automatic activation of those categories, discussed earlier in the section on interpersonal communication, should also result in the automatic activation of the associated evaluative reactions. Fiske and Pavelchak (1986) present data that indicate category-based evaluative responses are independent of how the individual members of that category are evaluated; thus the evaluation springs from the category directly and is not computed from an analysis of the features of the stimulus itself. Because social categories can become active automatically, it follows that the affect or evaluation stored in such constructs can become active automatically as well, with this evaluation having an influence over subsequent information processing (see Clark & Isen, 1982; Isen, 1984) without one being able to control or even be aware of this influence over one's thoughts and decisions.

In summary, whether a given model of the affect-cognition interface places the earliest source of affect at Paths A, B, or C of Fig. 2.1, all such models share the assumption that affect activation is a direct result of sensation or perception and does not require any conscious calculation or interpretation. The proposals of Zajonc (e.g., 1980), Leventhal (e.g., 1980), Fiske and Pavelchak (1986), Clark and Isen (1982; Isen, 1984), and Fazio et al. (1986) share the view that affect or evaluation may be often or even usually an uncontrollable reaction to an environmental stimulus, instead of necessarily the result of a controlled and deliberate interpretation of the stimulus event (e.g., Schachter & Singer, 1962; Weiner & Graham, 1984).

Consequences of Automatic Affect for Further Cognitive Processing

What are the consequences of automatic, preconscious evaluative processing for subsequent cognitive processing, such as is involved in judgments, memory, and behavior? Isen (1984) has recently reviewed a good deal of evidence supporting the idea that one's mental representations of people, places, and events are associated with each other in terms of how we evaluate them — the positive ones are associated with each other and the negative ones with each other. These memory linkages have been detected in many different ways. For example, Postman and Brown (1952) found that activation of the concept "good" made it easier to detect success-related words in a recognition threshold study, whereas activation of the concept "bad" made it easier to detect failure-related words. Johnson and Tversky (1983) showed that positive feelings induced by thinking about a positive event resulted in decreased estimates of the likelihood of several types of disasters and unpleasant events occurring, whereas induced negative feelings resulted in increased likelihood estimates.

Interestingly, although Johnson and Tversky (1983) varied the similarity between the event subjects thought about to produce the initial affective state and the event of which they judged the likelihood, the degree of similarity did not affect the results. For example, subjects' estimates of the probability of their getting cancer was greater than a control group's, whether they had read about someone who died of cancer or about someone who had perished in a fire. Just as in the Bargh, Litt, and Pratto (1986) and Fazio et al. (1986) studies, these results seem most parsimoniously explained by the activation of a global "good" or "bad" concept in memory; no matter what the nature or affective extremity of the activating event, the consequences are the same.

Isen, Shalker, Clark, and Karp (1978) found that when subjects had just experienced a minor good event (e.g., finding a dime in a pay-phone coin return), it was easier for them to recall positive events from their past. Isen (1984) concluded from such findings that in order for positive or negative feelings to serve as an effective retrieval cue, incoming information must be routinely and effortlessly encoded in terms of its evaluative or affective implications. In other words, information stored in memory is associatively linked with similarly evaluated information, through association with some general representation of goodness or badness.

Because this "good" or "bad" representation apparently can be activated automatically, outside of one's control and even awareness, with this activation then spreading to entire systems of similarly evaluated material in memory to have the kinds of pervasive influences on thought and behavior proposed by Clark and Isen (1982), a good deal of the influence over one's feelings, judgments, and memories would seem to be in the hands of the environment. Of course, as argued earlier, any judgments, decisions, or actions a person may make while these automatic evaluative influences were operating (which would be almost all the time) would be ultimately under that person's control (e.g., Logan & Cowan, 1984). But the *input* into those decisions may well be biased by the relative accessibility afforded to positive or to negative material by the automatic activation of the "good" or "bad" representation by some environmental event (Isen, 1984). And the fact that one is usually unaware of such automatic and preattentive influences over one's subsequent conscious thought processes makes it extremely difficult to adjust one's judgments to correct for the bias (Bargh, 1984).

"TO BE OR NOT TO BE CONTROLLED":
A CONCLUDING SERMONETTE

If one passively accepts the validity of interpretations and evaluations of oneself and other people that are automatically furnished by the perceptual mechanisms discussed in this chapter, one abdicates control over one's thoughts, feelings, decisions, and behavior based on them to the environment. Reliance on the effortless workings of the mind is adaptive and functional only when the interpretations automatically afforded correspond to reality. Unfortunately, this is not always the case, and unless we supervise and question the process to some extent we may be at the mercy of erroneous and maladaptive perceptual processes, such as may characterize the depressive (see Beck, 1976).

Consciousness in humans was a relatively late evolutionary development, and it developed for a good reason: To give us the means to be flexible and to adapt to changing environmental contingencies for which automatic patterns no longer serve us well. Thus, it is the nature of conscious, controlled processes to be able to override automatic processes when the two are in conflict (see Bargh, 1984;

Logan & Cowan, 1984). If one defaults on this control, one's judgments and behavioral choices can be influenced unduly by biases in the interpretations made for one by the perceptual system. Langer (e.g., 1978) makes exactly this point based on her work on "mindlessness"—that unless people question their assumptions about what is going on around them, they can easily be influenced to do things they wouldn't do if they were paying more attention.

This is not to say that automatic processing is "bad" or that people are "lazy" for relying on it. We have no choice but to rely on it, and without it the amount of attention it would require to do any of the well-learned things we as adults take for granted would overwhelm our limited attentional capacity; in Miller et al.'s (1960) example, we would be unable even to get out of bed in the morning. Automatic processing frees the limited attentional capacity to focus on the new, the unusual, the potentially dangerous, the most informative, and the most important events going on around us at any given time. The point is not that one should try to pay attention to everything that is happening, or to contemplate all of the ramifications and possible meanings of every event. Rather, the point is only that one should be aware and admit to the possibility that one might be biased without knowing it, and to take this into account when making the more important decisions concerning oneself, one's future, and the people in one's life.

ACKNOWLEDGMENTS

Preparation of this chapter was supported by Grant BNS-8404181 from the National Science Foundation. My thanks to Tory Higgins, Shelly Chaiken, and Felicia Pratto for their thoughtful comments on an earlier version of this manuscript.

REFERENCES

Anderson, N. H. (1968). Likableness ratings of 555 personality trait words. *Journal of Personality and Social Psychology, 9,* 272–279.

Bargh, J. A. (1984). Automatic and conscious processing of social information. In R. S. Wyer, Jr. & T. K. Srull (Eds.), *Handbook of social cognition* (Vol. 3, pp. 1–43). Hillsdale, NJ: Lawrence Erlbaum Associates.

Bargh, J. A., Bond, R. N., Lombardi, W. J., & Tota, M. E. (1986). The additive nature of chronic and temporary sources of construct accessibility. *Journal of Personality and Social Psychology, 50,* 869–878.

Bargh, J. A., Litt, J., & Pratto, F. (1986). *On the subconscious processing of affect: Evaluations need no semantic processing.* Unpublished manuscript, New York University.

Bargh, J. A., & Pietromonaco, P. (1982). Automatic information processing and social perception: The influence of trait information presented outside of conscious awareness on impression formation. *Journal of Personality and Social Psychology, 43,* 437–449.

Bargh, J. A., & Pratto, F. (1986). Individual construct accessibility and perceptual selection. *Journal of Experimental Social Psychology, 22,* 293–311.

Bargh, J. A., & Thein, R. (1985). Individual construct accessibility, person memory, and the recall-judgment link: The case of information overload. *Journal of Personality and Social Psychology, 49,* 1129–1146.

Bateson, G. (1972). *Steps to an ecology of mind.* San Francisco: Chandler.

Beck, A. T. (1976). *Cognitive therapy and the emotional disorders.* New York: International Universities Press.

Bower, G. H., Black, J. B., & Turner, T. J. (1979). Scripts in memory for text. *Cognitive Psychology, 11,* 177–220.

Bowers, K. S. (1985). On being unconsciously influenced and informed. In K. S. Bowers & D. Meichenbaum (Eds.), *The unconscious reconsidered.* New York: Wiley.

Bruner, J. S. (1957). On perceptual readiness. *Psychological Review, 64,* 123–152.

Bruner, J. S. (1958). Social psychology and perception. In E. E. Maccoby, T. M. Newcomb, & E. L. Hartley (Eds.), *Readings in social psychology* (3rd ed., pp. 85–94). New York: Holt, Rinehart & Winston.

Carroll, J. S., & Payne, J. W. (Eds.). (1976). *Cognition and social behavior.* Hillsdale, NJ: Lawrence Erlbaum Associates.

Chaiken, S. (1980). Heuristic versus systematic information processing and the use of source versus message cues in persuasion. *Journal of Personality and Social Psychology, 39,* 752–766.

Chaiken, S. (1987). The heuristic model of persuasion. In M. P. Zanna, J. M. Olson, & C. P. Herman (Eds.), *Social influence: The Ontario Symposium* (Vol. 5, pp. 3–39). Hillsdale, NJ: Lawrence Erlbaum Associates.

Clark, M. S., & Isen, A. M. (1982). Toward understanding the relationship between feeling states and social behavior. In A. H. Hastorf & A. M. Isen (Eds.), *Cognitive social psychology.* New York: Elsevier.

Cohen, C. E. (1981). Goals and schemata in person perception: Making sense from the stream of behavior. In N. Cantor & J. F. Kihlstrom (Eds.), *Personality, cognition, and social interaction* (pp. 45–68). Hillsdale, NJ: Lawrence Erlbaum Associates.

Corry, J. (1986, May 11). Is technology creating a reality of its own? *The New York Times,* pp. 33–34.

Csikszentmihalyi, M. (1975). *Beyond boredom and anxiety.* San Francisco: Jossey-Bass.

Dreyfus, H. L. (1972). *What computers can't do.* New York: Harper & Row.

Ekman, P., & Friesen, W. V. (1975). *Unmasking the face.* Englewood Cliffs, NJ: Prentice-Hall.

Epstein, S. (1977). Traits are alive and well. In D. Magnusson & N. S. Endler (Eds.), *Personality at the crossroads: Current issues in interactional psychology.* Hillsdale, NJ: Lawrence Erlbaum Associates.

Erdelyi, M. H. (1985). *Psychoanalysis: Freud's cognitive psychology.* New York: Freeman.

Fazio, R. H., Sanbonmatsu, D. M., Powell, M. C., & Kardes, F. R. (1986). On the automatic activation of attitudes. *Journal of Personality and Social Psychology, 50,* 229–238.

Fiske, S. T. (1982). Schema-triggered affect: Applications to social perception. In M. S. Clark & S. T. Fiske (Eds.), *Affect and cognition: The 17th annual Carnegie symposium on cognition* (pp. 55–78). Hillsdale, NJ: Lawrence Erlbaum Associates.

Fiske, S. T., & Pavelchak, M. A. (1986). Category-based versus piecemeal-based affective responses: Developments in schema-triggered affect. In R. M. Sorrentino & E. T. Higgins (Eds.), *Handbook of motivation and cognition* (pp. 167–203). New York: Guilford.

Gordon, P. C., & Holyoak, K. J. (1983). Implicit learning and generalization of the "mere exposure" effect. *Journal of Personality and Social Psychology, 45,* 492–500.

Hamilton, D. L. (1979). A cognitive-attributional analysis of stereotyping. In L. Berkowitz (Ed.), *Advances in experimental social psychology* (Vol. 12, pp. 53–84). New York: Academic Press.

Higgins, E. T., & Bargh, J. A. (1987). Social cognition and social perception. *Annual Review of Psychology, 38,* 369–425.

Higgins, E. T., Bargh, J. A., & Lombardi, W. (1985). Nature of priming effects on categorization. *Journal of Experimental Psychology: Learning, Memory, and Cognition, 11,* 59–69.

Higgins, E. T., Bond, R. N., Klein, R., & Strauman, T. (1986). Self-discrepancies and emotional vulnerability: How magnitude, accessibility, and type of discrepancy influence affect. *Journal of Personality and Social Psychology, 51,* 5–15.

Higgins, E. T., & King, G. (1981). Accessibility of social constructs: Information processing consequences of individual and contextual variability. In N. Cantor & J. F. Kihlstrom (Eds.), *Personality, cognition, and social interaction* (pp. 69–121). Hillsdale, NJ: Lawrence Erlbaum Associates.

Higgins, E. T., King, G. A., & Mavin, G. H. (1982). Individual construct accessibility and subjective impressions and recall. *Journal of Personality and Social Psychology, 43,* 35–47.

Higgins, E. T., Rholes, W. S., & Jones, C. R. (1977). Category accessibility and impression formation. *Journal of Experimental Social Psychology, 13,* 141–154.

Hoffman, M. L. (1986). Affect, cognition, and motivation. In R. M. Sorrentino & E. T. Higgins (Eds.), *Handbook of motivation and cognition* (pp. 244–280). New York: Guilford.

Isen, A. M. (1984). Toward understanding the role of affect in cognition. In R. S. Wyer, Jr., & T. K. Srull (Eds.), *Handbook of social cognition* (Vol. 3, pp. 179–236). Hillsdale, NJ: Lawrence Erlbaum Associates.

Isen, A. M., Shalker, T., Clark, M., & Karp, L. (1978). Affect, accessibility of material in memory and behavior: A cognitive loop? *Journal of Personality and Social Psychology, 36,* 1–12.

James, W. (1890). *Principles of psychology.* New York: Holt.

Johnson, E., & Tversky, A. (1983). Affect, generalization, and the perception of risk. *Journal of Personality and Social Psychology, 45,* 20–31.

Kahneman, D., & Tversky, A. (1973). On the psychology of prediction. *Psychological Review, 80,* 237–251.

Kaplan, S. (1976). Adaptation, structure, and knowledge. In G. T. Moore & R. G. Golledge (Eds.), *Environmental knowing.* Stroudsberg, PA: Dowden, Hutchinson & Ross.

Kuhn, T. S. (1962). *The structure of scientific revolutions.* Chicago: University of Chicago Press.

Lachman, R., Lachman, J. L., & Butterfield, E. C. (1979). *Cognitive psychology and information processing: An introduction.* Hillsdale, NJ: Lawrence Erlbaum Associates.

Langer, E. J. (1978). Rethinking the role of thought in social interaction. In J. H. Harvey, W. J. Ickes, & R. F. Kidd (Eds.), *New directions in attribution research* (Vol. 2, pp. 35–58). Hillsdale, NJ: Lawrence Erlbaum Associates.

Leventhal, H. A. (1980). Toward a comprehensive theory of emotion. In L. Berkowitz (Eds.), *Advances in experimental social psychology* (Vol. 13, pp. 139–207). New York: Academic Press.

Logan, G. D. (1980). Attention and automaticity in Stroop and priming tasks: Theory and data. *Cognitive Psychology, 12,* 523–553.

Logan, G. D., & Cowan, W. B. (1984). On the ability to inhibit thought and action: A theory of an act of control. *Psychological Review, 91,* 295–327.

Markus, H., & Smith, J. (1981). The influence of self-schemata on the perception of others. In N. Cantor & J. F. Kihlstrom (Eds.), *Personality, cognition, and social interaction* (pp. 233–262). Hillsdale, NJ: Lawrence Erlbaum Associates.

McCann, C. D., & Higgins, E. T. (1985). Individual differences in communication: Social cognitive determinants and consequences. In H. E. Sypher & J. L. Applegate (Eds.), *Communication by children and adults: Social cognitive and strategic processes* (pp. 172–210). Beverly Hills, CA: Sage.

Miller, G. A. (1956). The magical number seven, plus or minus two: Some limits on our capacity for processing information. *Psychological Review, 63,* 81–97.

Miller, G. A., Galanter, E., & Pribram, K. (1960). *Plans and the structure of behavior.* New York: Holt.

Neely, J. H. (1977). Semantic priming and retrieval from lexical memory: Roles of inhibitionless spreading activation and limited-capacity attention. *Journal of Experimental Psychology: General, 106,* 226–254.

Neisser, U. (1967). *Cognitive psychology.* New York: Appleton-Century-Crofts.

Nisbett, R., & Ross, L. (1980). *Human inference: Strategies and shortcomings of social judgment.* Englewood Cliffs, NJ: Prentice-Hall.

Nisbett, R. E., & Wilson, T. D. (1977). Telling more than we can know: Verbal reports on mental processes. *Psychological Review, 84,* 231–259.

Posner, M. I. (1978). *Chronometric explorations of mind.* Hillsdale, NJ: Lawrence Erlbaum Associates.

Posner, M. I., & Snyder, C. R. R. (1975). Attention and cognitive control. In R. L. Solso (Eds.), *Information processing and cognition: The Loyola symposium* (pp. 55–85). Hillsdale, NJ: Lawrence Erlbaum Associates.

Postman, L., & Brown, D. R. (1952). Perceptual consequences of success and failure. *Journal of Abnormal and Social Psychology, 47,* 213–221.

Sagi, A., & Hoffman, M. L. (1976). Empathic distress in newborns. *Developmental Psychology, 12,* 175–176.

Schachter, S., & Singer, J. L. (1962). Cognitive, social, and physiological determinants of emotional state. *Psychological Review, 69,* 379–399.

Schneider, W., & Fisk, A. D. (1982). Degree of consistent training: Improvements in search performance and automatic process development. *Perception & Psychophysics, 31,* 160–168.

Schneider, W., & Shiffrin, R. M. (1977). Controlled and automatic human information processing: I. Detection, search, and attention. *Psychological Review, 84,* 1–66.

Shallice, T. (1972). Dual functions of consciousness. *Psychological Review, 79,* 383–393.

Shiffrin, R. M., & Dumais, S. T. (1981). The development of automatism. In J. R. Anderson (Ed.), *Cognitive skills and their acquisition* (pp. 111–140). Hillsdale, NJ: Lawrence Erlbaum Associates.

Shiffrin, R. M., & Schneider, W. (1977). Controlled and automatic human information processing: II. Perceptual learning, automatic attending, and a general theory. *Psychological Review, 84,* 127–190.

Skinner, B. F. (1971). *Beyond freedom and dignity.* New York: Knopf.

Smith, E. R. (1984). Model of social inference processes. *Psychological Review, 91,* 392–413.

Sorrentino, R. M., & Short, J. C. (1986). Uncertainty orientation, motivation, and cognition. In R. M. Sorrentino & E. T. Higgins (Eds.), *Handbook of motivation and cognition* (pp. 379–403). New York: Guilford.

Srull, T. K., & Wyer, R. S., Jr. (1979). The role of category accessibility in the interpretation of information about persons: Some determinants and implications. *Journal of Personality and Social Psychology, 37,* 1660–1672.

Srull, T. K., & Wyer, R. S., Jr. (1980). Category accessibility and social perception: Some implications for the study of person memory and interpersonal judgments. *Journal of Personality and Social Psychology, 38,* 841–856.

Srull, T. K., & Wyer, R. S., Jr. (1986). The role of chronic and temporary goals in social information processing. In R. M. Sorrentino & E. T. Higgins (Eds.), *Handbook of motivation and cognition* (pp. 503–549). New York: Guilford.

Watson, J. B. (1919). *Psychology from the standpoint of a behaviorist.* Philadelphia: Lippincott.

Weiner, B., & Graham, S. (1984). An attributional approach to emotional development. In C. E. Izard, J. Kagan, & R. B. Zajonc (Eds.), *Emotions, cognition, and behavior* (pp. 167–191). New York: Cambridge University Press.

Werner, H. (1956). Microgenesis and aphasia. *Journal of Abnormal and Social Psychology, 52,* 347–353.

Winter, L., & Uleman, J. S. (1984). When are social judgments made? Evidence for the spontaneousness of trait inferences. *Journal of Personality and Social Psychology, 47,* 237–252.

Winter, L., Uleman, J. S., & Cunniff, C. (1985). How automatic are social judgments? *Journal of Personality and Social Psychology, 49,* 904–917.

Wyer, R. S., Jr., & Srull, T. K. (1986). Human cognition in its social context. *Psychological Review, 93,* 322–359.

Zajonc, R. B. (1980). Feeling and thinking: Preferences need no inferences. *American Psychologist, 35,* 151–175.

Zajonc, R. B. (1984). On the primacy of affect. *American Psychologist, 39,* 117–123.

Zajonc, R. B., & Markus, H. (1984). Affect and cognition: The hard interface. In C. E. Izard, J. Kagan, & R. B. Zajonc (Eds.), *Emotions, cognition, and behavior* (pp. 73–102). New York: Cambridge University Press.

Zajonc, R. B., Pietromonaco, P., & Bargh, J. (1982). Independence and interaction of affect and cognition. In M. S. Clark & S. T. Fiske (Eds.), *Affect and cognition: The 17th annual Carnegie symposium on cognition* (pp. 211–227). Hillsdale, NJ: Lawrence Erlbaum Associates.

Zukier, H. (1986). The paradigmatic and narrative modes in goal-guided inference. In R. M. Sorrentino & E. T. Higgins (Eds.), *Handbook of motivation and cognition* (pp. 465–502). New York: Guilford.

3 Schemas, Affect, and Communication

Walter H. Crockett
University of Kansas

We are often told that theory and research in social cognition take too rational a view of human behavior; that they minimize, where they do not ignore, the effects of feelings, motives, and general affective states. The criticism has some justification. Only recently have social psychologists followed the lead of cognitive theorists such as Mandler (1984) by bringing thought and affect together in their work. In this chapter, I describe how investigators who study the role of schemas in social communication have begun to relate that research to the study of affect.

SCHEMAS AND SOCIAL COGNITION[1]

A *schema* is a network of interrelated elements that defines a concept for some individual. Schemas are abstract representations of environmental regularities. There are schemas for any object of cognition, including physical objects, interpersonal traits, regular sequences of actions, patterns of interpersonal relations, and abstract concepts.

The nature of schemas is probably conveyed better by examples than by abstract definition. Consider the schema for *tree:* It includes a set of elements—roots, a trunk, limbs, and leaves—all falling in a specified pattern of relations to each other. The elements of this schema, *leaf,* for example, may constitute schemas in their own right, with their own set of elements in specified patterns of

---

[1]This discussion of the nature and functions of schemas relies heavily on the work of Rumelhart and Ortony (1978), Rumelhart (1980), and Mandler (1984).

relations to one another. Usually, however, when we focus on a more general schema like *tree*, we treat its subschemas as undifferentiated elements.

Now consider the schema for the verb, *help*. It requires at least two individuals, a goal, and a problem. The schema specifies the relations among those elements; in particular, one of the individuals assists the other in attaining the goal. The schema for the trait *helpful*, applies to a person who consistently enters into this relationship with regard to a variety of other individuals, goals, and problems.

Schemas such as *balance* apply to patterns of interpersonal relations, i.e., to the expectations that friends will agree with each other and enemies disagree. The schema, or "script" (Schank & Abelson, 1977) for *restaurant* refers to a sequence of related behaviors that occur among a set of people and objects (customers, waiters, cooks, dishes, food, and so on) in a particular setting.

It is important to distinguish between generic schemas and their "instantiations." The generic schema is the abstract pattern of elements and relations that characterizes the concept of *tree*, or *helpful*, or *balance*, or *restaurant script*. An instantiation occurs when the pattern is objectified in some object or event that we experience. We hold in memory both the generic schemas, with which we interpret and understand events, and concrete instantiations, which constitute our representations of particular events.

Relations Among Schemas

Commonly, some schemas are embedded in other schemas. The schemas for *roots, trunk, limbs, leaves,* and so on are embedded in the schema for *tree* which, in turn, is embedded in the schema for *forest*.

In addition to such hierarchical relations among schemas, there are also horizontal, implicational relations among them. The quality *helpful*, for example, may imply, for a given perceiver, *ethical*, or *conscientious*, or *trusting*, or even *foolish*. Similarly, the schema *tree* commonly carries implications about *birds, nests, hammocks, picnics, rakes,* and the like.

Any individual's cognitive system contains an immense number of such schemas. Each of these is a bounded unit, composed of a set of elements that are connected by a specific pattern of relations. Some schemas are shared, in general form, by people of similar backgrounds. Others are unique to a single person. They develop over time in correspondence with regularities in a person's experiences.

Schema-Based Inferences

Schemas permit at least three types of inferences: *default* inferences, inferences about future events, and inferences to other schemas.

Default inferences are those that an activated schema yields about unobserved events or relations. Suppose, for example, that we watch a woman enter a restaurant, talk to a waiter, eat her food, smile at the waiter, and pay her bill. We are likely to infer, from the restaurant script, that she also examined the menu and ordered a meal, that the waiter brought her the food, that she drank from the water glass, that the waiter presented her with the bill, and that she tipped the waiter *even though we observed none of the last half dozen events.* Again, when we learn that Harry and Dan are friends and that Harry favors gun control legislation, we infer from the balance schema that Dan also favors gun control. Or when we have observed an automobile crash, a skillful lawyer's suggestion causes us to infer from our schema about accidents that glass from a broken headlight was strewn on the pavement. In all three examples, because the events were viewed as instantiating a relevant schema (the *restaurant script,* the *balance schema,* the *car wreck schema*) information that was not actually observed could be inferred, by default, as something that must have occurred for the schema to apply.

There is abundant evidence that, after our representation of an event has remained in memory for a period of time, we have trouble distinguishing inferred information from observed (cf. Bower, Black, & Turner, 1979; Loftus & Zanni, 1975; Picek, Sherman, & Shiffrin, 1975). It should be noted that default inferences may be over-written by observed values. As is seen later, a mismatch between default expectations and an observed value serves to draw attention to relevant aspects of the stimulus situation in the interests, no doubt, of accounting for the situation.

Schemas also provide inferences about the specific content of future events. Having attributed the quality *helpful* to an acquaintance, for example, we can predict that person's actions in any number of concrete situations. Similarly, scripts predict how people will behave in situations that instantiate the script.

In addition, the implicational relations from one schema to another, as previously discussed, may yield expectations that go far beyond the province of the initially activated schema. Thus, if we attribute the quality *helpful* to a person and infer from that quality that she is *conscientious,* then we have available a set of expectations about how the person will act at her office where we have never seen her in action.

Because of inferences like these, our representations in memory of situations often elaborate considerably on what we have observed. No doubt we recognize that some of these inferences go beyond the information given; if so, the expectations may be held tentatively instead of confidently. But other inferences are likely to be indistinguishable in memory form observed events and the consequent expectations are as firm as those based on direct observation.

The Role of Schemas in Information Processing

There is a reciprocal relation between the stimuli we observe and the schemas we use to understand them. On the one hand, sensory representations commonly activate one or more schemas directly; such processing is often said to be *bottom-*

up, or data-driven. On the other hand, expectations from activated schemas may initiate a search for particular types of information; this increases the chances that stimuli that fit the schema will be processed and decreases the chances of processing irrelevant or contradictory stimuli. Such processing is termed *top-down,* or conceptually driven. Social cognition involves a continuous mixture of bottom-up and top-down processing. In Neisser's (1976) term, there is a *perceptual cycle* in which the schema directs attempts at exploration, which produces a sampling from the available information, which modifies the schema, which directs more attempts at exploration, and on and on.

Often, commonly experienced stimuli automatically activate appropriate schemas in long-term memory, without the aid of conscious attention. Indeed, well-practiced and complex schemas may "run off" outside of conscious awareness. The activation of these schemas, the monitoring of schema-relevant information, the organization of action schemas, and the production of an organized sequence of actions all take place with little or no conscious attention. As a result, when we are walking to work or driving to town, if the route is uncongested and accidents do not occur, we can let our attention flit from topic to topic, or can concentrate on some problem of interest, while the complex behaviors of walking or driving are organized almost completely outside of awareness. In other words, several distinct sequences of information-appraisal and behavioral response may be active at once, some requiring little or no reflective awareness, others involving detailed, focused processing.[2]

Often, ambiguous or uninterpretable events require conscious attention as we try to find a schema or a set of related schemas that will help us understand them. For example, garbled speech, an indecipherable photograph, or a piece of obscure poetry call for explicit, conscious processing. Even a pronoun without an obvious referent, in an otherwise sensible bit of discourse, demands extra attention, as the reader attempts to puzzle out the meaning of a passage (Clark & Haviland, 1977).

When inferences from an activated schema are violated, our attention is especially likely to focus on the unexpected aspects of the situation. For instance, subjects who encounter an unbalanced pattern of interpersonal relations devote more attention to it than to a balanced pattern (Sentis & Burnstein, 1979). Similarly, if subjects have attributed a personality trait to someone else and then observe actions that contradict their trait-based expectations, they pay special attention to the contradictory behavior (Hastie, 1980; O'Sullivan & Durso, 1984; White & Carlston, 1983). This concentrated attention on the unexpected (a) makes sure that the expectations were actually violated by the behavior and (b) begins the task of finding a schema that will make sense of the present observations and earlier ones, as well.

---

[2]The distinction between automatic and controlled processing, and the relevant research literature, is discussed comprehensively by Shiffrin (in press)

These circumstances—ambiguous information that defies understanding or unambiguous violation of a schema-based expectation—commonly promote the refinement of old schemas and the development of new ones. No doubt we first try to interpret the information in terms of the initial schema (in Piaget's, 1970, terms, we try to *assimilate* the information to the schema). If that proves impossible, or if still further contradictions are observed, we probably search our repertoire for a different schema that will account for these observations; this would appear to be another form of assimilation of information to our existing cognitions. When assimilation fails, we have two alternatives available: to give up any attempt at dealing effectively with this information or to develop new schemas that will account for it (in Piaget's terms, to *accommodate* our cognitive system to the intransigent information).

Whether or not a more effective set of schemas will actually be worked out probably depends on a number of factors. These include the complexity of the disconfirming events, the frequency with which we must deal with them, the flexibility of our schemas, whether our associates or wise counselors can suggest explanations that makes sense of the events, and the like.

Application to Inferences During Communication

Most of the preceding examples involve the process of communication, provided we think of communication in general terms, as the information that is transferred, explicitly or by inference, from one person to another during an interpersonal exchange. By that definition, the impressions we form of others or the way we construe a pattern of interaction are the products of communication; so, of course, are the interpretations we make of oral or written discourse.

In this model, the receiver of a communication is seen as an active interpreter of events, one who seeks to arrive at a schema or set of schemas that will provide an understanding of the events at hand. The schemas that are initially activated in this process will be a joint function of (a) the information that becomes available to the perceiver about the events and (b) stored schemas relevant to the persons, objects, and context. Depending on the goodness-of-fit of the schematic interpretation to the observed data, the initial schemas may be retained, modified, or replaced. Revision of an interpretation, and retesting it against observed information is likely to continue until (a) the situation (or the perceiver) goes away or (b) a schema or set of schemas is found that accounts for the available information.

These processes need not be conscious. As Clark (1978) remarked about discourse processing, "Most strategies (people) have available for building, testing, and registering interpretations are quick and efficient and carried out without awareness. Much of the process can never be introspected about" (p. 298). Some of the testing and modification of schematic representations, and some of the inferences that are drawn from activated schemas, will involve the use of conscious processes; much, perhaps most, of this cognitive activity will occur outside of awareness.

The Role of Schemas in Action

The preceding discussion examines the role of schemas in interpreting and understanding external events. Schemas also guide the actions we take in those situations. Which people we talk to at a party and about what; how we approach an acquaintance for assistance; the way we address a waiter, our employer, or an old friend all reflect our schema-based expectations about ourselves, other participants, and situational constraints.

Practiced action patterns in a familiar context often run off without much forethought or attention. Actions involving the attainment of some goal commonly involve considerable thought and the development of a plan of action. Enactment of the plan involves a cognitive–behavioral–perceptual cycle consisting of a sequence of actions, assessments of the effects of those actions, consequent adjustments of the plan, production of an additional sequence of actions, and so on. The determining role of schemas in this process should be obvious.

Compared to the mass of research on the processing of information from the social environment, not much work has been done on the organization and initiation of communicative actions. Berger (chapter 6, this volume) presents an insightful approach to this problem.

Use of the Concept in Theory and Research:
Some Cautionary Words

The general concept *schema* speaks to the organization of thought; it is silent about the content of thought. When schema theorists talk about the relations among elements of a schema, default inferences, perceiver's expectations, and the like, they do not specify (except in examples) the specific nature of the elements, inferences or expectations. Content only enters the discussion when the concept is applied to a particular empirical context.

Proper application of this concept to the study of some problem requires us to specify the content of the schema that interests us. We must identify its elements and the relations among those elements, and make clear the kinds of expectations the schema provides, its connections to other schemas, and so on. This may be no great task for very specific schemas such as that for the *eye* or for the trait *punctual*. It is a manageable task for scripts (cf. Bower, Black, & Turner, 1979; Galambos, 1983; Schank & Abelson, 1977), for the balance schema (Heider, 1958), for clusters of related traits in a higher order schema like extravert–introvert (Cantor & Mischel, 1979) as well as for shared stereotypes like "Jesus freak" (O'Sullivan & Durso, 1984).

But there are other contexts to which we would like to apply the concept where the content remains to be mapped out. Indeed, some of the most interesting potential applications of the concept—to international stereotypes, for example, or to negotiating schemas—are of this type. In many of these applications, the precise content and structure of the schemas is problematic; also problematic is whether that content and structure is generally shared among members of some group or largely idiosyncratic. In such circumstances, it is tempting to use the concept to offer a plausible explanation for a set of events without testing the explanation empirically. As Allport (1980) commented about a different concept, such usage "soothes away curiosity by the appearance of providing an explanation, even before the data have been obtained" (p. 121).

There is nothing wrong with proposing that people employ schemas that correspond to broad and general concepts. Indeed, there is a great deal to be said in favor of such application, provided the validity of the proposal is tested empirically, not merely assumed. Without such tests, we risk using the concept so loosely that, in explaining everything, we account for nothing.

AFFECT AND ITS RELATION TO COGNITION

An *affective orientation* is a positive or negative inclination toward some object or situation. I use the concept inclusively, to embrace what Clark and Isen (1982) call "feeling states" as well as orientations toward specific objects, ideas, or events. By this definition, physiological arousal need not accompany an affective orientation: The term can encompass preferences that involve little or no emotional component as well as those with some considerable degree of associated arousal. No doubt some level of arousal is associated with affective orientations more often than not.

There is a division of opinion over whether cognitive and emotive systems are unified (cf. Lazarus, 1968, 1982, 1984) or independent (cf. Tomkins, 1982; Zajonc, 1980, 1984). I adopt Bower's (1981) position, which assumes the dependence of the two systems. No doubt, in the real world, the effects of affect and cognition interact and reinforce each other. For the sake of exposition, however, I first review evidence that schemas influence affect, then consider the effects of affect upon the activation of schemas.

Effects of Schemas upon Affect

Schematic processes can influence affective ones in a variety of ways. The most obvious is the identification of a particular stimulus—a pointed gun, a snarling dog, a loved one's face, a sequence of musical chords—that has been conditioned to some emotional response. As Hoffman (1986) pointed out, all that is needed to elicit affect in this manner is registration of the stimulus event and a minimum of perceptual organization. Bargh (chapter 2, this volume) reviews a variety of evidence that such identification need not achieve consciousness to have both cognitive and affective consequences.

In the following, I discuss four other schema-based sources of affect: The interpretation of unexplained arousal, the interruption of ongoing schemas, the evaluation of stimuli with complex attributes, and the polarization of evaluations after thought. The last of these serves as an example of the need to identify the specific content of schemas in order to study their effects upon cognition.

The Interpretation of Arousal.   In what has become a classic experiment, Schachter and Singer (1962) induced states of autonomic arousal in such a way that subjects were unable to account for their aroused condition. Depending on the social context in which they were placed—in a waiting room with a colleague who was either irate or comically boisterous—the subjects interpreted their state either as a negative emotion—anger, or as a positive one—elation. Their subsequent behavior corresponded to the emotion they had attributed to themselves.

Thus, the emotion associated with an unexplained state of arousal appears to vary with one's assessment of cues in the social context. A major reason for this is the similarity across different emotions of the underlying physiological state that constitutes autonomic arousal. Except for one or two special cases, like sex, it appears that emotions as diverse as joy, sadness, elation, and anger share much the same physiological base. In the usual case, people are seldom in the dark about the cause of their aroused feelings: The preceding events (winning a prize, losing $10, receiving a welcome invitation, being snubbed) provide an unambiguous accounting for the arousal. But when contextual cues do not unequivocally point to one emotion or another, as in psychological experiments like the one just discussed, cues from the environment or shifts in the individual's intentional state often permit the construction of an appropriate emotional attribution (Mandler, 1984). Note, however, that contextual cues do not always activate a schema explicit enough to account for unexplained arousal: All of us have experienced situations in which we knew we were tense and aroused but did not know why and felt only vague anxiety, perhaps, or diffuse tension.

The Interruption of Schemas.   The idea that the interruption of a plan of action will produce an emotional response has a long and honored history in psychological theory and research (Dollard, Doob, Miller, Mowrer, & Sears, 1939; Freud, 1975; Lewin, 1935; Zeigarnik, 1927). Mandler (1984) has analyzed this phenomenon using a cognitive theory that employs schema as a central concept.

Interruption, in Mandler's terms, is any failure of a current structure to handle the available evidence or the requirements for action (1984). Application of the term extends from the disconfirmation of schema-based expectations to the disruption of an organized plan of action. Any form of interruption, Mandler proposes, produces arousal of the autonomic nervous system. The degree of arousal is expected to vary with (a) the degree of organization of the structure and (b) the magnitude of discrepancy between event and structure. The emotion associated with an interruption-induced arousal may vary from fear, to anger, to surprise, to humor depending on the context in which the interruption occurs. Thus, complete blockage of an organized sequence may produce rage or despair, the disconfirmation of an expectation by a new acquaintance may produce surprise or curiosity, the unexpectedly early solution of a difficult puzzle may lead to elation, and so on.

The effects of context in such cases are expected to operate in the same way as in the research by Schachter and Singer (1962): Interruption of a schema produces general arousal; the cognitive appraisal of the causes and consequences of the interruption yields the specific emotion that is experienced.

Evaluation of Stimuli with Complex Attributes. Fiske and Pavelchak (1986) proposed a theoretical model to account for the evaluations that are made from a complex set of information about another person. In such cases, the perceiver sometimes learns or infers that the person belongs to a socially defined category such as professor, salesman, extravert, or schizophrenic. A higher order schema is commonly associated with such categories; these schemas embrace, as part of their definitions a set of personality traits. The schema for extravert, for example, embraces traits such as outgoing, friendly, energetic, loud, humorous, active, and the like. In the Fiske–Pavelchak model, each personality trait that a perceiver employs to describe others is assumed to be linked to an affective tag, which may vary from positive through neutral to negative. Each category label is, itself, linked to an affective tag; the evaluation associated with the category will not necessarily be the average of the evaluations of the individual traits that the higher order schema subsumes.

The authors distinguish between *piecemeal* and *category-based* processing of information about others. In piecemeal processing, the separate items of information about a person are assessed individually; the overall evaluation of the person will then be an algebraic function of the affective tags that are linked to the separate items of information. Category-based processing occurs when the perceiver assigns the other person to some social category. So long as other information about that person is not obviously inconsistent with the category, the evaluation of the person will correspond to the affective tag of the category, not to the tags of the separate items. Category-based processing is said to be relatively rapid and subsequent recall for category-based information is good; piecemeal processing is slower and recall of the information is relatively poor (Fiske, 1982; Fiske & Beattie, 1982).

The implications of this model are then developed in an impressive set of hypotheses about the differential effects of category-based and piecemeal processing. The authors present an imaginative approach to resolving a number of theoretical problems in the study of person perception. More generally, they have taken a valuable step toward uniting cognitive and affective concepts in a theoretical framework that is similar to those of Bower (1981) and Clark and Isen (1982).

Polarization of Evaluations After Thought.   Tesser and his colleagues (e.g., Sadler & Tesser, 1973; Tesser & Conlee, 1975; Tesser & Cowan, 1977; Tesser & Leone, 1977) conducted a series of experiments on the effects of thinking about an experience upon the polarization of affect toward the object of the experience. A representative example of this work is the experiment by Tesser and Leone (1977). Subjects read a set of traits that was said to characterize either a particular person or a group of people and then recorded their evaluations of the person or group. Some subjects then thought about the person (or group) for 90 seconds; others performed a 90-second distractor task; and all subjects then recorded their evaluations of the person a second time. Those who spent the interval thinking about the other person's character produced second evaluations that were more polarized than their initial judgments; those who thought about a group, and also those who performed the distractor task, did not produce more polarized second evaluations.

Tesser (1980; Tesser & Leone, 1977) proposed that these results occurred because people have better-developed schemas about individuals than about groups. He argued that thought about a person induces polarization by (a) adding evaluatively consistent cognitions to what the person knows, (b) reinterpreting inconsistent cognitions, and (c) suppressing inconsistent cognitions. But these effects require a well-developed schema that can serve as a "blueprint" for such changes; without a schema concerning the traits of groups, thinking about a group's character does not produce polarization of evaluations. It should be clear that the results of Tesser's experiments did not reflect a difference between category-based and piecemeal processing. Whereas the Fiske–Pavelchak model pertains to immediate evaluations from a set of information, Tesser's effects occur when the perceiver mulls over a set of information after having made an initial evaluation.

Note that Tesser and his associates did not observe the nature of the schemas their subjects were using. Instead, they relied on well-established evidence that people have implicit theories of what traits go together in individual personalities (Rosenberg & Sedlak, 1972). In addition, Britton and Tesser (1982) showed that trait information is processed more efficiently about an individual than about a group. But research by Linville (1982; Linville & Jones, 1980) cast doubt on Tesser's interpretation by employing a measure of the structure of subjects' cognitions about people.

Using a modification of Scott's (1962) information-theory statistic, H, Linville (1982) obtained a measure of the complexity of college students' cognitions of young people and of the elderly. They held more complex cognitions about young adults than about the elderly. If this measure of complexity reflects the presence of better-developed schemas about young people than about the elderly, then by Tesser's reasoning these subjects should form more extreme impressions of a young person than of an old one. But Linville's results were just the opposite. When the same actions were ascribed to young adults as to elderly ones, impressions of the elderly were significantly more extreme than those of the young. Further, there was a significant inverse relation between the complexity of subjects' cognitions about the elderly and the extremeness of their impressions. Thus, the Linville results appear to contradict Tesser's interpretation.

The apparent contradiction is resolved when one examines the measure that Linville employed. As Judd and Lusk (1984) pointed out, this is a measure of the number of independent dimensions subjects employ in their judgments of young and old people. To repeat an earlier definition, a *schema* is a network of elements (e.g., people, objects, attributes, goals, beliefs, and the like) that are linked to one another by relations (e.g., implication, similarity, and so on) Clearly, Linville's measure does not correspond to that definition; instead, it reflects the number of independent dimensions along which elements of the schemas associated with young and old adults can be assessed.

Better examples of schemas are the kinds of categories Fiske and Pavelchak (1986) discussed. Thus, the schema for *professor* contains a number of traits, some patterns of behavior, a set of complementary roles, and a pattern of relations among those elements. Other categories contain other elements, all related to one another in more-or-less complex fashion. Brewer, Dull and Lui (1981) have shown that no single schema characterizes college students' impressions of the elderly; Schmidt and Boland (1986) concur; they identified a dozen distinct social categories that college students used to describe the elderly. Different categories evoked very different affective judgments. No doubt college students employ many more categories to describe young adults than old ones (O'Sullivan & Durso, 1984). Each such category connotes a cluster of related traits, beliefs, interests, goals, and other qualities, and a pattern of relations among those elements. That is, each category identifies a shared social schema.

Judd and Lusk (1984) pursued a similar line of thought by noting that Linville's (1982) measure referred to the number of independent dimensions underlying subjects' cognitions, but Tesser (1980) proposed that the effects of developed schemas were mediated by correlations among the elements of a schema. They hypothesized, therefore, that Linville's result (an inverse relation between the number of dimensions and polarization) would hold when the dimensions of a category were uncorrelated and Tesser's result (a direct relation between the number of dimensions and polarization) when the dimensions were correlated. The hypothesis was confirmed in both an experimental test and a multivariate analysis of attitudes toward sororities and rock bands.

These considerations lead to a slight modification of Tesser's (1980) position: When an observer categorizes another person in terms of a well-developed schema, further thought about the impression will produce polarization of the evaluation so long as the elements of the schema are linked with affective tags that point in the same direction. When a set of information may be ordered to many different subschemas (as when ambiguous information is attributed to "young adult" instead of to some more specific category) thinking about that person's characteristics will not produce polarization of the evaluation. Only when cues in the context or the experimenter's instructions prime a particular schema is thought-induced polarization likely to occur for a domain rich in subschemas. Millar and Tessar (in press) have also implicated commitment to a positive or negative impression as a determinant of the polarizing effect of thought.

Summary

A variety of ways have been demonstrated by which schematic processing evokes affect. The simplest of these is the identification, sometimes without conscious awareness, of a stimulus that is directly associated with an emotional response; the basis of such associations may be either innate or conditioned. More complex relations between schemas and affect include the use of contextual cues to find a schema that explains an undifferentiated state of arousal for which no explanation was previously available.

Interruption of an ongoing schema also appears to evoke affect; its magnitude depends on the importance of the interrupted task and the degree of disruption; the specific affect that is experienced will vary with the context that surrounds the interruption. A fourth linkage between schemas and affect is postulated by Fiske and Pavelchak (1986), who propose that each element of a category, as well as the category label, is linked to an affective tag; these authors then trace out the differential effects of processing the information in terms of the category as a unit, as compared to processing in terms of the individual elements. Finally, Tesser's (1980) results suggest that thinking about a person who fits a well-developed schema may produce increased polarization of one's attitude toward that person.

Some of these evoked affective states may be mild ones; others may be intense; in either case, activation of a particular schema, or processing of a set of information in the light of a schema has been shown to evoke affective responses in the perceiver. One problem that has plagued previous research on these problems has been the failure to identify the elements of schemas and their relations. Another problem is to specify how the connection between schemas and affect takes place; let us turn to a discussion of that problem.

Theoretical Account of the Connection Between Schemas and Affect

Clearly, any model that proposes to explain the connection between schemas and affect should also work for the reverse connection, between affect and schemas. The Fiske—Pavelchak model previously described, operates in the first direction only, although it could easily be modified to account for affect-schema connections. Such a modification would make the model very similar to those developed by Bower (1981) and by Clark and Isen (1982). I summarize Bower's model here.

Bower (1981) extended associative network theory (e.g., Anderson, 1983; Anderson & Bower, 1973) from a model that includes only cognitions and the relations among them to one that includes both cognitive and affective components. Associative network theories propose that human knowledge can be represented as a network of "nodes," corresponding to concepts, and "links," or associations among the concepts. A concept is said to enter consciousness when its "activation" exceeds a certain level, either by the presentation of the corresponding stimulus or by activation from an associated concept. Activation is presumed to spread from one node to another along the links between nodes in the network. Thus, the activation of one or more related nodes can initiate the activation of the entire pattern as a unit. The use of schemas as units of tightly linked nodes was proposed by Anderson (1980).[3]

Bower's modification represents each emotion, as well as each cognition, as a node in memory. Linked to each emotion node are autonomic reactions, standard behaviors for expressing the emotion, descriptions of situations that evoke the emotion, verbal labels assigned to it, and propositions describing events in the person's life when the emotions were aroused. Also linked to positive or negative emotions, as appropriate, are those concepts and schemas with evaluative connotations. Thinking about events or schemas that are linked to an emotion node increases the likelihood that the associated affect will be activated.

Thus, if a trait such as *helpful* is linked to a positive emotion node, then attributing that trait to another person will render the evaluation of that person more positive by virtue of the activation from the associated emotion. Similarly, a particular emotion will be inferred to account for a general, unexplained state of autonomic arousal provided cues in the context activate schemas that are unequivocally linked to a particular emotion node. Likewise, the review of a well-developed schema that has been instantiated in an impression of another person will polarize the evalution of that person provided the emotion nodes that are linked to the elements of that schema are predominantly positive or negative.

EFFECTS OF AFFECTIVE ORIENTATIONS ON SCHEMAS[4]

There is abundant evidence that emotional experiences are often memorable ones. Brown and Kulik (1977) described the detailed "flashbulb memories" that people commonly retain of the circumstances surrounding unexpected and emotionally involving events. Matlin (1983) comments that after the details of an event have faded from memory we can often still recall our emotional reaction to

---

[3]See Anderson (1984) for a succinct summary of associative network theory and a comparison of four such theories to one another.

[4]Isen (1984) and Hoffman (1986) have recently reviewed at length the effects of affect upon cognition; the present review is a selective one.

the event. But the question to be addressed in this section is not whether affect is memorable but how it affects (a) the kinds of schemas a person employs and (b) the effectiveness with which the person employs them.

Effects of Affect on the Kinds of Schemas Employed

Left to themselves, people are more likely to access positive rather than negative material. Matlin and Stang (1978), for example, reviewed 52 studies in which people recalled items that varied in pleasantness; in 39 of these, significantly more pleasant items were recalled than unpleasant ones; furthermore, pleasant items appeared earlier in the recalled lists than unpleasant ones.

Varying affective experiences above or below the somewhat positive norm affects the schemas that people employ to interpret experienced events. Thus, compared to the ratings of control groups, subjects who are feeling happy or elated rate ambiguous scenes positively and those who are angry or depressed rate the same scenes negatively (Forest, Clark, Mills, & Isen, 1979). Schiffenbauer (1974) observed parallel effects of positive and negative emotions on ratings of other people's ambiguous facial expressions.

Similar effects are found for recall of events from memory, although the effects differ with the quality of the affect. Teasdale and Fogarty (1979) induced happy or sad emotions and then asked subjects to recall either happy or sad events after being prompted by a neutral word; reaction times were faster when the valence of the events they were to recall matched their mood. There is substantial evidence that positive affect induces the recall of positively valenced material (Bartlett et al., 1982; Bower et al., 1982; Isen et al., 1978; Nasby & Yando, 1982; Natale & Hantas, 1982; Teasdale, Taylor, & Fogarty, 1980). Negative affect also promotes the recall of negative material, but the extent of affect-congruent recall is much less for negative than for positive affect. The probable reason is people's motivation to maintain a generally positive mood (Hoffman, 1986; Isen, Shalker, Clark, & Karp, 1978); one way of altering a negative mood to a positive one is to recall positive material (Zillmann, chapter 8, this volume).

Yet another important connection between affect and cognition involves processes pertaining to the person's self. Hoffman (1986), Zajonc (1980), and others have commented on the intimate relationship between the self and affect. On the one hand, threats to the self arouse negative affect and support for the self produces positive affect. Conversely, intense emotional reactions of any sort commonly come to be associated with the individual's self-concept.

The associative network model previously outlined accounts readily for these effecfs. When a particular emotion is activated, subthreshold activation will occur at its associated nodes; among the nodes receiving such activation will be those representing the schemas and events associated with that emotion node. Thus, schemas and other cognitive materials that are tagged with that emotion will be primed for both the identification of mood-congruent stimulus material and for the recall of congruent material from memory.

Arousal and the Effectivenss of Schematic Processing

Yerkes and Dodson (1908) postulated an inverted-U relation between arousal and performance. Both very low and very high levels of arousal were said to produce low efficiency; moderate arousal was said to produce optimal efficiency. Further, Yerkes and Dodson proposed that the optimal level of arousal would vary inversely with the complexity of the task: for simple tasks, a high level of arousal may be optimal; for complex tasks the optimal arousal level will be lower. Easterbrook (1959) proposed that the mechanism underlying the Yerkes–Dodson Law is that increased arousal diminishes the range of cues people attend to; that is, at low levels of arousal, people attend to irrelevant cues, which diminishes performance while, at high levels of arousal, they ignore relevant cues, which also diminishes performance.

Tests of the Yerkes–Dodson Law make things look much more muddled than the law predicts. For one thing, there are cognitive mechanisms that can modulate the effects of arousal so that the effects on attention of intense anxiety, say, are not as great as one would expect (Broadbent, 1971; Eysenck, 1982). On the other hand, undertaking a task is itself arousing, so that what should be low-arousal conditions may be transformed by a subject's self-directed intention into moderate-arousal conditions.

Second, different sources of arousal affect different processes differently. Eysenck (1984) suggests that virtually all sorts of arousal increase attentional selectivity and most sorts also increase speed at the expense of accuracy. However, different kinds of arousal have different effects on other processes. For example, high incentives decrease distractibility but high anxiety increase it; noise and anxiety at high levels decrease attentional capacity, whereas incentive increases it. These and other complexities demonstrate that no functional relationship as simple as the Yerkes–Dodson Law is adequate to describe the effects of arousal in general on cognitive performance.

Nevertheless, very high levels of arousal do diminish the quality of performance on complex tasks. Very little recent work has extended the study of this problem to the field of social cognition. Rosenbach, Crockett, and Wapner (1973) presented ambivalent information about a person to subjects who held a strong affective orientation, either positive or negative, toward that person; subjects selected elements from the information that matched their positive or negative orientation and ignored elements that were of incongruent valence. In addition, subjects who were not emotionally involved with the person employed relatively high-level schemas to unify the bivalent information in an organized impression, but emotionally involved subjects formed one-sided positive or negative impressions of the other person. These results may be seen as an example of the deleterious effects of strong emotion on people's use of complex schemas to deal with complex phenomena.

The effects of different kinds of emotions, and of variations in such emotions, on cognitive processes need to be studied across a range of content. And this research should examine not only the effects of emotional arousal on the processing of stimulus information or the retrieval of information from memory, but also its effects on the initiation and performance of communicative acts.

SUMMARY AND CONCLUSIONS

There is a growing body of literature that ties the use of social schemas to the experience of affect. The effects operate in both directions; no doubt the two types of effects interact, as well. One theoretical model to account for these reciprocal effects proposes that various emotions are represented by nodes in memory that are linked both to cognitive structures, including schemas, and to autonomic responses and expressive behaviors. Activation of the emotion nodes will then facilitate activation of associated cognitive structures and vice versa.

Schemas influence affect in a variety of ways. The identification of objects that have been conditioned to an emotional response will evoke the relevant emotion; indeed, familiar objects that have not previously been conditioned to emotional responses tend to evoke positive affect (Zajonc, 1968). Unexplained states of arousal may lead to the self-attribution of either positive or negative emotions, depending on cues in the surrounding context. The disruption of an ongoing schema is itself arousing; the emotion associated with such arousal may be either positive or negative, depending on cues in the surrounding context. Finally, thinking about one's impression of a person who is categorized by a well-developed schema produces a polarization of affect, provided the schema's constituent elements share the same general evaluation.

Conversely, affective orientations influence the kinds of schemas that are applied to ambiguous patterns of stimuli or that are recalled from memory. It is not necessary for the affect to be intense for effects upon cognition to occur. Clark and Isen (1982) pointed out that "feeling states" have pronounced effects on thought and actions (see also Sypher & Sypher, this volume). "Unlike strong emotion, these states do not interrupt our thought and behavior; rather, they gently color and redirect ongoing thoughts and actions, influencing what will happen next but almost without notice and certainly without changing the context or basic activity" (Isen, 1984, pp. 186–187). Of course, intense emotions also affect thought and actions at least as greatly as do affect-free feeling states.

Beyond this, it appears that strong arousal interferes with the effective employment of complex schematic structures. Such interference probably reflects a progressive narrowing of attention as arousal increases, supplemented by an increase in the speed and intensity of responses and a decrease in their accuracy.

Whether these effects of intense arousal are general across all types of emotions, which schematic and communication processes they effect, and how their effects are mediated remains to be explored in detail.

REFERENCES

Allport, D. A. (1980). Attention and performance. In G. Claxton (Ed.), *Cognitive psychology: New directions*. London: Routledge & Kegan Paul.

Anderson, J. R. (1980). Concepts, propositions, and schemata: What are the cognitive units? In J. H. Flowers (Ed.), *Nebraska symposium on motivation* (Vol. 28, pp. 241–275). Lincoln, NE: University of Nebraska Press.

Anderson, J. R. (1983). A spreading activation theory of memory. *Journal of Verbal Learning and Verbal Behavior, 22,* 261–295.

Anderson, J. R. (1984). Spreading activation. In J. R. Anderson & S. M. Kosslyn (Eds.), *Tutorials in learning and memory* (pp. 105–144). San Francisco: W. H. Freeman.

Anderson. J. R., & Bower, G. H. (1973). *Human associative memory*. Washington, DC: Hemisphere Press.

Bower, G. H. (1981). Mood and memory. *American Psychologist, 36,* 129–148.

Bower, G. H., Black, J. B. & Turner, T. J. (1979). Scripts in memory for text. *Cognitive psychology, 11,* 177–220.

Brewer, M. B., Dull, V., & Lui, L. (1981). Perceptions of the elderly: Stereotypes as prototypes. *Journal of Personality and Social Psychology, 41,* 656–670.

Britton, B. K., & Tesser, A. (1982). Effects of prior knowledge on use of cognitive capacity in three complex cognitive tasks. *Journal of Verbal Learning and Verbal Behavior, 24,* 421–436.

Broadbent, D. E. (1971). *Decision and stress*. London: Academic Press.

Brown, R., & Kulik, J. (1977). Flashbulb messages. *Cognition, 5,* 73–99.

Cantor, N., & Mischel, W. (1979). Prototypes in person perception. In L. Berkowitz (Ed.), *Advances in experimental social psychology* (Vol. 12). New York: Academic Press.

Clark, H. H. (1978). Inferring what is meant. In W. J. M. Levelt & G. B. Flores d'Arcais (Eds.), *Studies in the perception of language*. New York: Wiley.

Clark, H. H., & Haviland, S. E. (1977). Comprehension and the given-new contract. In R. O. Freedle (Ed.), *Discourse production and comprehension*. Norwood, NJ: Ablex.

Clark, M. S., & Isen, A. M. (1982). Toward understanding the relationship between feeling states and social behavior. In A. Hastorf & A. M. Isen (Eds.), *Cognitive social psychology*. Amsterdam: Elsevier-North Holland.

Dollard, J., Doob, L., Miller, N. E., Mowrer, O. H., & Sears, R. (1939). *Frustration and aggression* New Haven: Yale University Press.

Easterbrook, J. A. (1959). The effect of emotion on cue utilization and the organization of behavior. *Psychological Review, 66,* 183–201.

Eysenck, M. W. (1982). *Attention and arousal: Cognition and performance*. Berlin: Springer.

Eysenck, M. W. (1984). *A handbook of cognitive psychology*. Hillsdale, NJ: Lawrence Erlbaum Associates.

Fiske, S. T. (1982). Schema-triggered affect: Applications to social perception. In M. S. Clark & S. T. Fiske (Eds.), *Affect and cognition. The 17th annual Carnegie Symposium on Cognition*. Hillsdale, NJ: Lawrence Erlbaum Associates.

Fiske, S. T., & Beattie, A. E. (1982, September). *Two modes of processing affect in social cognition*. Paper presented at the American Psychological Association, Washington, DC.

Fiske, S. T., & Pavelchak, M. A. (1986). Category-based versus piecemeal-based affective responses: Developments in schema-triggered affect. In R. M. Sorrentino & E. T. Higgins (Eds.), *Handbook of motivation and cognition: Foundations of social behavior.* New York: Guildford.

Forest, D., Clark, M. S., Mills, J., & Isen, A. M. (1979). Helping as a function of feeling state and nature of the helping behavior. *Motivation and Emotion, 3,* 161–169.

Freud, S. (1975). *Inhibitions, symptoms, and anxiety.* (Vol. 20). London: Hogarth Press.

Galambos, J. A. (1983). Normative studies of six characteristics of our knowledge of common activities. *Behavior Research Methods and Instrumentation, 15,* 327–340.

Hastie, R. (1980). Memory for behavioral information that confirms or contradicts a personity impression. In R. Hastie, T. M. Ostrom, E. B. Ebbesen, R. S. Wyer, D. L. Hamilton, & D. E. Carlston, (Eds.), *Person memory: The cognitive basis of social perception.* Hillsdale, NJ: Lawrence Erlbaum Associates.

Heider, F. (1958). *The psychology of interpersonal relations.* New York: Wiley.

Hoffman, M. L. (1986). Affect, cognition, and motivation. In R. M. Sorrentino & E. T. Higgins (Eds.), *Handbook of motivation and cognition: Foundations of social behavior.* New York: Guildford.

Isen, A. M. (1984). Toward understanding the role of affect in cognition. In R. W. Wyer & T. Srull (Eds.), *Handbook of social cognition.* Hillsdale, NJ: Lawrence Erlbaum Associates.

Isen, A. M., Shalker, T. E., Clark, M., & Karp, L. (1978). Affect, accessibility of material in memory, and behavior: A cognitive loop? *Journal of personality and social psychology, 36,* 1–12.

Judd, C. M., & Lusk, C. M. (1984). Knowledge structures and evaluative judgments: Effects of structural variables on judgment extremity. *Journal of Personality and Social Psychology, 46,* 331–338.

Lazarus, R. S. (1968). Emotions and adaptation: Conceptual and empirical relations. In W. J. Arnold (Ed.), *Nebraska Symposium on Motivation.* Lincoln, NE: University of Nebraska Press.

Lazarus, R. S. (1982). Thoughts on the relations between emotion and cognition. *American Psychologist, 37,* 1019–1024.

Lazarus, R. S. (1984). On the primacy of cognition. *American Psychologist, 39,* 124–129.

Lewin, K. (1935). *A dynamic theory of personality.* New York: McGraw-Hill.

Linville, P. W. (1982). The complexity-extremity effect and age-based stereotyping. *Journal of Personality and Social Psychology, 42,* 193–211.

Linville, P. W., & Jones, E. E. (1980). Polarized appraisals of outgroup members. *Journal of Personality and Social Psychology, 38,* 689–703.

Loftus, E. F., & Zanni, G. (1975). Eyewitness testimony: The influence of the wording of a question. *Bulletin of the Psychonomic Society, 5,* 86–88.

Mandler, G. (1984). *Mind and body: Psychology of emotion and stress.* New York: Norton.

Matlin, M. W. (1983). *Cognition.* New York: Holt, Rinehart & Winston.

Matlin, M. W., & Stang, D. J. (1978). *The Polyanna principle: Selectivity in language, memory, and thought.* Cambridge, MA: Schenkman.

Millar, M. G., & Tesser, A. (in press). Thought-induced attitude change: The effects of schema structure and commitment. *Journal of Personality and Social Psychology.*

Neisser, U. (1976). *Cognition and reality.* San Francisco: Freeman.

O'Sullivan, C. S., & Durso, F. T. (1984). Effect of schema-incongruent information on memory for stereotypical attributes. *Journal of Personality and Social Psychology, 47,* 55–70.

Piaget, J. (1970). Piaget's theory. In P. Mussen (Ed.). *Carmichael's manual of child psychology* (Vol. 1). London: Routledge & Kegan Paul.

Picek, J. S., Sherman, S. J., & Shiffrin, R. M. (1975). Cognitive organization and encoding of social structures. *Journal of Personality and Social Psychology, 31,* 758–768.

Rosenbach, D., Crockett, W. H., & Wapner, S. (1973). Developmental level, emotional involvement, and the resolution of inconsistgency in impression formation. *Developmental Psychology, 9,* 120–130.

Rosenberg, S., & Sedlak, A. (1972). Structural representations of implicit personality theory. In L. Berkowitz (Ed.), *Advances in experimental social psychology* (Vol. 6, pp. 114–147). New York: Academic Press.

Rumelhart, D. E. (1980). Schemata: The building blocks of cognition. In R. Spiro, B. Bruce, & W. Brewer (Eds.) *Theoretical issues in reading comprehension* (pp. 249–291). Hillsdale, NJ: Lawrence Erlbaum Associates.

Rumelhart, D. E., & Ortony, A. (1978). The representation of knowledge in memory. In R. C. Anderson, R. J. Spiro, & W. E. Montague (Eds.), *Schooling and the acquisition of knowledge.* Hillsdale, NJ: Lawrence Erlbaum Associates.

Sadler, O., & Tesser, A. (1973). Some effects of salience and time upon interpersonal hostility and attraction during social interaction *Sociometry, 36,* 99–112.

Schachter, S., & Singer, J. E. (1962). Cognitive, social, and psychological determinants of emotional state. *Psychological Review, 69,* 379–399.

Schank, R., & Abelson, R. (1977). *Scripts, plans, goals, and understanding: An inquiry into human knowledge structures.* Hillsdale, NJ: Lawrence Erlbaum Associates.

Schiffenbauer, A. (1974). Effects of observer's emotional state on judgments of the emotional state of others. *Journal of Personality and Social Psychology, 30,* 31–35.

Schmidt, D. F., & Boland, S. M. (1986). *The structure of perceptions of older adults: Evidence for multiple stereotypes.* Unpublished manuscript, Washington University, St. Louis, MO.

Scott, W. A. (1962). Cognitive complexity and cognitive flexibility. *Sociometry, 25,* 405–414.

Sentis, K. P., & Burnstein, E. (1979). Remembering schema-oconsistent information: Effects of a balance schema on recognition memory. *Journal of Personality and Social Psychology, 37,* 2200–2211.

Shiffrin, R. M. (in press). Attention. In R. C. Atkinson, R. J. Herrnstein, G. Lindzey, & R. D. Luce (Eds.), *Stevens' handbook of experimental psychology,* (2nd ed., pp. 314–354). New York: Wiley.

Teasdale, J. D., & Fogarty, S. J. (1979). Differential effects of induced mood on retrieval of pleasant and unpleasant affects from episodic memory. *Journal of Abnormal Psychology, 88,* 248–257.

Tesser, A. (1980). Self-generated attitude change. In L. Berkowitz (Ed.), *Advances in experimental social psychology,* (Vol. 11, pp. 85–117). New York: Academic Press.

Tesser, A., & Conlee, M. C. (1975). Some effects of time and thought on attitude polarization. *Journal of Personality and Social Psychology, 31,* 262–270.

Tesser, A., & Cowan, C. L. (1977). Some attitudinal and cognitive consequences of thought. *Journal of Research in Personality, 11,* 216–226.

Tesser, A., & Leone, C. (1977). Cognitive schemas and thought as determinants of attitude change. *Journal of Experimental Social Psychology, 13,* 340–356.

Tomkins, S. S. (1982). Affect theory. In P. Ekman (Ed.), *Emotion in the human face* (2nd ed., pp. 127–161). Cambridge, England: Cambridge University Press.

White, J. V., & Carlston, D. E. (1983). Consequences of schemata for attention, impressions, and recall in complex social interactions. *Journal of Personality and Social Psychology, 45,* 538–549.

Yerkes, R. M., & Dodson, D. (1908). The relation of strength of stimulus to rapidity of habit formation. *Journal of Comparative and Neurological Psychology, 18,* 459–482.

Zajonc, R. B. (1968). The attitudinal effects of mere exposure. *Journal of Personality and Social Psychology, 9,* 1–27.

Zajonc, R. B. (1980). Feeling and thinking: Preferences need no inferences. *American Psychologist, 35,* 151–175.

Zajonc, R. B. (1984). On the primacy of affect. *American Psychologist, 39,* 102–103.

Zeigarnik, B. (1927). Das Behalten erledigter und unerledigter Handlungen. *Psychologische Forschung, 9,* 1–85.

4

Motivation and Affect in Interpersonal Relations: The Role of Personal Orientations and Discrepancies

C. Douglas McCann
York University

E. Tory Higgins
New York University

> *Affect dominates social interaction, and it is the major currency in which social interaction is transacted.*
> —Zajonc, 1980, p. 153

Recent developments in several areas of psychology have highlighted a concern with the relation between affect and cognition. Although traditional research has tended to focus on one or the other of these factors, there is growing recognition that further progress depends on more precise specification of the relation between them. This concern is, of course, not new (e.g., Cannon, 1927; Freud, 1923/1961; James, 1890/1948). What has changed, however, is the realization that understanding their interrelation is not only useful but necessary (see Sorrentino & Higgins, 1986).

This issue has received increasing attention in a number of areas. Researchers in social psychology, for example, have evidenced an accelerating interest in cognitive analyses of social behavior and perception (Fiske, 1982; Hastie, Ostrom, Ebbesen, Wyer, Hamilton, & Carlston, 1980; Higgins, Herman, & Zanna 1981; Isen, 1984; Wyer & Srull, 1984, Vol. 1, 2, & 3). This interest in social cognition, or the processes involved in knowing self and others, has increasingly focused on the role of affect in such phenomena and its relation to cognitive processes (see Bower, 1981; Buck, 1985; Higgins, Kuiper, & Olson, 1981; Markus & Zajonc, 1985; Showers & Cantor, 1985; Sorrentino & Higgins, 1986). This has raised a variety of issues including the primacy or independence of the two types of systems (e.g., Lazarus, 1982, 1984; Zajonc, 1980, 1984).

Similar concerns have recently been manifested in clinical psychology.

Clinical psychologists, of course, traditionally have been interested in affect and cognition, or more precisely, disturbances in affect and cognition. The recent clinical literature has also shown an increasing interest in information-processing models of dysfunctional behavior (e.g., Beck, 1976) and the relation between cognitive and affective factors in psychopathology and psychotherapy (e.g., Coyne & Gotlib, 1983; Gotlib & McCann, 1984; Greenberg & Safran, 1984; Ingram, 1984).

A final area, whose theoretical and empirical efforts relate to an examination of affect and cognition, is the study of interpersonal relationships. The study of interpersonal relationships has recently evidenced a resurgence of interest (e.g., Brehm, 1985; Duck, 1982, 1984; Duck & Gilmour, 1981a, 1981b, 1981c; Kelley, 1979; Kelley et al., 1983). This research orientation has taken as an explicit focus what is implied in the beginning quotation. That is, interpersonal relations are seen to be replete with affect and are, therefore, a natural environment in which to explore affect both as a causal and consequent factor.

Traditional research in this area focused on the determinants of affect associated with interpersonal attraction and with affect as a "transaction commodity" (e.g., Gaelick, Bodenhausen, & Wyer, 1985; Gottman, 1979; Noller, 1985; Pike & Sillars, 1985). Other recent formulations have turned to a specification of how interaction engenders affect and the role played by cognitive factors in this process (e.g., Abelson, 1983; Berscheid, 1983; Kelley, 1984).

Even from this brief review, it is clear that an examination of the relation between affective and cognitive factors is central to the work in a variety of areas of psychology. This literature suggests a convergence of interests, as well as the fact that an appropriate avenue for further exploration of the relation between affect and cognition would be in the context of interpersonal relations. To do so in this chapter we draw upon and integrate formulations derived from social cognition, clinical psychology, and research on close relations. We present two frameworks for considering the link between affect and cognition: one derived from our previous work on the "communication-game" model of interpersonal communication (e.g., Higgins, 1981; McCann & Higgins, 1984) and the other derived from "self-discrepancy" theory (e.g., Higgins, Klein, & Strauman, 1985; Higgins, McCann, Gavin & Foxall, 1986).

The communication-game model focuses on the goal-oriented nature of interpersonal interaction. Although the model considers affect implicitly in terms of the various affect-relevant goals that guide message production (e.g., social relationship goals, face goals, etc.), we integrate it with recent work in other areas that make more salient the affective implications of interpersonal events that facilitate or inhibit goal attainment. In these models, affective experience is seen to result from the incongruence or discrepancy between goal-based expectancies and what actually happens in an interaction episode. Thus, quality and intensity of affective experience is seen to depend on the discrepancy between expected (or imagined) events and actually experienced events (e.g., Ableson, 1983; Berscheid, 1983; Kelley, 1984; Mandler, 1975; Srull & Wyer, 1986). In the second part of this chapter we focus on the implications of another type of discrepancy for affective experience. More specifically, we focus on the implications of self-discrepancy theory (Higgins, 1985) for affective experience in interpersonal relations (Higgins, McCann, Gavin, & Foxall, 1986). Recent models of the self have suggested the existence of multiple selves (e.g., Greenwald & Pratkanis, 1984; Higgins, 1985; Kihlstrom & Cantor, 1981; Markus & Nurius, 1986). Although this idea is not new (e.g., James, 1890/1948, self-discrepancy theory specifically addresses the implications of discrepancy between different ''selves'' or self-state representations for emotional experience. Previous work by Higgins and his colleagues (e.g., Higgins, Bond, Klein, & Strauman, 1986) suggests that individuals' vulnerability to different kinds of discomfort is a function of the type and degree of self-discrepancies they possess. In the second part of this chapter we extend this formulation to individuals' experience of specific emotions in their interpersonal relations with significant others.

GOAL-ORIENTED INTERACTION AND AFFECT

Interest in specifying the variables that influence how individuals interact with others in their social environment has led students of social interaction to examine a wide variety of factors ranging from relatively impersonal role and normative prescriptions to the very personal constructions of social reality. Common to these approaches, however, is the search for those explanatory concepts that can account for both the diversity and consistency evidenced in everyday social interaction.

In this section, we focus on one such concept, social goals. In the present context, the term *social goals* refers to the interpersonal objectives that individuals pursue in their interactions with others (McCann, Breckler, & Devine, 1986). While having obvious implications for social behavior, social goals also are seen to have direct and indirect social–cognitive effects and are linked to affective experiences through their associations with interpersonal relations and expectancies.

Recent formulations of social behavior have emphasized the strategic nature of social interaction. From this perspective, interpersonal behavior is enacted in pursuit of specific personal objectives (e.g., Argyle & Kendon, 1967; Athay & Darley, 1981; Goffman, 1959; Higgins, 1981; McCann & Hancock, 1983; McCann & Higgins, 1984; Miller, Galanter, & Pribram, 1960). Although the concept of goal has been invoked in analyses of a wide variety of substantive issues much of its current interest derives from its implications for social behavior and social cognition (see Cohen, 1981; McCann & Higgins, 1984; Srull & Wyer, 1986; Zukier, 1986). We illustrate this focus by considering our own recent research on the communication game.

The Communication Game

Communication is intimately involved in all forms of interpersonal interaction. Surprisingly, social psychologists have shown a relative lack of interest in this phenomenon except for work on information transmission and persuasion (see Higgins, 1981; Kraut & Higgins, 1984; McGuire, 1969, 1985). Interpersonal communication is multipurposed, however, and serves not only to transmit information but also to establish and maintain relationships between participants (Blumer, 1961; Garfinkel, 1967; Gumperz & Hymes, 1972; Hawes, 1973; Watzlawick, Beavin, & Jackson, 1967). In the communication game, interpersonal communication is conceptualized as purposeful social interaction occurring within a socially defined context, involving interdependent social roles and conventional rules, strategies, and tactics for making decisions and obtaining various goals. In previous accounts of this model (Higgins, 1981; McCann & Higgins, 1984) we have detailed the rules of the communication game that individuals follow in their interpersonal relations.

Much of our recent research has been devoted to an examination of the implications of these rules for interpersonal behavior and social cognition (Higgins, Fondacaro, & McCann, 1981; Higgins & McCann, 1984; Higgins, McCann, & Fondacaro, 1982; Higgins & Rholes, 1978; McCann & Hancock, 1983). According to the communication game, the specific rules that individuals follow in any particular communicative interaction is a function both of transitory context-driven emphases as well as chronic individual differences in personal goal orientation (e.g., McCann & Higgins, 1984).

This latter point (i.e., transitory and chronic differences in goal emphasis) can be illustrated with reference to Communicator Rule 1 (that communicators should take the audience's or recipient's characteristics into account when delivering a message). Past research has indicated that individuals will modify their messages by taking into account the informational and attitudinal characteristics of their audience (Flavell, Botkin, Fry, Wright, & Jarvis, 1968; Glucksberg, Krauss, & Higgins, 1975; Higgins & Rholes, 1978; Manis, Cornell, & Moore, 1974; Newtson & Czerlinsky, 1974). In one study, we demonstrated that the nature of the message modification exhibited by communicators was dependent on the temporary activation of either ''interpretive'' or ''descriptive'' goals (Higgins, McCann, & Fondacaro, 1982).

In two subsequent studies, we examined the impact of *chronic* individual differences in personal goal orientation on rule-following behavior. McCann and Hancock (1983), for example, demonstrated that it was especially the pragmatically oriented high self-monitor individuals (relative to low self-monitors) who tailored their messages to suit audience characteristics. In a later study, we demonstrated the impact of both contextual and individual difference factors in showing that high authoritarians tuned their messages to suit the attitudes of especially high status (vs. equal status) recipients, whereas low authoritarians did not show this pattern (Higgins & McCann, 1984).

The implications of this view of communicative interaction can be extended to social interaction more generally. This generalization is based upon the observations that interpersonal interactions are rule governed (e.g., Argyle & Henderson, 1984; Harre & Secord, 1972) and that individuals engage in relationships with particular goals or objectives in mind (e.g., McClintock, 1983). These goals are seen to activate cognitive representations of interpersonal strategies, in script-like form, that contain information regarding "organized action sequences" and contingency plans (e.g., Miller et al., 1960; Rule, Bisanz, & Kohn, 1985; Schank & Abelson, 1977). Kihlstrom and Cantor (1981), for example, suggest that such organized action sequences may be part of the information stored in procedural memory. Recent work has examined the representational nature of only a relatively small number of such goal-related structures (e.g., Rule et al., 1985). But the issue is of clear relevance to work in many areas, such as the remedial scripts people use following social embarrassment (e.g., Edelman, 1985; Modigliani, 1968, 1971). Our knowledge about these issues, however, is limited by the predominately speculative nature of the social goal taxonomies that have been developed thus far. This issue is considered next.

Varieties of Social Goals and Their Effects.   It is clear that individuals enter into interpersonal interactions in order to achieve a variety of social goals. Such personal objectives have been the subject of a great deal of theoretical and empirical interest (see Berger, chapter 6, this volume). Beginning with Festinger's (1954) classic work on social comparison, it has been suggested that one of the most important bases of affiliative tendencies is the individual's concern with the accuracy of his or her conception of social reality (see also Schachter, 1959). In addition to social reality goals, interpersonal interaction initiates, defines, and maintains social relationships (Reusch & Bateson, 1968; Watzlawick et al., 1967), and is enacted in the service of face (Goffman, 1967), ingratiation (Jones, 1964), task (Bales & Slater, 1955; Festinger, 1950), persuasion (Schank & Abelson, 1977), and entertainment goals (Higgins, Fondacaro, & McCann, 1981; Tubbs & Moss, 1977). Although this list of interpersonal objectives is not meant to be exhaustive (see for example, the work on resource theory, Foa & Foa, 1975), it should be clear that this concept has attracted a great deal of attention and has been applied to the analysis of many substantive issues.

To date, however, our knowledge of the nature and structure of social-interaction objectives has been largely speculative in nature or has focused on a restricted range of goals whose relation to everyday interaction remains unclear (e.g., Hastie, Park, & Weber, 1984). One of us recently conducted a study designed to examine in a preliminary fashion the nature and structure of individuals' cognitive representation of everyday social goals (McCann, Breckler, & Devine, 1986). In order to obtain a set of stimulus materials to use in this research we asked 70 undergraduate students at Ohio State University to list all the social goals they most often pursue in dyadic interactions with others. Subjects were given 15 minutes to complete their list and only those goals listed by at least 10% of the sample were retained for further use. Two judges then grouped the interaction goals into distinct categories, supplying labels descriptive of the goals in each category. The 20 social goals obtained through this procedure are listed in Table 4.1.

Our next objective was to examine the structure of subjects' cognitive representations of these social goals. A second sample of subjects were given the 20 social goals and were asked to make judgments regarding their similarity by sorting them into categories according to their similarity of purpose. The resulting similarity indices were analyzed by means of metric multidimensional scaling (Kruskal & Wish, 1978; Young & Lewyckyi, 1979), the results of which indicated that a three-dimensional solution was optimal. The social goals and their stimulus coordinates on the three dimensions are given in Table 4.1.

The scaling solution was interpreted by examining the ordering of the social goals along each of the three dimensions. The first dimension appeared to reflect a "social reality" versus "sociability" focus. The goals on this dimension varied from checking ideas and obtaining information at one extreme to being sociable and making acquaintances at the other. The second dimension was interpreted as a "self" (Me) versus "relationship" (We) focus. The goals varied at one extreme from persuading others, creating an impression, and avoiding being bored to the other extreme of giving and getting help, and maintaining friendships. Social interaction objectives on the third dimension reflected a "task" versus "social manipulation" focus. The goals varied at one extreme from getting a job done and obtaining information to the other extreme of getting approval and creating an impression. Thus the three-dimensional solution reflects a highly interpretable representation of the dimensions underlying subjects cognitive representations of their social goals.

The results of this study as well as studies by others suggest that individuals have clearly defined sets of personal objectives that they orient toward in everyday social interaction. According to the formulations presented here and elsewhere (see for example, Athay & Darley, 1981), individuals engage in interpersonal interaction in order to pursue these types of general objectives. Although several empirical and speculative taxonomies and dimensional analyses have been advanced, differentiation is typically made among objectives relating to self-interest ("Me"), relational focus ("We"), and task achievement (e.g., Clark, 1979). This literature seems to omit, however, entertainment (i.e., sociability) and social reality goals (e.g., McCann et al., 1986).

A communicator's social goals are also important from the point of view of

TABLE 4.1
Social Goal Dimensions

Dimension One		Dimension Two		Dimension Three	
1.8137	Check ideas	1.7186	Persuade others	1.7400	Job done
1.7442	Obtain information	1.3023	Create an impression	1.2073	Obtain information
1.5977	Express opinion	1.2401	Avoid being bored	0.7872	Avoid being bored
1.5577	Job done	1.0249	Get a date	0.7642	Learn of others
1.2937	Persuade others	0.7886	Get approval	0.1846	Give help
0.9969	Get advice	0.7820	Job done	0.0746	Be sociable
0.8516	Get help	0.6479	Obtain information	0.0540	Have fun
0.5011	Give help	0.4096	Check ideas	0.0532	Get a date
0.4611	Get approval	0.3546	Be sociable	0.0270	Make acquaintance
0.0659	Share ideas	0.2254	Make acquaintance	0.0020	Get advice
0.0517	Express emotion	0.0919	Avoid alone	-0.0020	Check ideas
-0.1304	Create an impression	-0.2391	Express opinion	-0.0193	Maintain friendship
-0.7714	Maintain friendship	-0.2566	Share ideas	-0.0305	Get help
-1.2273	Learn of others	-0.5467	Have fun	-0.0769	Avoid alone
-1.3021	Avoid being bored	-1.0868	Get advice	-0.1733	Share ideas
-1.3955	Avoid alone	-1.2412	Learn of others	-0.4946	Express emotion
-1.4424	Have fun	-1.2273	Maintain friendship	-0.7349	Express opinion
-1.5219	Get a date	-1.2657	Express emotion	-0.8059	Persuade others
-1.5386	Be sociable	-1.2922	Get help	-1.1526	Create impression
-1.6057	Make acquaintance	-1.4165	Give help	-1.4060	Get approval

the interaction partner. The recipients of a social exchange attempt to decode the actions of their partner in order to infer intentionality and dispositions. Holmes (1981), for example, distinguishes between the observer's assessment of micro- and macro-motives (such as trust and cooperation) and the implications of such assessments for the future course of the relationship. In addition to behavioral effects, social goals have both direct and indirect social-cognitive consequences, which we now briefly consider.

Direct and Indirect Social–Cognitive Consequences.   Much of the current interest in social goals or personal objectives derives from evidence of their effects on the processing of social information about others. This current interest was preceded by the early work of Jones and Thibaut (1958) on "inferential sets" and the work of Zajonc (1960) on "cognitive tuning."

More contemporary formulations are provided by Cohen (1981), Srull and Wyer, (1986), and Zuckier (1986). Cohen (1981), for example, suggests that social goals are largely responsible for the activation of particular schemata that are then utilized in the processing of social information (see also Wyer & Srull, 1980). Thus, the activation of some specific social goal is seen to influence the way in which social information is processed by engaging a relevant schema (see also, Taylor & Crocker, 1981).

Although this research has been limited by the somewhat impoverished set of social goals examined and its removal from the context of social interaction (e.g., Hastie et al., 1984; McCann et al., 1986), it has served to emphasize the importance of such social goals for social information processing. Although a comprehensive review of this literature is beyond the scope of this chapter (see Srull & Wyer, 1986), it is clear that social goals can have direct effects on the encoding, representation, and retrieval of social information.

The research testing the communication game model was specifically designed to examine how individual's social goals in a social-interaction context might also have indirect effects on social–cognitive processes (e.g., Higgins & Rholes, 1978; McCann & Hancock, 1983; McCann & Higgins, 1984). In this case, social goals are not seen to influence directly social information processing as in the research just documented, but are seen to influence rule-following social behavior that in turn impacts on memory, attitudes, and social judgment. To illustrate, McCann and Hancock (1983) had high and low self-monitors communicate about a target to an audience who purportedly either liked or disliked that person. Previous research had indicated that subjects in such a context would tend to modify their messages about the target person to suit their audience's attitude (Higgins & Rholes, 1978). McCann and Hancock, however, suggested that such message modification would be a function of both audience characteristics and personal goal orientation.

High self-monitors are known to be the type of individual who take a pragmatic or strategic orientation toward social interaction (e.g., Snyder, 1979). They are responsive to situational cues regarding appropriate behavior and will manage their behavior accordingly. Low self-monitors, on the other hand, do not alter their behavior or beliefs to suit the context. Thus, it was expected that high self-monitors would tailor their messages to suit the characteristics of their audience but low self-monitors would not.

The results supported this prediction; high self-monitors communicating to an audience who liked the target person characterized him in a more positive manner than did high self-monitors communicating to an audience who disliked the target person. No such pattern was observed for low self-monitors. As in our previous studies, potential social–cognitive effects of such message modification were also examined. A consideration of the information processing factors underlying social encoding (e.g., Higgins & Rholes, 1978) suggested that subjects' verbal encodings of the stimulus information would influence their own subsequent impressions of the target person. The results supported this prediction. Thus, high self-monitors who communicated to an audience who liked the target person ended up with a more positive impression of him than subjects who talked to someone who disliked him. No such effects were observed for low-self monitors.

Other research examining the communication game has indicated similar effects of message modification on subjects' reconstruction of the initial target person information as well as on subjects' own attitudes toward the target person (Higgins & McCann, 1984; Higgins & Rholes, 1978). In addition, these social–cognitive consequences have been found to increase significantly over time. Thus, the tendency for subjects' message-modification effects to show up in their memory for the initial target person information increases from brief to long delay periods (see Higgins & McCann, 1984; Higgins & Rholes, 1978). Our research has also indicated that these social–cognitive effects are due to the communicative behavior engaged in by subjects and not to social conformity, experimental demand, cognitive dissonance effects, nor to communicative intent alone (see Higgins & McCann, 1984; Higgins & Rholes, 1978).

It is clear, then, that the social goals or personal objectives operative in any particular social context can have important effects on social behavior, social–cognitive processes, and attitudes toward others. More recently, Higgins and Stangor (1986) have described such social-cognitive effects as "perceiver context-adaptation effects" in which perceivers actively (although not necessarily consciously) modify their encoding of target information as a function of contextual goals and/or the audience with which they communicate. In these communication situations, subjects modify their messages based upon contextual cues salient in the immediate situation. These context-based modifications have demonstratable influence on subjects' subsequent memory, impressions and attitudes, and these effects tend to increase over time. Thus, individuals' memory and evaluations are based in part on their context-induced judgments and verbal encoding rather than solely on the original stimulus information itself. The important thing to note here is that communicators fail to adjust their memories and attitudes sufficiently for the effects of such goal-directed and "context-biased" processes.

These effects are, however, only part of the range of effects that social goals can have. Social goals have also been implicated in affective experience, especially within social relationships. In the next section we review recent formulations in this area.

Social Goals and Affect

Several formulations of affect and emotions have been developed that serve to integrate the concept of social goals, as defined previously, with affective or emotional experience (e.g., Abelson, 1983; Berscheid, 1983; Kelley, 1984; Mandler, 1975; Srull & Wyer, 1986; Tversky & Kahneman, 1981). In these formulations, affect and emotion are viewed both as resulting from and resulting in social-goal activation.

Berscheid (1983) has recently adapted and extended Mandler's (1975) formulation of emotion in terms of affective experience in interpersonal relations. She suggests that interpersonal relationships can be characterized by the extent to which the goals of the interactants are "meshed." Thus, in close relations with significant others, individuals are often dependent on others for the successful completion of their own personal goals and plans. These other individuals, therefore, are often in a position to facilitate or inhibit the successful completion of an actor's goal-oriented behavioral sequences (both immediate and long term).

The sequence of behavior engaged in by individuals is often simultaneously organized in terms of both intra- and intersequential chains. Two individuals are meshed to the extent to which there are many necessary interchain connections between the sequences of behavior each must engage in for their own goal attainment. The more intermeshed the behavioral sequences are, the greater potential there exists for faciliatory and inhibitory actions on the part of the interaction partners, and thus the greater potential there is for positive and negative affective experience.

In effect, and in accordance with Mandler's (1975) view, the quality of affective experience is derived from the implications of the partner's behavior for the actor's personal control. Those actions on the part of the partner that serve to facilitate goal attainment induce arousal interpreted as positive affective experiences, whereas those that interrupt or inhibit goal attainment result in negative affective experiences. Emotional intensity is considered to be a result of such factors as: (a) the degree of organization of the behavioral sequence, (b) the discrepancy between the interrupting event and the interrupted sequence, (c) the availability of alternative behaviors, (d) the place of the interruption in the behavior sequence, and (d) the extent to which the organized behavior sequence is disrupted. Thus, the actions of others that serve to disrupt the organized action routines initiated by the actor result in the experience of positive or negative emotions. In relationships in which no interruptions occur the partners should experience emotional quiescence (but see Buck, 1985). Srull and Wyer (1986) have recently extended this model and have formalized its predictions regarding the quality and intensity of affect.

The formulations proposed by Abelson (1983) and Tversky and Kahneman (1981) overlap both with one another and those just outlined. These models, however, are somewhat more precise in generating predictions regarding differential quality of affective experience. Here we focus on Abelson's ideas given their explicit reference to interpersonal relations.

According to Abelson (1983) affect or emotion is experienced whenever "alternative constructions of events with sharply different hedonic import for an individual are concurrently mentally exercised" (p. 46). The term *mentally exercised* includes both mental simulations of potential events and "recognition" of the actual state of affairs. Consistent with our previous discussion, interpersonal behavior is viewed as a system of behavioral events in which individuals pursue particular plans or goals that lead them to engage in organized action routines. Goals and outcomes are linked through a process of participant action and the contribution of "causal instrumentality" that refers, in part, to the actions of other participants.

Thus, interpersonal interaction consists of a sequence of goals, action, causal instrumentality, and outcome. Reality can be discrepant from the imagined sequence anywhere along this causal chain and affective experience is seen to be dependent on where and what type of divergence occurs. A couple of examples serve to illustrate this view. Consider first a situation in which an individual engages in a behavior for which a positive outcome is anticipated. According to Abelson's formulation, if the goal, action, and causal instrumentality are fixed but the actual outcome is negative, the actor will experience "disappointment." In a similar context, if goal and actions are fixed but if the causal instrumentality and outcome diverge in a negative way from those anticipated, "anger" and "frustration" will result. Although we cannot do full justice to the complexity of the model, it is worth noting that the location and type of discrepancy are the parameters that produce intensity and quality of affect.

The models reviewed thus far have primarily addressed the antecedent status of social goals with respect to affective experience. This causal relationship, however, is not one of unidirectionality and some authors have dealt with affect as a contributing factor to social-goal activation (e.g., Carver & Scheier, 1981; Hoffman, 1986; Kelley, 1984). A brief summary of Kelley's perspective on this issue serves as an illustration.

Kelley (1984) suggests that an individual's causal environment consists of discriminable situations that have significance for the individual's well-being. These he refers to as *interest-relevant* situations. He suggests that individuals have developed internal systems (i.e., intersituational processes) that serve, among other things, to identify the nature of the experienced interest-relevant situations and to orient the organism to upcoming situations.

In terms of the present concerns, affect is seen to be one of the most important of these intersituational processes. Affective experiences are functional and adaptive in that they mark prior experience and orient or motivate the organism to respond adaptively to forthcoming situations. Accordingly, affect may serve to motivate particular social goals that function to adaptively orient the organism to the future. For example, in Roseman's (1979) terms, anger may activate the goal of vengence, fear of avoidance, and joy of maintenance (see Kelley, 1984).

It is clearly inappropriate to draw unidirectional causal links between affect and cognition or social goals. We have attempted to present formulations regarding social goals and affective experience from a variety of sources and the resulting picture achieves some clarity. It should be obvious, however, that much work remains to be done in order to specify the exact nature of their interrelation in the context of interpersonal relations.

Summary and Implications

In the preceding section we presented empirical and theoretical work from several diverse areas that relate to our concern with the relation between affect and cognition in interpersonal relationships. Interpersonal behavior was conceptualized as being primarily goal-oriented in nature in which chronic and transitory concerns orient individuals toward particular objectives in their interpersonal relations. Although having obvious implications for social behavior, the activation of social goals is also seen to influence social–cognitive processes in both direct and indirect ways that in turn impact on memory and affect.

The formulations we have presented are intended to be heuristic but much remains to be filled in. A couple of examples serve to make this point. The various formulations we have discussed differ in level of abstraction. Some conceptualizations of social goals and plans seem to refer to ''life-long'' aspirations, whereas others refer to goals operating at the level of particular interaction episodes. We have provided some descriptive analysis of the types of goals individuals pursue in everyday dyadic interaction but much work remains to be done in this area. Another source of ambiguity relates to the overlap (or lack thereof) between the notions of affect, emotion, mood, and feeling states. Some formulations appear to distinguish only between their positive and negative quality while others subcategorize each of these domains.

The approaches just outlined appear to have clear relevance to a variety of substantive issues. For example, it would appear to be important to examine goal orientation from a developmental perspective, both in terms of individual and relationship development. Relationships are seen to develop through a series of discriminable stages (e.g., La Gaipa, 1977; Levine & Moreland, 1982; Levinger, 1983), and it seems reasonable to suggest that the personal goals emphasized by the participants in a relationship would vary with relationship stage. This suggestion is clearly consistent with the work on social penetration and self-disclosure (e.g., Altman & Taylor, 1973). In addition, some research suggests that individual social development is related to differential goal emphasis. For example, adolescence has been characterized as a stage of life in which consensual validation or social-reality goals are emphasized (e.g., Duck, 1981; see also Higgins & Parsons, 1983).

A final area of relevance relates to current work in psychopathology. Social-interaction factors have been implicated in the etiology and maintenance of depressive episodes (Coates & Wortman, 1980; Coyne, 1976). Although these models achieve some precision in specifying the objectives of the depressive's interaction partner, much less is known about what the depressives themselves are trying to obtain. It is possible that one could examine the interpersonal orientation characteristically adopted by depressed and non-depressed individuals by utilizing the dyadic social goals just described and comparing the dimensions underlying depressed and non-depressed individuals' social-goal orientations. Such a perspective might contribute to our understanding of the nature of the "downward depressive spiral" (Coyne, 1976).

Although we have provided one perspective on the relation between affect and cognition in interpersonal relations, this does not exhaust the range of potential perspectives. In the next section we examine this relation in the context of another social–cognitive approach—self-discrepancy theory.

SELF-DISCREPANCY AND AFFECT

This chapter focuses on the relation between affect and cognition in interpersonal relations by considering the implications of two forms of discrepancy. In the preceding section we examined this issue by invoking the concept of social goals and the discrepancy between expected (i.e., goal-related) and experienced interpersonal events. In this section we detail the implications of another type of discrepancy, self-discrepancy, for affective experience. This chronic form of intrapersonal discrepancy has its origins in as well as consequences for, interpersonal relationships.

Self-Discrepancy Theory

Self-discrepancy theory (see Higgins, 1985; Higgins, Bond, Klein, & Strauman, 1986; Higgins, Klein, & Strauman, 1985; Higgins, Strauman, & Klein, 1986) derives from an attempt to systematize and extend the implications of two classic observations about the self: (a) self-concept (i.e., perceived actual self-state) and self-guides (i.e., perceived potential self-states) are situated in and are the result of social processes; and (b) there exists different kinds of self-guides that have psychological reality (e.g., Allport, 1955; Cooley, 1902/1964; James, 1890 /1948; Mead, 1934). In this section, we focus on the implications of the theory for affect in social relationships and present the results of a recent study examining this issue (Higgins, McCann, Gavin, & Foxall, 1986).

Domains of the Self and Standpoints on the Self.   Previous work in psychology suggests the existence of three discriminable and important self-domains or types of self-states (e.g., Colby, 1968; Freud, 1923/1961; James, 1890/1948; Rogers, 1961). In self-discrepancy theory, these three domains of the self are defined as (Higgins, 1985):

1. *Actual Self:* A person's representation of the attributes that someone (self or other) believes the person actually possesses.
2. *Ideal Self:* A person's representation of the attributes that someone (self or other) would like the person, ideally to possess; i.e., someone's hopes, wishes, or goals for the person.
3. *Ought Self:* A person's representation of the attributes that someone (self or other) believes the person ought to possess; i.e., someone's beliefs about the duties, responsibilities, and obligations for the person.

Self-discrepancy theory proposes that it is also necessary to distinguish self-states along another cognitive dimension—"standpoints on the self." The notion of standpoints has been seen as an important consideration by others working in the areas of self and affect (e.g., DeRivera, 1977; Freud, 1915/1957; Kelley, 1952; Lewin, 1935; Turner, 1956). There are two basic standpoints on the self, where a standpoint on the self is a point of view or position from which a person can be judged that reflects a set of attitudes or values—a person's "own" personal standpoint and the standpoint of some significant "other" (e.g., mother, father, closest friend).

Type of Self-Discrepancy and Kind of Emotional Vulnerability.   The model proposes that different types of self-discrepancy result in different qualities of discomfort or affective experience. Research to date has focused on four particular combinations of "domain" and "standpoint": actual/own versus ideal/own, actual/own versus ideal/other, actual/own versus ought/own, and actual/own versus ought/other. These four types of discrepancy all involve the fact that an individual's self-perceived attributes are discrepant from his or her relevant self-guides for these attributes. Although sharing this similarity, they differ in terms of their implications for emotional vulnerability.

All actual/ideal discrepancies involve perceived absence of positive outcomes. An actual/own:ideal/own discrepancy reflects the fact that an individual believes that he or she has failed to live up to his or her own hopes and goals. An actual/own:ideal/other discrepancy involves the fact that an individual believes that he or she has failed to live up to the hopes and goals that he or she believes a significant other holds for him or her. Both types of discrepancy, involving loss of or absence of desired outcome, should elicit sorrow, feeling down, or more generally "dejection." Although both lead to dejection, the type of dejection should differ depending on standpoint. Thus, actual/own:ideal/own discrepancy should be associated with disappointment and dissatisfaction whereas actual/own:ideal/other discrepancy should be associated with shame and embarrassment.

In contrast, actual:ought discrepancies involve the perceived presence of negative outcomes, and thus lead to "agitation" or anxiety related affect. An actual/own:ought/other discrepancy reflects the fact that an individual believes that he or she has not lived up to the prescribed duties and obligations set for him or her by some significant other that could lead to punishment or sanctions by that other. This type of discrepancy is associated with fear, threat, and agitation. An actual/own:ought/own discrepancy reflects an individual's belief that he or she has not met their own standard with regard to duty and obligation, which can lead to self-punishment. This type of discrepancy is seen to be related to guilt and self-contempt.

The research conducted to date has supported these predictions (e.g., Higgins, Bond, Klein, & Strauman, 1986; Higgins, Klein, & Strauman, 1984, 1985; Higgins, Strauman, & Klein, 1984, Higgins, Strauman & Klein 1986). Although a comprehensive review of this research is beyond the scope of this chapter, a brief summary of a couple of experiments will serve to illustrate this point.

Higgins, Bond, Klein, and Strauman (1986) conducted two studies to examine whether the type of emotional change experienced by individuals was influenced by the *magnitude* and *accessibility* of the different types of self-discrepancies they possessed. Subjects in both studies were administered a measure of self-discrepancy several weeks before participating in an experimental session. Of primary interest in these studies were the implications of actual:ought versus actual:ideal discrepancies.

Study One was designed to determine if the type of discomfort that resulted from focusing on a negative event varied according to the type of self-discrepancy that was predominant for an individual. Subjects were instructed (through a guided imagery technique) to focus on either a positive event (e.g., you just received an A in an important course) or a negative (e.g., you just received a D in an important course) event. Subjects were then asked to complete a mood inventory assessing dejection and agitation and were given a writing-speed test that had been shown to be sensitive to mood (i.e., slower writing speeds with increases in sadness). The results were consistent with the predictions of the model. Subjects with a predominant actual:ideal discrepancy (i.e., high actual:ideal discrepancy and low actual:ought discrepancy) felt more dejected and wrote slower after the imagined negative event than after the imagined positive event, whereas subjects with a predominant actual:ought discrepancy tended to be more agitated and write faster after the imagined negative event.

In Study Two, subjects were selected who were either high in both types of discrepancies or low in both. Half of each group were then asked to discuss their own and their parents' hopes and goals for them (i.e., Ideal priming) and the other half were asked to discuss their own and their parents' beliefs concerning their duties and obligations (i.e., Ought priming). The discussion conditions were designed to make accessible either Ideal or Ought discrepancies (see Bargh, chapter 2, this volume: Higgins & King 1981). Subjects were then given a mood questionnaire to assess dejection and agitation. The results indicated, as predicted, that for high-discrepancy subjects only, the Ideal priming manipulation induced increased dejection and the Ought priming induced agitation.

Self-Discrepancy and Affect in Relationships.   To date, research testing the implications of self-discrepancy theory has focused exclusively on the implications of self-discrepancies for an individual's general affective state. But the model also has implications for affective reactions in specific interpersonal relations. Thus far in our review, interpersonal relations have been connected with affect in terms of the dimension of "standpoints" on the self. This dimension reflects the literature suggesting that individuals' cognitive representations of self are partially determined through processes such as reflective appraisal derived from relationships with significant others (for example, see Damon, 1983 and Shantz, 1983, for reviews). Support for this position in the context of self-discrepancy theory comes from results demonstrating both that actual/own:ideal/other discrepancy and actual/own:ought/other discrepancy have implications for an individual's general affective state.

Interpersonal relations, however, can be associated with self-discrepancies in another important way. To the extent that individuals believe that they are not living up to the standards (i.e., oughts or ideals) that they believe a significant other holds for them, they should experience discomfort specifically in that relationship. Moreover, the quality of their discomfort should depend on the type of standard that they believe they are discrepant from and should be unique to the relationship assessed in that particular self-guide (e.g., dejection in relations with father should be uniquely related to actual/own:ideal/father discrepancy). In a recent study (Higgins, McCann, Gavin, & Foxall, 1986) we examined this hypothesis in the context of parent–child relationships.

In this study we asked 94 undergraduates[1] at York University to complete a series of questionnaires. For all subjects, the first questionnaire completed was the "Selves" questionnaire and the last two questionnaires were the "Emo-

---

[1]Some subjects in the study failed to complete all measures. In fact, subjects who were living in single-parent families were told not to complete the "Selves" measure from the standpoint of the absent parent. For each correlational analysis we used a pairwise deletion procedure, so that the *n*'s for the analyses varied from 73 to 93. Significance levels are based on the appropriate sample size of that analysis.

tions'' measures described here. These measures provided the data relevant to the hypotheses. Between these two sets of questionnaires, subjects were asked to complete several additional questionnaires, which took about 45 minutes to fill out. These filler questionnaires helped to disguise the specific purpose of the research.

In the Selves questionnaire subjects were asked to list the attributes associated with their actual, ought, and ideal self-states from three standpoints (i.e., own, mother, and father). On the basis of these attribute lists the following self-discrepancy scores were calculated for each subject (see Higgins, Bond, Klein, & Strauman, 1986, for a complete discussion of the method for calculating discrepancy scores): actual/own:ideal/own, actual/own:ought/own, actual/own:ought/mother, actual/own:ideal/mother, actual/own:ideal/father, and actual/own:ought/father. There were two versions of the Emotions questionnaire (i.e., mother and father relationship) in which subjects were asked to indicate how often their relationship with their mother/father elicited in them each of 60 emotions (on 5-point scales ranging from ''almost never'' to ''almost always''). Embedded in these measures were items related specifically to dejection and agitation.[2] In order to calculate separate dejection and agitation scores we summed the rating for each type of emotion (for both scales, alpha coefficient = .90). These emotion scores were then correlated with subjects' self-discrepancies as described later.

We conducted several analyses to examine the relations between the various self-discrepancies and reported affect. The first analysis indicated, as expected, that actual/own:ideal/mother and actual/own:ideal/father discrepancy scores were significantly related to the dejection experienced in each of those relationships separately (r's = .31, $p < .002$, and .41, $p < .0001$, respectively), and that actual/own:ought/mother and actual/own:ought/father scores were associated with reported agitation in each of those relationships separately (r's = .36, $p < .0001$, and .39, $p < .0001$, respectively). Thus, as predicted by the model, affective experience in interpersonal relations with significant others was significantly related to the discrepancies between actual self-states and self-guides attributed to those significant others.

We also conducted several partial-correlation analyses to examine the uniqueness of these relations. In the first analysis, we partialled out the contribution of general emotional vulnerability due to discrepancies involving the subjects' ''own'' standpoint (i.e., partialling actual/own:ideal/own out of the correlations between actual/own:ideal/other discrepancies and reported dejection in

---

[2]The dejection items used were: disappointed, happy, satisfied, sad, depressed, regretful, lonely, hopeless, self-blaming. The agitation items were: restless, fearful, agitated, panicky, tense, uneasy, irritable, on edge, apprehensive, relaxed, and terrified. For each scale the scoring of some items was reversed (e.g., happy, optimistic, relaxed) so that higher scale scores always indicated feeling more negative.

mother and father relationships and partialling actual/own:ought own out of the correlations between actual/own:ought/other and reported agitation). The correlations remained significant in all cases: actual/own:ideal/mother with dejection in mother relationship, $r = .19$, $p < .04$; actual/own:ideal/father with dejection in father relationship $r = .34$, $p < .002$; actual/own:ought/mother with agitation in relationship with mother, $r = .25$, $p < .01$; and actual /own:ought/father with agitation in relationship with father, $r = .29$, $p < .006$. In a second partial correlation analysis, we again examined the relations between self-discrepancies and affect predicted by the model this time partialling out the contribution of the self-discrepancy derived from the same domain of self but from the other parent's standpoint. The results of these analyses provide further support for the predictions of self-discrepancy theory: the correlation between actual/own:ideal/mother and dejection in relationship with mother, partialling out actual/own:ideal/father discrepancy, was, $r = .15$, $p < .10$; the correlation between actual/own:ideal/father and dejection in father relationship, partialling out actual/own:ideal/mother discrepancy was, $r = .32$, $p < .003$; the correlation between actual/own:ought/mother and agitation in mother relationship, partialling out actual/own:ought/father discrepancy was, $r = .25$, $p < .02$; and the correlation between actual/own:ought/father and agitation in that relationship partialling out actual/own:ought/mother discrepancy was, $r = .25$, $p < .02$.

Although the results just reported provide support for the predicted relations between self-discrepancy and affect in interpersonal relationships, further evidence is required to support the specificity of the relations predicted by the model. As just described, self-discrepancy theory not only relates self-discrepancy to affect but, in addition, it explicitly relates specific discrepancies to specific affective experience in specific relationships. Thus, for example, actual/own:ideal/father discrepancies should be uniquely related to experienced dejection in relationship with father and vice versa. We examined the specificity of the obtained relations by conducting four sets of semi-partial correlations analyses (see Table 4.2).

In the first column of Table 4.2 we report the significance levels of several analyses conducted to examine the specificity of the predictions made by self-discrepancy theory. In examining Target Specificity, from the predicted relations (e.g., actual/own:ideal/mother discrepancy with dejection in relationship with mother) we semi-partial out of the self-discrepancy the contribution of the same discrepancy from other parent's standpoint (i.e., actual/own:ideal/father) and we semi-partialled out of the theoretically related affect (i.e., dejection in relationship with mother) the contribution of the same type of affect but as experienced in relations with the other parent (i.e., dejection in relationship with father). We conducted parallel analyses for the other three relations indicated in the top half of the first column of Table 4.2. These results provide strong support for the predictions just described with regard to Target Specificity.

In the bottom half of the first column we report the results of parallel analyses

TABLE 4.2
Specificity of Relations Between Self-Discrepancy[a]
and Affect in Relationship

Analysis	Model Predictions	Alternative Predictions
Target Specificity	Actual/own: Ideal/mother (Actual/own: Ideal/father)[b] with mother dejection[c] (father dejection)**	Actual/own: Ideal/mother (Actual/own: Ideal/father) with father dejection (mother dejection), n.s.
	Actual/own: Ought/mother (Actual/own: Ought/father) with mother agitation (father agitation)**	Actual/own: Ought/mother (Actual/own: Ought/father) with father agitation (mother agitation), n.s.
	Actual/own: Ideal/father (Actual/own: Ideal/mother) with father dejection (mother dejection)***	Actual/own: Ideal/father (Actual/own: Ideal/mother) with mother dejection (father dejection), n.s.
	Actual/own: Ought/father (Actual/own: Ought/mother) with father agitation (mother agitation)**	Actual/own: Ought/father (Actual/own: Ought/mother) with mother agitation (father agitation), n.s.
Affective Specificity	Actual Own: Ideal/mother (Actual: Ought/mother) with mother dejection (mother agitation)**	Actual/own: Ideal/mother (Actual/own: Ought/mother) with mother agitation (mother dejection), n.s.
	Actual/own: Ought/mother (Actual/own: Ideal mother) with mother agitation (mother dejection)*	Actual/own: Ought/mother (Actual/own: Ideal/mother) with mother dejection (mother agitation)*
	Actual/own: Ideal/father (Actual/own: Ought/father) with father dejection (father agitation)**	Actual/own: Ideal father (Actual/own: Ought/father) with father agitation (father dejection), n.s.
	Actual/own: Ought/father (Actual/own: Ideal/father) with father agitation (father dejection)*	Actual/own: Ought/father (Actual/own: Ideal/father) with father dejection (father agitation), n.s.

[a]* = $p < .10$, ** = $p < .05$, *** = $p < .01$, all others = n.s.

[b]Terms in parentheses indicate what has been partialled out of the preceding concept.

[c]The terms *mother dejection, father dejection, mother agitation,* and *father agitation,* refer to specific emotion reported as experienced in relationship with the identified parent.

examining Affective Specificity. In order to examine Affective Specificity we again examined the predictions of the model (e.g., actual/own:ideal/mother discrepancy with dejection in relationship with mother) this time semi-partialling out of the self-discrepancy the contribution of the self-discrepancy derived from same standpoint and other domain (i.e., actual/own:ought/mother) and semi-partialling out of the affect (i.e., dejection) the contribution of the other affect (i.e., agitation) as experienced in relationship with same parent (i.e., mother). Parallel analyses were conducted for the other three predictions indicated in the bottom half of the first column of Table 4.2. Again, the results of these analyses provide strong support for the specificity of the predictions of the model as previously described.

Finally, in an attempt to provide more converging evidence regarding the specificity of the relations predicted by the model we conducted two other sets of semi-partial correlational analyses. In the second column of Table 4.2 we report the significance of the relations that would be assumed to hold true if our assumptions regarding Target and Affective Specificity were false. In seven of eight cases, the alternative predictions do not result in significant correlations, again providing support for the specificity of the relations between self-discrepancy and experienced affect in interpersonal relationships.

Summary and Implications

In this section we review literature and data suggesting the implications of another form of discrepancy for affective experience in interpersonal relationships. Here, the important discrepancy is between an individual's actual self-state and the standards he or she believes that others hold for them. We have shown that different forms of such discrepancies have effects on the intensity and quality of affect reported in these relationships. The data we report in this section are preliminary, but are supportive of the theoretical links we outline between cognition and affect. We also believe that such affective reactions will have implications for the nature of the interpersonal interactions that ensue, especially when we can assume that the presence of the significant other will serve to increase the *accessibility* of the discrepancy that leads to the emotional discomfort. This latter point is the subject of some of our current research efforts.

These results also suggest a couple of other avenues for future research. The interpersonal affective implications of self-discrepancies should depend upon the relevance or importance of the relationship. This could be examined both by comparing distinct types of relationships and significant others (e.g., lover vs. casual friend) and by examining longitudinally the implications of self-discrepancies for affective experience as the relationships evolve into more intimate forms. One last avenue for future research is perhaps the most intriguing of all. Individuals can be classified according to the type of discrepancy that is most dominant for them, as an individual difference measure, (see Higgins, Bond,

Klein, & Strauman, 1986). Relationships can be thought of as being composed of two persons whose dominant discrepancies may be either congruent or incongruent. Although we have already demonstrated the implications of *intraindividual* self-discrepancy for affective reactions in the relationship, it is a logical next step to consider the implications of interindividual discrepancy (i.e., the discrepancy between discrepancies) for affective experience in relationships. This seems fertile ground for extending our knowledge about such matters and we are currently examining this issue.

CONCLUDING COMMENTS

As indicated in the quotation with which we began this chapter, affective reactions dominate interpersonal relations. Our interactions with others are the primary source of our most intense pleasure and our most intense pain. A concern with an explication of the factors that elicit positive and negative emotions is clearly an important issue in many areas of psychological investigation. This interest is, in part, a reaction to the limitations inherent in exclusively cognitive orientations to human behavior and, in part, a function of increasing interest in the nature of interpersonal relations themselves. To date, most analyses of affect in interpersonal relations have focused on how interpersonal discrepancy or conflict results in interpersonal problems and negative affect for the conflicting partners. In this chapter, we have focused on the role played by "intrapersonal" discrepancy. This has necessitated a consideration of, on a more general level, the relations between affect and cognition, with each considered both as an initiating and derivative factor.

We have reviewed and integrated research in social cognition, clinical psychology, and personal relations and have outlined the role played by two types of intrapersonal discrepancies for affective experience in interpersonal relations: (a) the discrepancy between an individual's orientation to (or expectancy for) interaction episodes and actual events; and (b) the discrepancy between an individual's beliefs about his or her actual self and the beliefs attributed to significant others concerning his or her potential self. In both cases, affective and cognitive factors are linked.

The first type of discrepancy explicitly implicates the behavior of interaction partners in terms of the degree to which they are perceived to inhibit or facilitate the attainment of an individual's goals. In this way it incorporates an emphasis of the role played by "exogenous" factors in affective experience. The second type of discrepancy just outlined focuses primarily on "endogenous" factors dealing with the relation among self-state representations (actual and potential). Although described separately for ease of presentation, the distinction between these exogeneous and endogenous factors is a difficult one to make. In fact, the two are likely related and this provides a final avenue for future research. Expectations for the relationship and particular interaction episodes may be influenced by personal guides (i.e., ideals and oughts), and actual experience may be interpreted in terms of the personal guides or standards made accessible by the relationship. Thus, the two types of intrapersonal discrepancies may have a mutual influence. Clarifying the precise nature of this interaction is an exciting challenge for future research.

ACKNOWLEDGMENTS

Preparation of this manuscript was facilitated by a National Sciences and Engineering Research Council of Canada Grant (#A0575) to the first author and a National Institute of Mental Health Grant (#MH39429) to the second author. This manuscript has benefited from the comments of Douglas Gavin, Kathy Foxall, Barbara Dominic, Mary Blakely, and Harry Coyle.

REFERENCES

Abelson, R. P. (1983). Whatever became of consistency theory. *Personality and Social Psychology Bulletin, 9*, 35–54.

Allport, G. W. (1955). *Becoming*. New Haven, CT: Yale University Press.

Altman, I., & Taylor, D. A. (1973). *Social penetration: The development of interpersonal relationships*. New York: Holt, Rinehart & Winston.

Argyle, M., & Henderson, M. (1984). The rules of friendship. *Journal of Social and Personal Relationships, 1*, 211–237.

Argyle, M., & Kendon, A. (1967). The experimental analysis of social performance. In L. Berkowitz (Ed.), *Advances in experimental psychology* (Vol. 3, pp. 55–99). New York: Academic Press.

Athay, M., & Darley, J. M. (1981). Toward an interaction-centered theory of personality. In N. Cantor & J. F. Kihlstrom (Eds.), *Personality, cognition, and social interaction* (pp. 281–308). Hillsdale, NJ: Lawrence Erlbaum Associates.

Bales, R. F., & Slater, P. (1955). Role differentiation in small groups. In T. Parsons & R. F. Bales (Eds.), *Family, socialization and interaction processes*. (pp. 259–306). Glencoe, IL: Free Press.

Beck, A. T. (1976). *Cognitive therapy and the emotional disorders*. New York: International Universities Press.

Berscheid, E. (1983). Emotion. In H. H. Kelley, E. Berscheid, A. Christensen, J. H. Harvey, T. L. Huston, G. Levinger, E. McClintock, L. A. Peplau, & D. R. Peterson (Eds.), *Close relationships*. (pp. 110–169). New York: Freeman.

Blumer, H. (1962). Society as symbolic interaction. In A. M. Rose (Ed.), *Human behavior and social processes* (pp. 139–148). London: Routledge & Kegan Paul.

Bower, G. H. (1981). Emotional mood and memory. *American Psychologist, 36*, 129–148.

Brehm, S. S. (1985). *Intimate relationships*. New York: Random House.

Buck, R. (1985). Prime theory: An integrated view of motivation and emotion. *Psychological Review, 92*, 389–413.

Cannon, W. B. (1927). The James–Lange theory of emotion: A critical examination and an alternative theory. *American Journal of Psychology, 39*, 106–124.

Carver, C. S., & Scheier, M. F. (1981). *Attention and self-regulation: A control theory approach to human behavior*. New York: Springer-Verlag.

Clark, R. A. (1979). The impact of self interest and desire for liking on the selection of communicative strategies. *Communication Monographs, 46,* 257–273.

Coates, D., & Wortman, C. B. (1980). Depression maintenance and interpersonal control. In A. Baum & J. E. Singer (Eds.), *Advances in environmental psychology: Applications of personal control* (Vol. 2, pp. 149–182). Hillsdale, NJ: Lawrence Erlbaum Associates.

Cohen, C. E. (1981). Goals and schemas in person perception: Making sense out of the stream of behavior. In N. Cantor & J. F. Kihlstrom (Eds.), *Personality, cognition, and social behavior* (pp. 45–68). Hillsdale, NJ: Lawrence Erlbaum Associates.

Colby, K. M. (1968). A programmable theory of cognition and affect in individual personal belief systems. In R. P. Abelson, B. Aronson, W. J. McGuire, T. M. Newcomb, M. J. Rosenberg, & P. H. Tannenbaum (Eds.), *Theories of cognitive consistency: A source book* (pp. 520–525). Chicago: Rand McNally.

Cooley, C. H. (1964). *Human nature and the social order.* New York: Schocken Books. (Original publication, 1902)

Coyne, J. C. (1976). Toward an interactional description of depression. *Psychiatry, 39,* 28–40.

Coyne, J. C., & Gotlib, I. H. (1983). The role of cognition in depression: A critical appraisal. *Psychological Bulletin, 94,* 472–505.

Damon, W. (1983). *Social and personality development.* New York: Norton.

DeRivera, J. (1977). A structural theory of the emotions. *Psychological Issues, 10,* 4, Monograph 40.

Duck, S. (1981). Toward a research map for the study of relationship breakdown. In S. Duck & R. Gilmour (Eds.), *Personal relationships 3: Personal relationships in disorder* (pp. 1–30). New York: Academic Press.

Duck, S. (Ed.). (1982). *Personal relationships 4: Dissolving personal relationships.* New York: Academic Press.

Duck, S. (Ed.). (1984). *Personal relationships 5: Repairing personal relationships.* New York: Academic Press.

Duck, S., & Gilmour, R. (Eds.). (1981a). *Personal relationships 1: Studying personal reltionships.* New York: Academic Press.

Duck, S., & Gilmour, R. (Eds.). (1981b). *Personal relationships 2: Developing personal relationships.* New York: Academic Press.

Duck, S., & Gilmour, R. (Eds.). (1981c). *Personal relationships 3: Personal relationships in disorder.* New York: Academic Press.

Edelman, R. J. (1985). Social embarrassment: An analysis of the process. *Journal of Social and Personal Relationships, 2,* 195–213.

Festinger, L. (1950). Informal social communication. *Psychological Review, 57,* 271–282.

Festinger, L. (1954). A theory of social comparison processes. *Human Relations, 7,* 117–140.

Fiske, S. T. (1982). Schema-triggered affect: Applications to social perception. In M. S. Clark & S. T. Fiske (Eds.), *Affect and cognition: The 17th Annual Carnegie-Mellon Symposium on Cognition* (pp. 55–78). Hillsdale, NJ: Lawrence Erlbaum Associates.

Flavell, J. H., Botkin, P. T., Fry, C. L., Wright, J. W., & Jarvis, P. (1968). *The development of role-taking and communication skills in children.* New York: Wiley.

Foa, U. G., & Foa, E. B. (1975). *Resource theory of social exchange.* Morristown, NJ: General Learning Press.

Freud, S. (1957). In J. Strachey (Ed. and Trans.), *Instincts and their vicissitudes. Standard edition of the complete psychological works of Sigmund Freud.* (Vol. 14, pp. 117–140). London: Hogarth Press. (Original publication, 1915).

Freud, S. (1961). The ego and the id. In J. Strachey (Ed. and Trans.), *Standard edition of the complete psychological works of Sigmund Freud* (Vol. 19, pp. 19–27) London: Hogarth. (Original publication, 1923).

Gaelick, L., Bodenhausen, G. V., & Wyer, R. S. Jr., (1985). Emotional communication in close relationships. *Journal of Personality and Social Psychology, 49,* 1246–1265.

Garfinkel, H. (1967). *Studies in ethnomethodology.* Englewood Cliffs, NJ: Prentice-Hall.

Glucksberg, S., Krauss, R. M., & Higgins, E. T. (1975). The development of referential communication skills. In F. Horowitz, E. Hetherinton, S. Scarr-Salapetek, & G. Siegel (Eds.), *Review of child development research* (Vol. 4, pp. 305–345). Chicago: University of Chicago Press.

Goffman, E. (1959). *The presentation of self in everyday life.* Garden City, NY: Doubleday.

Goffman, E. (1967). *Interaction ritual: Essays on face-to-face behavior.* Garden City, NY: Doubleday.

Gotlib, I. H., & McCann, C. D. (1984). Construct accessibility and depression: An examination of cognitive and affective factors. *Journal of Personality and Social Psychology, 47,* 427–439.

Gottman, J. M. (1979). *Marital interaction: Experimental investigations.* New York: Academic Press.

Greenberg, L. S., & Safran, J. D. (1984). Integrating affect and cognition: A perspective on the process of therapeutic change. *Cognitive Therapy and Research, 8,* 559–578.

Greenwald, A. G., & Pratkanis, A. R. (1984). In R. S. Wyer, Jr. & T. K. Srull (Eds.), *Handbook of social cognition* (Vol. 3., pp. 129–178). Hillsdale, NJ: Lawrence Erlbaum Associates.

Gumperz, J. J., & Hymes, D. (Eds.). (1972). *Directions in sociolinquistics: The ethnography of communication.* New York: Holt, Rinehart & Winston.

Harre, R., & Secord, P. F. (1972). *The explanation of social behavior.* Totowa, NJ: Rowman & Littlefield.

Hastie, R., Ostrom, T. M., Ebbesen, E. B., Wyer, R. S. Jr., Hamilton, D. L., & Carlston, D. E. (Eds.). (1980). *Person memory: The cognitive basis of social perception.* Hillsdale, NJ: Lawrence Erlbaum Associates.

Hastie, R., Park, B., & Weber, R. (1984). Social memory. In R. S. Wyer, Jr. & T. K. Srull (Eds.), *Handbook of social cognition* (Vol. 2, pp. 151–212). Hillsdale, NJ: Lawrence Erlbaum Associates.

Hawes, L. C. (1973). Elements of a model for communication processes. *Quarterly Journal of Speech, 59,* 11–21.

Higgins, E. T. (1981). The "communication game": Implications for social cognition and persuasion. In E. T. Higgins, C. P. Herman, & M. P. Zanna, (Eds.), *Social cognition: The Ontario symposium* (Vol. 1, pp. 343–392). Hillsdale, NJ: Lawrence Erlbaum Associates.

Higgins, E. T. (1985). *Self-concept discrepancy: A theory relating self and affect.* Unpublished manuscript, New York University.

Higgins, E. T., Bond, R. N., Klein, R., & Strauman, T. (1986). Self-discrepancies and emotional vulnerability: How magnitude, accessibility, and type of discrepancy influence affect. *Journal of Personality and Social Psychology, 51,* 5–15.

Higgins, E. T., Fondacaro, R., & McCann, C. D. (1981). Rules and roles: The "communication-game" and speaker-listener processes. In W. P. Dickson (Ed.), *Children's oral communication skills* (pp. 289–312). New York: Academic Press.

Higgins, E. T., Herman, C. P., & Zanna, M. P. (1981). *Social cognition: The Ontario symposium* (Vol. 1). Hillsdale, NJ: Lawrence Erlbaum Associates.

Higgins, E. T., & King, G. A. (1981). Accessibility of social constructs: Information processing consequences of individual and contextual variability. In N. Cantor & J. F. Kihlstrom (Eds.), *Personality, cognition, and social interaction.* Hillsdale, NJ: Lawrence Erlbaum Associates.

Higgins, E. T., Klein, R., & Strauman, T. (1984). *Emotional change as a function of changes in the accessibility of discrepant self-concepts.* Unpublished manuscript, New York University.

Higgins, E. T., Klein, R., & Strauman, T. (1985). Self-concept discrepancy theory: A psychological model for distinguishing among different aspects of depression and anxiety. *Social Cognition, 3,* 51–76.

Higgins, E. T., Kuiper, N. A., & Olson, J. (1981). Social cognition: A need to get personal. In E. T. Higgins, C. P. Herman, & M. P. Zanna (Eds.), *Social cognition: The Ontario symposium* (Vol. 1, pp. 395–420). Hillsdale, NJ: Lawrence Erlbaum Associates.

Higgins, E. T., & McCann, C. D. (1984). Social encoding and subsequent attitudes, impressions, and memory: "Context driven" and motivational aspects of processing. *Journal of Personality and Social Psychology, 47,* 26–39.

Higgins, E. T., McCann, C. D., & Fondacaro, R. (1982). The "communication game": Goal-directed encoding and cognitive consequences. *Social Cognition, 1,* 21–37.

Higgins, E. T., McCann, C. D., Gavin, D. R., & Foxall, K. (1986). *Self-concept discrepancy and affect in relationships.* Unpublished manuscript, York University.

Higgins, E. T., & Parsons, J. E. (1983). Stages as subcultures: Social-cognitive development and the social life of the child. In E. T. Higgins, W. W. Hartup, & D. N. Ruble (Eds.), *Social cognition and social development: A sociocultural perspective* (pp. 15–62). New York: Cambridge University Press.

Higgins, E. T., & Rholes, W. S. (1978). "Saying is believing": Effects of message modification on memory and liking for the person described. *Journal of Experimental Social Psychology, 14,* 363–378.

Higgins, E. T., & Stangor, C. (1986). Context-driven social judgment and memory: When "behavior engulfs the field" in reconstructive memory. In D. Bar-Tal & A. Kruglanski (Eds.), *Social psychology of knowledge* (pp. 42–75). Cambridge England: Cambridge University Press.

Higgins, E. T., Strauman, T., & Klein, R. (1984). *Self-concept discrepancies and emotional problems.* Unpublished manuscript, New York University.

Higgins, E. T., Strauman, T., & Klein, R. (1986). Standards and the process of self-evaluations: Multiple affects from multiple stage. In R. M. Sorrentino & E. T. Higgins (Eds.), *Handbook of motivation and cognition: Foundations of social behavior* (pp. 23–63). New York: Guilford Press.

Hoffman, M. (1986). Affect, cognition and motivation. In R. M. Sorrentino & E. T. Higgins (Eds.), *Handbook of motivation and cognition: Foundations of social behavior* (pp. 244–280). New York: Guilford Press.

Holmes, J. G. (1981). The exchange process in close relationships: Microbehavior and macromotives. In M. J. Lerner & S. C. Lerner (Eds.), *The justice motive in social behavior: Adapting to times of scarcity and change* (pp. 261–284). New York: Plenum Press.

Ingram, R. E. (1984). Toward an information-processing analysis of depression. *Cognitive Therapy and Research, 8,* 443–478.

Isen, A. M. (1984). Toward understanding the role of affect in cognition. In R. S. Wyer & T. K. Srull (Ed.), *Handbook of social cognition* (Vol. 3, pp. 179–236). Hillsdale NJ: Lawrence Erlbaum Associates.

James, W. (1948). *Psychology.* New York: The World Publishing Co. (Originally published 1890)

Jones, E. E. (1964). *Ingratiation: A social-psychological approach.* New York: Appleton-Century-Crofts.

Jones, E. E., & Thibaut, J. W. (1958). Interaction goals as a bases of inference in interpersonal perception. In R. Taguiri & L. Petrullo (Eds.), *Person perception and interpersonal behavior* (pp. 151–178). Stanford, CA: Stanford University Press.

Kelley, H. H. (1952). Two functions of reference groups. In G. Swanson, T. M. Newcomb, & E. L. Hartley (Eds.), *Readings in social psychology* (pp. 132–154). New York: Wiley.

Kelley, H. H. (1979). *Personal relationships: Their structures and processes.* Hillsdale, NJ: Lawrence Erlbaum Associates.

Kelley, H. H. (1984). Affect in interpersonal relations. In P. Shaver (Ed.), *Review of personality and social psychology: Emotions, relationships and health* (Vol. 5, pp. 89–115). Beverly Hills: Sage.

Kelley, H. H., Berscheid, E., Christensen, A., Harvey, J. H., Huston, T. L., Levinger, G., McClintock, E., Peplau, L. A., & Peterson, D. R. (Eds.). (1983). *Close relationships.* New York: Freeman.

Kihlstrom, J. F., & Cantor, N. (1981). Mental representations of the self. In L. Berkowitz (Ed.), *Advances in experimental social psychology* (Vol. 17, pp. 1–47). New York: Academic Press.

Kraut, R. E., & Higgins, E. T. (1984). Communication and social cognition. In R. S. Wyer & T. K. Srull (Eds.), *Handbook of social cognition* (Vol. 3, pp. 87–128). Hillsdale, NJ: Lawrence Erlbaum Associates.

Kruskal, J. B., & Wish, M. (1978). *Multidimensional scaling.* Beverly Hills: Sage.

La Gaipa, J. J. (1977). Testing a multidimensional approach to friendship. In S. Duck (Ed.), *Theory and practice in interpersonal attraction* (pp. 249–270). New York: Academic Press.

Lazarus, R. S. (1982). Thoughts on the relations between emotion and cognition. *American Psychologist, 37,* 1019–1024.

Lazarus, R. S. (1984). On the primacy of cognition. *American Psychologist, 39,* 124–129.

Levine, J., & Moreland, R. (1982). Socialization in small groups: Temporal changes in individual-group relations. In L. Berkowitz (Ed.), *Advances in experimental social psychology* (Vol. 15, pp. 137–193). New York: Academic Press.

Levinger, G. (1983). Development and change. In H. H. Kelley, E. Berscheid, A. Christensen, J. H. Harvey, T. L. Huston, G. Levinger, E. McClintock, L. A. Peplau, & D. R. Peterson, (Eds.), *Close relationships* (pp. 315–359). New York: Freeman.

Lewin, K. (1935). *A dynamic theory of personality.* New York: McGraw-Hill.

Manis, M., Cornell, S. D., & Moore, J. C. (1974). Transmission of attitude-relevant information through a communication chain. *Journal of Personality and Social Psychology, 30,* 81–94.

Mandler, G. (1975). *Mind and emotion.* New York: Wiley.

Markus, H., & Nurius, P. (1986). Possible selves. *American Psychologist, 41,* 954–969.

Markus, H., & Zajonc, R. B. (1985). The cognitive perspective in social psychology. In G. Lindzey & E. Aronson (Eds.), *Handbook of social psychology* (3rd ed., Vol. 1, pp. 137–230). New York: Random House.

McCann, C. D., & Hancock, R. D. (1983). Self-monitoring in communicative interactions: Social cognitive consequences of goal-directed message modification. *Journal of Experimental Social Psychology, 19,* 109–121.

McCann, C. D., & Higgins, E. T. (1984). Individual differences in communication: Social cognitive determinants and consequences. In H. E. Sypher & J. L. Applegate (Eds.), *Understanding interpersonal communication: Social cognitive and strategic processes in children and adults* (pp. 172–210). Beverly Hills: Sage.

McCann, C. D., Breckler, S. J., & Devine, P. G. (1986). *Social goals: The nature and structure of interaction objectives.* Unpublished manuscript, York University.

McClintock, E. (1983). Interaction. In H. H. Kelley, E. Berscheid, A. Christensen, J. H. Harvey, T. L. Huston, G. Levinger, E. McClintock, L. A. Peplau, & D. R. Peterson (Eds.), *Close relationships* (pp. 68–109). New York: Freeman.

McGuire, W. J. (1969). The nature of attitudes and attitude change. In G. Lindzey & E. Aronson (Eds.), *Handbook of social psychology* (2nd ed., pp. 136–314). Reading, MA: Addison-Wesley.

McGuire, W. J. (1985). Attitudes and attitude change. In G. Lindzey & E. Aronson (Eds.), *Handbook of social psychology* (3rd ed., Vol. 2, pp. 233–346). New York: Random House.

Mead, G. H. (1934). *Mind, self, and society.* Chicago: University of Chicago Press.

Miller, G. A., Galanter, E., & Pribram, K. H. (1960). *Plans and the structure of behavior.* New York: Holt.

Modigliani, A. (1968). Embarrassment and embarrassibility. *Sociomety, 31,* 313–326.

Modigliani, A. (1971). Embarrassment, facework, and eye contact: - Testing a theory of embarrassment. *Journal of Personality and Social Psychology, 17,* 15–24.

Newtson, D., & Czerlinsky, T. (1974). Adjustment of attitude communications for contrasts by extreme audiences. *Journal of Personality and Social Psychology, 30,* 829–837.

Noller, P. (1985). Negative communications in marriage. *Journal of Social and Personal Relationships, 2,* 289–301.

Pike, G. R., & Sillars, A. L. (1985). Reciprocity of marital communication. *Journal of Social and Personal Relationships, 2,* 303–324.

Reusch, J., & Bateson, G. (1968). *Communication: The social matrix of psychiatry.* New York: Norton.

Rogers, C. R. (1961). *On becoming a person.* Boston: Houghton Mifflin.

Roseman, J. J. (1979). *Cognitive aspects of emotions and emotional behavior.* Paper presented at the Annual Convention of the American Psychological Association, New York.

Rule, B. G., Bisanz, G. L., & Kohn, M. (1985). Anatomy of a persuasion schema: Target, goals and strategies. *Journal of Personality and Social Psychology, 48,* 1123–1140.

Schachter, S. (1959). *The psychology of affiliation.* Stanford, CA: Stanford University Press.

Schachter, S., & Singer, J. E. (1962). Cognitive, social and physiological determinants of emotional state. *Psychological Review, 69,* 379–399.

Schank, R., & Abelson, R. (1977). *Scripts, plans, goals, and understanding.* Hillsdale, NJ: Lawrence Erlbaum Associates.

Shantz, C. U. (1983). Social cognition. In P. H. Mussen (Ed.), *Handbook of child psychology* (4th ed., Vol. 3, pp. 497–549). New York: Wiley.

Showers, C., & Cantor, N. (1985). Social cognition: A look at motivated strategies. In M. R. Rosenzweig & L. W. Porter (Ed.), *Annual Review of Psychology* (Vol. 36, pp. 275–305). New York: Annual Reviews.

Snyder, M. (1979). Self-monitoring processes. In L. Berkowitz (Ed.), *Advances in experimental social psychology* (Vol. 12, pp. 86–128). New York: Academic Press.

Sorrentino, R. M., & Higgins, E. T. (1986). *Handbook of motivation and cognition: Foundations of social behavior.* New York: Guilford Press.

Srull, T. K., & Wyer, R. S., Jr. (1986). The role of chronic and temporary goals in social information processing. In R. M. Sorrentino & E. T. Higgins (Eds.), *Handbook of motivation and cognition: Foundations of social behavior* (pp. 503–549). New York: Guilford Press.

Taylor, S. E., & Crocker, J. (1981). Schematic bases of information processing. In E. T. Higgins, C. P. Herman, & M. P. Zanna (Eds.), *Social cognition: The Ontario symposium* (Vol. 1, pp. 89–134). Hillsdale, NJ: Lawrence Erlbaum Associates.

Tubbs, S. L., & Moss, S. (1977). *Human communication* (2nd ed.). New York: Random House.

Turner, R. H. (1956). Role-taking, role standpoint, and reference group behavior. *American Journal of Sociology, 61,* 316–328.

Tversky, A., & Kahneman, D. (1981). The framing of decisions and the psychology of choice. *Science, 211,* 453–458.

Watzlawick, P., Beavin, J. H., & Jackson, D. D. (1967). *Pragmatics of human communication.* New York: Norton.

Wyer, R. S., Jr., & Srull, T. K. (1980). The processing of social stimulus information: A conceptual integration. In R. Hastie, T. M. Ostrom, E. B. Ebbesen, R. S. Wyer, Jr., D. L. Hamilton, & D. E. Carlston (Eds.), *Person memory: The cognitive basis of social perception* (pp. 227–300). Hillsdale, NJ: Lawrence Erlbaum Associates.

Wyer, R. S., Jr., & Srull, T. K. (1984). *Handbook of social cognition.* (Vols. 1, 2, & 3). Hillsdale, NJ: Lawrence Erlbaum Associates.

Young, F. W., & Lewyckyi, R. (1979). *ALSCAL user's guide.* Chapel Hill, NC: Institute for Research in the Social Sciences.

Zajonc, R. B. (1960). The process of cognitive tuning and communication. *Journal of Abnormal and Social Psychology, 61,* 159–167.

Zajonc, R. B. (1980). Feeling and thinking: Preferences need no inferences. *American Psychologist, 34,* 151–175.

Zajonc, R. B. (1984). On the primacy of affect. *American Psychologist, 39,* 117–123.

Zuckier, H. (1986). The paradigmatic and narrative modes in goal-guided inference. In R. M. Sorrentino & E. T. Higgins, (Eds.), *Handbook of motivation and cognition: Foundations of social behavior* (pp. 465–502). New York: Guilford Press.

5 Affect and Message Generation

Howard E. Sypher
Beverly Davenport Sypher
University of Kentucky

Any conceptualization of human communication and its attendent social cognitive foundations should be able to account for the effects of individuals' internal affective states, even though most fail to do so. Admittedly, these effects are complex and communicative behavior can be influenced in a variety of ways by relatively subtle to relatively intense affect-laden cues. But only recently have a number of efforts been directed toward understanding the role of communication and affect. Some of this research looks at affect and the effects of persuasive messages on a communicator (e.g., Petty, Cacioppo, & Kasmer, this volume). Other research also reviewed in this volume and elsewhere explores the impact of more intense affective stimuli (e.g., Zillmann, this volume).

A great deal of recent research has shown that even mild forms of positive (and perhaps negative) affect can have important effects on decision making, judgments, and a variety of cognitive processes (Isen & Daubman, 1984; Isen & Means, 1983; Isen & Shalker, 1982; Johnson & Tversky, 1983). This research indicates that mild positive affect can serve as a retrieval cue for other positive material in memory, can affect judgments of various kinds, and can even influence respondents' willingness to take different types of risks. Indeed, the link between affect and cognitive processing appears reasonably well substantiated in the psychological literature. In the field of communication there are equally substantial and varying arguments regarding the central role of social cognition and communication. And although affect and social cognition have been linked, there is very little work focusing on the nature and extent of this relationship.

Given the relatively well documented relationship between cognitive structure and communication and the equally impressive literature linking affect and cognitive structure (e.g., Isen & Means, 1983; Isen & Shalker, 1982) it is somewhat surprising that the relationship of mild forms of affect to message generation has been largely unexplored.

Following a review of research focusing on recent social psychological research on affect and communication, this chapter sketches the findings of two exploratory studies designed to investigate the relationship between affect, cognitive differentiation, and persuasive message generation. The research reviewed here deals with the effects of mild positive affect and its potential influence on impression formation, personal judgments, and communicative behavior.

AFFECT AND COGNITIVE STRUCTURE

In a series of studies Isen and her colleagues have suggested that affect influences not only memory but cognitive organization and the consequences of this organization (Isen & Daubman, 1984). In several investigations Isen and her co-workers found that induced affective states led to a tendency to simplify decision making in problem-solving situations. However, Isen also found that individuals in the positive affect group tended to recheck stimulus information less often, and although they were faster in solving problems, they were also susceptible to greater error. These results led Isen to suggest that although happy individuals may be more efficient, they also may be more distractable. Other research indicates that affect may result in multiple encoding and retrieval because the cued positive material may come from a wide range of stimuli (e.g., Bousfield, 1944; Isen, Johnson, Mertz, & Robinson, 1984).

Isen's research has employed a variety of creative ways of inducing affect. In some studies people were given free gifts, seated in comfortable surroundings and served refreshments, told they had performed particularly well on some task, or were asked to recall pleasant situations.

Isen's conclusions that affective state may influence the way in which items or units are grouped appears interesting in a variety of ways. Of special interest to us is her contention that the cognitive context induced in a positive affective state may be more complex and lead to multiple interpretions, retrieval, and encodings.

The notion that positive affect can enhance performance also appears to receive support from other work that has shown that good mood results in speedier information processing and makes things come to mind faster in decision-making tasks (Isen, Means, Patrick, & Nowicki, 1982; Masters, Bardin, & Ford, 1979). Similarly, work by Fiske and Taylor (1984) suggests that positive moods are more likely than negative moods to facilitate many kinds of behavior.

Of course, on the flip side there is a great deal of literature that shows that strong affect, such as that associated with strong emotions or arousal, can interrupt/disrupt ongoing cognitive processes (e.g., Maslach, 1979; Marshall & Zimbardo, 1979). So, mood or affect does not always enhance performance; indeed it can be repressive. Pfeiffer (1973), for example, has shown that certain communicative content may produce emotional blocks. These blocks are thought to be produced by emotional arousal that interferes with one's ability to listen to messages or even prevents one from recognizing message content. Mandler (1975) noted that when information is processed it goes through *meaning analysis* (a kind of semantic network integration). If this content is tagged with some kind of highly undesirable affective label then persons may avoid it or equally uncomfortable related information. So, what we have here is the possibility that particular areas in memory may be affected by the degree to which the information sought is threatening or unpleasant. Davis (1982) also suggests that unpleasant information may be encoded and stored in ways that make it more difficult to access. In a similar and possibly related vein, other work has shown that affect-laden schemata may result in a tendency to rely on information-processing short cuts (Delia, 1972; Hamilton, 1982; H. Sypher & Waltman, 1983).

COGNITIVE STRUCTURE AND COMMUNICATION:
THE CONSTRUCTIVIST APPROACH

A great deal of recent research in communication evidences a relationship between cognitive structure and message generation (see O'Keefe & Sypher, 1981). However this work, for the most part, has focused little attention on the the linkage between cognition, communication, and affect. Constructivist research in particular has documented an impressive array of findings linking cognitive differentiation with a variety of communication and communication-related abilities (persuasion, perspective-taking, comforting strategies, etc.). In most of this work, more cognitively differentiated persons were able to generate relatively large numbers of sophisticated messages in persuasive contexts and proved to be better social perspective takers. This research in communication appears to document a cognitive structure–communicative performance link.

In a number of studies (see Delia, O'Keefe, & O'Keefe, 1982) we and our colleagues have conducted research exploring these links. Drawing on early research by Crockett and his colleagues (Crockett, 1965; Crockett, Gonyea, & Delia, 1970; Crockett, Mahood, & Press, 1975) and influenced by the early work of Kelly (1955), a number of researchers in communication have sought to explore links between cognitive organization/structure and communicative behavior, especially the production of person-centered messages. Traditionally, these researchers have argued that developed cognitive systems contribute to the generation of more listener-adapted messages, and more recently, the argument has been that differentiated individuals develop more sophisticated messages that attend to their more complex intentions and goals (O'Keefe & Delia, 1982). This research tradition in communication has been labeled the *constructivist approach.*

In research operating from a somewhat different theoretical stance to Linville (1982a, 1982b), recent constructivist work in communication has focused on the consequences of informational or cognitive complexity. In this line of research, attempts have been made to explore the relationship between cognitive differentiation or complexity and communicative behavior or its antecedents (see Burleson & Waltman, in press; Delia, O'Keefe, & O'Keefe, 1982; O'Keefe & Sypher, 1981). This research has also begun to explore the relationship between cognitive differentiation and outcome variables in longitudinal studies with children and their mothers (Applegate, Burke, Burleson, Delia, & Kline, 1984) and with employees in large organizations (e.g., B. Sypher & Zorn, 1986). What appears relatively neglected at this point are efforts to examine in any detail the manner in which cognitive differentiation or organization can be influenced by affective reactions and in turn can influence message generation. In some ways this seems especially surprising because this work has been heavily influenced by Kelly (1955) whose theory of personal constructs emphasizes affect.

The constructivist line of work has employed a variety of free-response data-collection techniques to examine cognitive structure and communicative behavior and has focused on impressions of hypothetical (H. Sypher & D. O'Keefe, 1980) and real others (B. Sypher & Zorn, 1986), the analysis of written messages in hypothetical contexts (H. Sypher, Witt, & B. Sypher, 1986) and examined audio and videotaped persuasive situations (Applegate, 1982). At times, researchers have also employed rating scales (B. Sypher & H. Sypher, 1983), checklists (H. Sypher, Witt, & B. Sypher, 1986), and naturalistic methods (Applegate & Delia, 1980). However, our primary tool for the analysis of cognitive organization or complexity has been Crockett's (1965) Role Category Questionnaire (RCQ) of cognitive differentiation. This measure utilizes from two to eight role figures and requires the respondent to describe the qualities of these role figures (e.g., liked other, disliked other) in a free response format (see Crockett, Press, Delia, & Kenny, 1974, for a description of the coding procedures).

In employing the RCQ, we have almost exclusively sought to identify systematic individual differences in differentiation, integration, comprehensiveness, or some other aspect derived from structural analysis of impressions. Again, for the most part, these analyses have tended to ignore other interesting and important aspects of these impressions, especially affective dimensions. Although these analyses of known and unknown others have seemingly obvious affective qualities, this work has for the most part explored other dimensional aspects.

Despite potential shortcomings, this research has yielded a number of interesting and important findings. These analyses of impressions of known and unknown others have consistently resulted in individual differences in impression complexity, integration, and abstractness. This line of work has led to the claim that individuals vary in the extent to which they have relatively developed systems for conceptualizing others and their behavior. Further research has shown that these individual differences in cognitive system development relate to message generation abilities, especially in persuasive (O'Keefe & Delia, 1979) and comforting contexts (Burleson, 1984). Indeed, it may be that these individuals have greater or disproportinate accessibility of information, perhaps due to greater richness in the original trace (Ozier, 1980) or possibly to a general interest in others as a kind of "person orientation."

These findings suggest that information disproportionately accessible in memory will have a disproportionate impact on impression-formation processes and possibly on message generation that relies on these impressions. This argument is not new, and we have elsewhere posited an "availability" interpretation of the RCQ (H. Sypher & Applegate, 1984; see also O'Keefe & Delia, 1982) derived from the work of Tversky and Kahneman (1973). However, in this chapter we employ the term *accessibility* (see the distinction outlined by Higgins & King, 1981). In their original work, Tversky and Kahneman only examined individuals' estimates of event likelihood. However, in this chapter we have expanded on their conceptualization, employed the term *accessibility,* and applied it to persuasive message generation (see a similar argument by Reyes, Thompson, & Bower, 1980). Relevant to this discussion, we contend that mildly positive affect induced by thinking about liked others or positively described others is also likely to enhance recall of relevant (and related positively valenced) material in impressions and could enhance one's ability to develop persuasive messages.

We need not look far in the literature to see that people consistently describe liked (as opposed to disliked) individuals in a more differentiated fashion (Crockett, 1965; Crockett, Press, & Gonyea, 1968: Horsfall, 1969; B. Sypher & Zorn, 1985; H. Sypher & Waltman, 1983; Waltman & H. Sypher, 1986; Wicker, 1969). This consistent finding has usually been explained in terms of a "frequency-of-interaction" or "avoidance" hypothesis as opposed to a "vigilance" hypothesis. A frequency-of-interaction interpretation suggests that persons tend to have more complex cognitive systems for those they know well because they interact with them more often and have more behavioral and trait information upon which to make judgments or discriminations. Or conversely, persons are said to have less differentiated systems for disliked others because they tend to avoid them or to think about them less often. Interestingly, we have been unable to identify any research that directly links impression complexity to frequency of interaction.

Without downplaying the importance of differences in amount of interaction, it also seems plausible that impression tasks might be influenced by differences in information accessibility. That is, positive qualities, positive behaviors, positive trait terms, and so on, might be easier to access than negative qualities or that arousal might differentially influence memory (Clark, Milberg, & Ross, 1983). The linkages utilized in recall might be stronger because they receive more use. Indeed, there is some evidence that "positivity biases" exist in various appraisal processes, and we may have a situation where the pool of frequently accessed positive qualities is larger and richer or more interconnected than its converse negative pool. It appears feasible that this differential richness in domains may account for differences in the descriptions of liked and disliked others without regard to frequency of interaction. Previous research (Matlin & Stang, 1978) has shown that pleasant items tend to be better recalled than unpleasant items.

In some recent and detailed analyses of the content of impressions, B. Sypher and Zorn (1985) found, not too surprisingly, that liked others are described not only more differentially but with a very large proportion of positively valenced traits or constructs. More specifically, the results of this study showed descriptions of liked others contained proportionately fewer negative qualities than were found in descriptions of disliked others. Furthermore, the constructs used in the impressions of liked others were more tightly organized than those in impressions of disliked others.

Quite to the point, Isen and her coworkers have concluded that postive affect impacts on cognitive content and complexity and thus influences cognitive organization and interpretation. We suggest that a further link to communicative behavior, or more precisely message generation, needs to be explored. Indeed, we see this as a logical extension of ongoing work in communication and cognitive social psychology (see especially, Fiske & Pavelchak's, 1986 research on schema-triggered affect).

In the remainder of this chapter we report the results of initial explorations into the relationship of mild positive affect and message generation. This investigation is obviously tentative and preliminary, but we feel the results are suggestive. In the first part of this work we have attempted to examine the extent to which mild positive affect (or possibly "passive priming," although we recognize current definitional disputes) can influence impression formation and message generation.

AN INVESTIGATION OF MESSAGE GENERATION
AND AFFECT

In this study we had respondents (undergraduate student volunteers at a large southern university) either describe a liked or a disliked peer ($n = 54$) or form an impression of an unknown other ($n = 46$). The unknown other was described in all positive or a combination of positive and negative traits that taken together are approximately neutral in overall evaluation by Andersons' (1968) normative ratings. In the known-other condition, the respondents were asked to indicate on a 7-point scale how often they interacted with this peer (from several times a day to every few months). At a later session the respondents were asked to reread their original impression and then to utilize this information in a persuasive task.

To control for frequency-of-interaction effects and to vary priming conditions, some were given their impression of the known (liked or disliked) other, and some were given their impression of the unknown other to reread when generating a persuasive message. They were to persuade a known or unknown other to contribute money to the Red Cross. This task was then coded for the number of messages generated according to procedures outlined by O'Keefe and Delia (1979). Interrater reliability for all the codings was high (exceeding .90) and consistent with reliabilites reported in related literature.

Obviously, this line of work implies an assumption that affect and cognition are interrelated, and although it may be that in some cases affective and cognitive processes are independent, we leave these concerns to others (see Zajonc, Pietromonaco, & Bargh, 1982 for more detail).

Results

The results of this study are not unequivocal, but they are in the expected direction and do provide support for our contention that affect and cognition are related at least in terms of message generation. First respondents tended to write more differentiated impressions of liked others than disliked others ($t = 4.98$, $p < .01$). This is not surprising because much of the previously reviewed research supports this tendency. Second, respondents who were asked to reread their impressions of liked others tended to generate more arguments in the persuasive message task than respondents who were asked to direct their efforts toward persuading a disliked other ($t = 3.09$, $p<.01$).

Third, we found no significant differences in impression complexity for respondents who were asked to form an impression of an unknown other (Randy C.) who was described with either all-positive or an equal number of positive and negative traits (resulting in normative neutrality). Obviously, this result failed to support our previously hypothesized link between mild positive affect and impression formation. However, a number of other possible factors may be responsible, so we are not yet dussuaded of the possible hypothesized link.

Fourth, respondents who received the all-positive trait information and were asked to review their impression failed to generate more arguments in a persuasive task (the Red Cross letter) than did respondents who received mixed trait information. This result also failed to support our contention that mildly positive affect can positively influence message generation. Again, this finding should be considered very tentative because a number of questions might be asked about the extent to which mildly positive affect was introduced in this procedure. Remember, respondents only were asked to reread positive descriptions they had written themselves. We may have a procedural rather than conceptual problem in substantiating our claims.

Finally, the design of the study involving known others allowed us to examine the relationship between frequency of interaction, impression complexity, and message generation. An examination of the zero-order correlations among these variables is very illuminating. The correlation between impression complexity of the liked other and frequency of interaction was .24. The correlation between message generation and frequency of interaction was .25, whereas the correlation between impression complexity of the liked other and message generation was .28. Although the correlations are not very strong, they are clearly consistent in direction.

Hence, on the face of it, frequency of interaction appears to play a significant part in this process. However, an interesting thing happens when frequency of interaction is statistically paritalled. Contrary to what one might suspect, the correlation between impression complexity of the liked other and message generation goes up slightly to .31. So it appears, at least in this data, that frequency of interaction was acting as a supressor variable.

Discussion

On the whole, the results reported here provide mixed support for our hypothesized link between mildly positive affect and message generation. Obviously, we feel hesitant to make any strong statements at this point because a number of other factors may be involved. For example, we provided respondents with only a limited number of communicative situations. One situation can hardly be expected to be representative of the variety of persuasive contexts one encounters in social interaction.

We probably need to employ other ways of inducing mild affect. It seems entirely likely that positive affect was not induced in the unknown-other situation. The stimuli used in this study may have been too weak, impoverished, or pallid. For instance, we might have had respondents experience a pleasant event or informed them that they had done especially well on some task. These forms of inducing mild affect have been used in past studies.

Another possibility involves the importance that the respondents attached to the task. Bower and Cohen (1982) contend that the intensity of any emotion is highly dependent on the importance of the stimulus. In this study, known others (especially liked others) were probably seen as more important and hence generated somewhat more intense affect. Epstein (1982) makes a similar argument concerning the role of perceived significance in eliciting emotions.

The most interesting results centered on the possible influence of affect with known others. The findings of this study seem to suggest that we have a much richer conceptual domain for known-liked others, and this larger pool of positively valenced material may be beneficial in generating persuasive messages. Certainly, there is recent research (B. Sypher & Zorn, 1985) that suggests linkages in positively vaenced impressions are more tightly organized and thus likely to be more easily retrievable. We should be careful however, not to equate message production capabilities with persuasive skill. There are still questions of message quality, strategic message placement, and so on, to be handled.

Interestingly, these results showed a general failure to support a frequency-of-interaction or avoidance interpretation for differences between the complexity of impressions for liked and disliked others. This is somewhat puzzling because a great deal of previous work has posited such a relationship. Again, given the tentative nature of the present study we do not make much of this. However, it does suggest that future research should take into account other explanations for these well-documented differences in descriptions of liked and disliked others.

SUMMARY

In this chapter we have not speculated on the extent to which affect is a primary innate biological motivating mechanism. Nor have we argued for the primacy of cognition. Some of the other chapters in this volume touch more on these issues.

What we do contend is that affect plays a very important, but often neglected role in human communicative conduct. Indeed, in this chapter we only scratched the surface of what promises to be a very fertile area of work.

The interrelationship of cognition, communication, and affect are of obvious importance but their theoretical and empirical linkages remain somewhat of a puzzle. Several theoretical explanations involving spreading activation and semantic network models of memory have been offered. Bower and Cohen (1982) suggest that feelings can cause certain stimuli to become more salient, evoke deeper processing, and lead to better memory. They also contend that emotion influences a number of judgmental processes. Similar theoretical conceptualizations have been offered by others.

For the most part, communication researchers have ignored the role of affect. We, like a number of scholars in related fields, have focused our primary attention on cognitive functioning without regard to affect. Indeed, on the surface it appears we have ignored part of our rhetorical heritage. However, although rhetorical theorists have maintained an interest in the role of pathos or affect, the line of work we outline here is distinct in that it focuses on the influence of affect on the communicator and not the influence of emotional appeals on audience members or their attitudes. Similarly, most psychological work in this area focuses on the influence of affect on a communicator's persuasability, attitudes, and so on.

Historically, the role of emotion has received a great deal of attention in examinations of the universal recognition of emotions and nonverbal behavior. And although considerable work has been done in the area of nonverbal communication and emotion, especially facial expression (e.g., Ekman, 1982) with few notable exceptions (see Trevarthon, 1984) the relationship between verbal communication and affect continues to be ignored.

The results of the investigation reported here and our associated speculations do not stand alone. The role that affect plays in message production, persuasive behavior, listening, and so on has not received the attention it deserves. Future research efforts will no doubt begin to examine these and other aspects of communicative behavior. We see this research and related work in other areas of communication (some represented in this volume) as part of a growing chorus of researchers focusing on the interrelationship of affect, cognition, and communication.

REFERENCES

Anderson, N. H. (1968). Likeablenss ratings of 555 personality-trait words. *Journal of Personality and Social Psychology, 9,* 272–279.

Applegate, J. L. (1982). The impact of construct system development on communication and impression formation in persuasive contexts. *Communication Monographs, 49,* 277–289.

Applegate, J. L., Burke, J. A., Burleson, B. R., Delia, J. G., & Kline, S. L. (1984). Reflection-enhancing parental communication. In I. E. Sigel (Ed.), *Parent-child interaction* (pp. 107–142). Hillsdale, NJ: Lawrence Erlbaum Associates.

Applegate, J. L., & Delia, J. G. (1980). Person-centered speech, psychological development, and the contexts of language usuage. In R. St. Clair & H. Giles (Eds.), *The social and psychological contexts of language* (245–282). Hillsdale, NJ: Lawrence Erlbaum Associates.

Bousfield, W. A. (1944). An empirical study of the production of affectively toned items. *Journal of General Psychology, 30,* 205–215.

Bower, G. H., & Cohen, P. R. (1982). Emotional influences in memory and thinking: Data and theory. In M. S. Clark & S. T. Fiske (Eds.), *Affect and cognition* (pp. 291–331). Hillsdale, NJ: Lawrence Erlbaum Associates.

Burleson, B. R. (1984). Comforting communication. In H. E. Sypher & J. L. Applegate (Eds.), *Communication by children and adults: Social cognitive and strategic processes* (pp. 63–104). Beverly Hills, CA: Sage.

Burleson, B. R., & Waltman, M. E. (in press). The Role Category Questionnaire Measure of cognitive complexity. In C. H. Tardy (Eds.), *Instrumentation in communication research.* Norwood, NJ: Ablex.

Clark, M. S., Milberg, S., & Ross, J. (1983). Arousal cues arousal-related material in memory: Implications for understanding effects of mood on memory. *Journal of Learning and Verbal Behavior, 22,* 633–649.

Crockett, W. H. (1965). Cognitive complexity and impression formation. In B. A. Maher (Ed.), *Progress in experimental personality research* (Vol. 2, pp. 47–90). New York: Academic Press.

Crockett, W. H., Gonyea, A. H., & Delia, J. G. (1970). Cognitive complexity and the formation of impressions from abstract qualities or from concrete behaviors. *Proceedings of the 78th Annual Convention of the American Psychological Association, 5,* 375–376.

Crockett, W. H., Mahood, S. M., & Press, A. N. (1975). Impressions of a speaker as a function of set to understand or to evaluate, cognitive complexity, and of prior attitudes. *Journal of Personality, 43,* 168–178.

Crockett, W. H., Press, A. N., Delia, J. G., & Kenny, C. T. (1974). *Structural analysis of the organization of written impressions.* Unpublished manuscript, University of Kansas.

Crockett, W. H., Press, A. N., & Gonyea, A. T. (1968, August). *Affective stimulus value, discrimination among others, and measures of cognitive complexity.* Paper presented at meeting of the Eastern Psychological Association Washington, DC.

Davis, D. (1982). Determinants of responsiveness in dyadic interactions. In W. Ickes & E. Knowles (Eds.), *Personality, roles, and social behavior* (pp. 85–139). New York: Springer-Verlag.

Delia, J. G. (1972). Dialects and the effects of stereotypes on interpersonal attraction and cognitive processes in impression formation. *Quarterly Journal of Speech, 58,* 285–297.

Delia, J. G., O'Keefe, B. J., & O'Keefe, D. J. (1982). The constructivist approach to communication. In F. E. X. Dance (Ed.), *Human communication theory* (pp. 147–191). New York: Harper & Row.

Ekman, P. (1982). Methods of measuring facial action. In K. Scherer & P. Ekman (Eds.), *Handbook of methods in nonverbal behavior research* (pp. 45–90). Cambridge: Cambridge University Press.

Epstein, S. (1982). A research paradigm for the study of personality and emotions. In M. M. Page (Ed.), *Nebraska symposium on motivation, 1982* (pp. 46–67). Lincoln, NE: University of Nebraska Press.

Fiske, S. T., & Pavelchak, M. A. (1986). Category-based versus piece-meal base affect responses: Developments in schema-triggered affect. In R. M. Sorrentino & E. T. Higgins (Eds.), *Handbook of motivation and cognition: Foundations of social behavior* (pp. 167–203). New York: Guilford.

Fiske, S. T., & Taylor, S. E. (1984). *Social cognition.* Reading, MA: Addison-Wesley.

Hamilton, D. L. (1982). *Cognitive processes in stereotyping and intergroup behavior.* Hillsdale, NJ: Lawrence Erlbaum Associates.

Higgins, E. T., & King, G. A. (1981). Accessibility of social constructs: Information-processing consequences of individual and contextual variablity. In N. Cantor & J. F. Kihlstrom (Eds.), *Personality, cognition, and social interaction.* Hillsdale, NJ: Lawrence Erlbaum Associates.

Horsfall, R. A. (1969). *A comparison of two cognitive complexity measures.* Unpublished doctoral dissertation, The Johns Hopkins University, Baltimore, MD.

Isen, A. M., & Daubman, K. A. (1984). The influence of affect on categorization. *Journal of Personality and Social Psychology, 47,* 1206–1217.

Isen, A. M., Johnson, M. M. S., Mertz, E., & Robinson, G. F. (1984). *The influence of positive affect on the unusualness of word associations.* Unpublished manuscript, University of Maryland.

Isen, A. M., & Means, B. (1983). Positive affect as a variable in decision making. *Social Cognition, 2,* 18–31.

Isen, A. M., Means, B., Patrick, R., & Nowicki, G. (1982). Some factors influencing decision-making strategy and risk taking. In M. S. Clark & S. T. Fiske (Eds.), *Affect and cognition* (pp. 243–261). Hillsdale, NJ: Lawrence Erlbaum Associates.

Isen, A. M., & Shalker, T. E. (1982). The effect of feeling state on evaluation of positive, neutral, and negative stimuli: When you "accentuate the postive," do you "eliminate the negative?" *Social Psychology Quarterly, 45,* 58–63.

Johnson, E. J., & Tversky, A. (1983). Affect generalization and the perception of risk. *Journal of Personality and Social Psychology, 45,* 20–31.

Kelly, G. A. (1955). *A theory of personality.* New York: Norton.

Linville, P. W. (1982a). Affective consequences of complexity regarding the self and others. In M. S. Clark & S. T. Fiske (Eds.), *Affect and cognition* (pp. 71–109). Hillsdale, NJ: Lawrence Erlbaum Associates.

Linville, P. W. (1982b). The complexity-extremity effect and age-based stereotyping. *Journal of Personality and Social Psychology, 42,* 193–211.

Mandler, G. (1975). *Mind and emotion.* New York: Wiley.

Marshall, G. D., & Zimbardo, P. G. (1979). Affective consequences of inadequately explained physiological arousal. *Journal of Personality and Social Psychology, 37,* 953–969.

Maslach, C. (1979). Negative emotional biasing of unexplained arousal. *Journal of Personality and Social Psychology, 37,* 953–969.

Masters, J. C., Bardin, R. C., & Ford, M. E. (1979). Affective states, expressive behavior and learning in children. *Journal of Personality and Social Psychology, 37,* 380–391.

Matlin, M. W., & Stang, D. J. (1978). *The Pollyanna principle: Selectivity in language, memory, and thought.* Cambridge, MA: Schenkman.

O'Keefe, B. J., & Delia, J. G. (1979). Construct comprehensiveness and cognitive complexity as predictors of the number and strategic adaption of arguments and appeals in a persuasive message. *Communication Monographs, 46,* 231–240.

O'Keefe, B. J., & Delia, J. G. (1982). Impression formation and message production. In M. E. Roloff & C. R. Berger (Eds.), *Social cognition and communication* (pp. 33–72). Beverly Hills, CA: Sage.

O'Keefe, D. J., & Sypher, H. E. (1981). Cognitive complexity measures and the relationship of cognitive complexity to communication. *Human Communication Research, 8,* 72–92.

Ozier, M. (1980). Individual differences in free recall: When some people remember better than others. In G. H. Bower (Ed.), *The psychology of learning and motivation* (pp. 310–358). New York: Academic Press.

Pfeiffer, J. W. (1973). Conditions which hinder communication. In J. W. Pfeiffer & J. E. Jones (Eds.), *The 1973 annual handbook for group facilitators* (pp. 45–62). Iowa City: University Associates.

Reyes, R. M., Thompson, W. C., & Bower, G. H. (1980). Judgmental biases resulting from differing availabilities of arguments. *Journal of Personality and Social Psychology, 39,* 2–12.

Sypher, B. D., & Sypher, H. E. (1983). Self-monitoring and communication in an organizational setting. *Personality and Social Psychology Bulletin, 9,* 297–304.

Sypher, B. D., & Zorn, T. E. (1985, November). *Salient communication related constructs in descriptions of 'liked' coworkers.* Paper presented at the meeting of the Speech Communication Association, Chicago, IL.

Sypher, B. D., & Zorn, T. E. (1986). Communication-related abilities and upward mobility: A longitudinal investigation. *Human Communication Research, 12,* 420–431.

Sypher, H. E., & Applegate, J. L. (1984). Organizing communication behavior: The role of Schemas and constructs. In R. Bostrom (Ed.), *Communication yearbook 8* (pp. 310–329). Beverly Hills, CA: Sage.

Sypher, H. E., & O'Keefe, D. J. (1980, May). *The comparative validity of several cognitive complexity measures as predictors of communication relevant abilities.* Paper presented at the meeting of the International Communication Association, Acapulco, Mexico.

Sypher, H. E., & Waltman, M. E. (1983, November). *Dialect-cued social stereotypes: Differential utilization of base-rate information.* Paper presented at the meeting of the Speech Communication Association, Washington, DC.

Sypher, H. E., Witt, D. E., & Sypher, B. D. (1986). The comparative validity of three measures of cognitive differentiation as predictors of written communication ability. *Communication Monographs, 53,* 376–382.

Trevarthon, C. (1984). Emotions in infancy: Regulators of contact and relationships with persons. In K. Scherer & P. Ekman (Eds.), *Approaches to emotion* (pp. 129–157). Hillsdale, NJ: Lawrence Erlbaum Associates.

Tversky, A., & Kahneman, D. (1973). Availability: A Heuristic for judging frequency and probability. *Cognitive Psychology, 5,* 207–232.

Walman, M. E., & Sypher, H. E. (1986). *Cognitive differentiation and the perception of older persons: Vigilance or frequency of interaction.* Unpublished manuscript, Department of Communication, University of Tulsa.

Wicker, A. (1969). Cognitive complexity, school size and participation in school behavior settings: A test of the frequency of interaction hypothesis. *Journal of Educational Psychology, 60,* 200–203.

Zajonc, R. B., Pietromonaco, P., & Bargh, J. (1982). Independence and interaction of affect and cognition. In M. S. Clark & S. T. Fiske (Eds.), *Affect and cognition* (pp. 211–227). Hillsdale, NJ: Lawrence Erlbaum Associates.

6 Planning, Affect, and Social Action Generation

Charles R. Berger
Northwestern University

Miller, Galanter, and Pribram (1960) attempted to fill the gap between cognition and action with their Test-Operate-Test-Exit (TOTE) units. They argued that goal-directed action could be accounted for by the hierachical organization of these units. In this work, plans were accorded a central role in the production of actions instrumental to goal achievement. Since publication of this work, cognitive scientists and artificial intelligence researchers have found the plan construct to be of use in developing both explanations for human action and computer software designed to produce intelligent behavior. Artificial intelligence (AI) researchers have implemented planners to: guide robot arms (Sacerdoti, 1977), produce speech acts (Cohen & Perrault, 1979), organize sequences of errands (Hayes-Roth & Hayes-Roth, 1979) and understand action sequences (Schank, 1982; Schank & Abelson, 1977; Schmidt, 1976; Wilensky, 1981, 1983). Bruce (1980) has argued that goal and plan recognition are central to story understanding and Hobbs and Evans (1980) have shown how conversations can be viewed from a planning perspective. Some philosophers have also shown interest in the role that plans play in the production of human action. Brand (1984) sees plans as pivotal to the generation of intentional action; although he notes that plans themselves cannot provide a complete explanation for such action.

Interestingly, social psychologists identified with the social–cognition research enterprise have shown relatively little interest in action production; even though they have embraced such cognitive constructs as scripts (Abelson, 1976, 1981; Schank, 1982; Schank & Abelson, 1977) that have actional implications. Taylor and Crocker (1981) argue that scripts are one type of event schema and that one function played by such schemata is the production of action. Nevertheless, where the script construct has been employed in social psychological research, e.g. Langer's work on "mindlessness" (Langer, 1978; Langer, Blank, & Chanowitz, 1978; Langer & Weinman, 1981), it has been invoked to explain certain experimental outcomes. There has been little concern shown for the ways in which scripts or plans themselves drive social actions. This state of affairs is somewhat reminiscent of the late 1960s when attitude-change researchers became concerned with the relationship between attitudes and behavior only after hundreds of studies were reported in which attitudes were assessed through questionnaire responses (Wicker, 1969). The ensuing "crisis" spawned Fishbein and Ajzen's (1975) work on attitude-behavior consistency.

Lest history repeat itself, it is imperative that those interested in the relationships between cognition and communication focus their attention not only on the link between cognitive structures and the interpretation of the social actions of self and others, but also the role that cognitive structures play in driving human action. One might, of course, argue that the social–cognition research concerning social judgment and decision making (Kahneman, Slovic, & Tversky, 1982; Nisbett & Ross, 1980) does concern itself with the relationship between cognition and action. However, such assertions miss the point. In order for persons to act in social situations, it is not enough to reach a particular decision or to make a judgment. Persons must have available to them the procedural knowledge necessary to reach their goals; whatever those goals may be. It is one thing to decide that one is attracted to another person; it is quite another to know how to ask that person out for a date, as any young teenager will attest. It is the domain of procedural knowledge that has received short shrift in contemporary social–cognition research. The aim of this chapter is to begin to redress this imbalance.

Wilensky (1981, 1983) has argued that plans are implicated in both the understanding of actions and their production; although the two processes differ. In the case of understanding, persons derive explanations for others' conduct by inferring what their goals are and the plans they are employing to reach those goals. Thus, we have little difficulty understanding the following passage, even though the actor's goals and plans are not spelled out in detail:

> John went to the store. After he returned home, he microwaved a "Lean Cuisine" and consumed it with great gusto.

If we ask what John's goal was in this situation and why he did what he did, our understanding of mundane goals and plans enables us to construct a plausible explanation for John's actions.

The role played by plans in the generation of social action is the reverse of the understanding process. Goals are generated and then plans are constructed to reach them. This chapter focuses on this latter process; although at points the analysis presented has implications for action understanding. The first section of the chapter addresses a number of issues related to the development of planning theory. Given the current state of knowledge in this area, it is not possible to present a fully developed formal theory, however. The second section of the chapter reports some of our research that has examined the relationship between plans and social action.

TOWARD A THEORY OF PLANNING

What is a Plan?

Before considering the outlines of a theory of planning, a working definition of the plan construct is needed. Toward this end, it is fruitful to examine alternative definitions of plans that have been offered in the past. The following are a number of such definitions:

1. A *Plan is any hierarchial process in the organism that can control the order in which a sequence of operations is to be performed. . .* Moreover, we also use the term *Plan* to designate a rough sketch of some course of action, just the major topic headings in the outline, as well as the completely detailed specification of every detailed operation. (Miller, Galanter, & Pribram, 1960, pp. 16–17)

2. A plan is made up of general information about how actors achieve goals. A plan explains how a given state or event was prerequisite for, or derivative from, another state or event. . . Plans describe the set of choices that a person has when he sets out to accomplish a goal. . . A plan is a series of projected actions to realize a goal. (Schank & Abelson, 1977, pp. 70–71)

3. Planning concerns the process by which people select a course of action— deciding what they want, formulating and revising plans, dealing with problems and adversity, making choices, and eventually performing some action. (Wilensky, 1983, p. 2)

4. Planning includes assessing a situation, deciding what goals to pursue, creating plans to secure these goals, and executing plans. (Wilensky, 1983, p.5)

These definitions of *plans* and *planning* share a number of commonalities. First, definitions 2 and 4 explicitly mention the fact that the desire to achieve goals motivates the instantiation or fabrication of plans. Moreover, Miller et al. (1960) discuss the importance of goal-directed activity to the planning process. Second, the first two definitions emphasize the fact that plans consist of series of actions that can be performed to achieve goals. Third, the first two definitions highlight the general nature of planning knowledge. Schank and Abelson (1977) make the point that plans are the progenitors of scripts and that plans embody more general knowledge than their offspring. Finally, definitions 2 and 3 mention the notion of choice in plans and planning activity. Plans may include alternative paths from which the social actor can choose.

On the basis of these definitions, the following definition of the plan construct is offered:

> A plan specifies the actions that are necessary for the attainment of a goal or several goals. Plans vary in their levels of abstraction. Highly abstract plans can spawn more detailed plans. Plans can contain alternative paths for goal attainment from which the social actor can choose.

This definition embodies the general features of the definitions previously cited. However, it is worth noting that the definition proffered here as well as those just cited fail to mention the role played by affect in the planning process or how affect is related to plans themselves. In general, those interested in planning have virtually ignored the role that affect plays in planning; although Miller et al. (1960) devoted some discussion to the issue. Instead of trying to integrate affective dimensions into the definition of *plan,* the role played by affect in the planning process is discussed later in this section.

Goal Dynamics

Typically, social interactions involve simultaneous striving for a number of goals. For example, when a person attempts to persuade a friend to go with him or her to a movie, in addition to the obvious goal of influencing the friend the person may have the goal of maintaining their relationship. Of course, in any given situation, certain goals may be more important than others; although less important goals may set limits on how more important goals are pursued. Thus, the desire to maintain the friendship may limit the range of persuasion plans that can be deployed in the example situation previously discussed. Interaction goals may be either explicit or implicit; thus, social actors and actresses may be more or less aware of them. As interaction sequences unfold, the initial goals of the participants may be modified in a number of different ways. We now consider some of these possibilities.

Goal Dissolution.   As interactions progress, the persons involved in them may be unable to articulate the goals they held before entering the interaction. This phenomenon is little different from the situation in which persons set out for another room only to find that upon arrival they are unable to remember why they came to the room in the first place. Norman (1981) provides many examples of such action slips and attempts to explain why various types of slips occur. Goal dissolution may be followed by the creation of new goals during the interaction; that is, persons can enter conversations to accomplish one goal, but end up accomplishing another and not be able to articulate their original goal.

Goal Parlaying.   Another type of alteration of interaction goals concerns the situation in which a person enters an interaction to accomplish a particular goal but ultimately accomplishes a different but related goal. For example, a person may enter a conversation with another in order to try to develop a friendship; however, as the interaction progresses, and it becomes obvious that the friendship goal is being reached, the individual may raise the interaction ante by redefining the goal of the interaction such that the aim becomes one of developing a lover relationship with the other person. This situation is different from the goal dissolution sequence just discussed because the interactant remembers quite clearly what the original goal was; moreover, in the case of goal parlaying, the goals involved must somehow be related. Substitution of a new goal after dissolution involves the development of goals that are not necessarily related to previous ones.

Thwarted Goals.   Interaction goals may be altered because they are blocked in some way. Such thwarting can arise from at least two conceptually different sources. First, persons involved in interactions may have incompatible goals and experience goal conflict. Second, interactants may have compatible goals but because of the intrusion of a variety of factors, they are unable to reach them. For example, the persons themselves may not have the communication skills necessary to reach their goals or the social situation may be such that they are constrained from reaching their goals. The mere presence of other persons in the social situation may act as such a constraint.

Berger and Kellermann (1986) have reported findings that are relevant to the issue of goal incompatibility. In this study, persons were given specific interaction goals to achieve in their conversations with others. One member of each dyad was asked to find out as much as possible about his or her conversational partner during the course of an initial interaction. These High Seekers were paired with persons who were given either compatible or incompatible interaction goals. In the compatible cases, some partners were instructed to reveal as much as they could about themselves during the course of the interaction (High Revealers), while others were told to have a normal conversation (Normals). In the incompatible situation, the High Seekers were paired with persons who were told to reveal as little as possible about themselves (Low Revealers). Numerous verbal and nonverbal interaction indices were computed from the videotapes of the interactions. In addition, judges rated a number of aspects of the behavior of the interactants.

Manipulation checks revealed that High Seekers faced with Low Revealers reported significantly more difficulty in reaching their conversational goal than did High Seekers paired with either High Revealers or Normals. Thus, the experimental inductions created the desired effects. Comparisons of the three groups of High Seekers revealed that there were no significant changes in question-asking rate over the course of the 5-minute interactions; thus, thwarted High

Seekers asked no more or no fewer questions than did High Seekers whose goals were compatible with their partners' goals. However, High Seekers paired with Low Revealers did alter other aspects of their behavior in response to the thwarting offered by their reticent partners. When compared with the High Seekers in the compatible conditions, thwarted High Seekers tended to: (a) interrupt their partners less, (b) *not* answer questions about themselves, (c) utter fewer statements about themselves, (d) use more verbal backchannels, and (e) show fewer positive headnods. With the exception of the last class of behaviors, the other verbal and nonverbal behaviors on the list are aimed at either refocusing the conversation on the partner (not answer questions about self and utter fewer statements about self) or trying to increase the partner's level of responsiveness (interrupting less and increasing the use of verbal backchannels). Showing fewer positive headnods is inconsistent with these goals; however, this particular finding may be the result of the leakage of negative affect created by the frustrating behavior of the Low Revealers.

The findings of this study not only show how persons may compensate for failure by deploying a variety of tactical variations in their behavior, they also suggest that failure to reach interaction goals can provide considerable information about persons' planning capabilities. When persons are immediately successful at reaching their interaction goals, relatively little is learned about the breadth and depth of their planning repertoires. When persons fail to reach their interaction goals, however, they are forced to modify their current plan in some way, for example, access a new plan from a long-term store or fabricate an entirely new plan on-line. In any case, goal failure is likely to expose the extent of individuals' planning knowledge and their abilities to use that knowledge to organize their actions for further goal-seeking attempts. Of course, the astute social actor or actress knows when it is futile to continue to pursue a thwarted goal; thus, continued attempts to achieve a goal in the face of failure may not necessarily indicate the actions of an optimal planner.

The discussion presented in this section has not addressed the question of what specific goals persons typically pursue in social interaction situations. Rather, the focus has been upon the processes by which goals are modified and reformulated. In order to construct a useful theory of planning, it is necessary to tackle the problem of describing systematically the kinds of goals that social actors and actresses try to attain. Fortunately, McCann and Higgins (this volume) report the findings of initial studies designed to delineate the social goals for which persons strive. Ultimately, the findings of this line of research might be integrated with the process concerns discussed in this section.

Plan Formation

As indicated previously, plans needed to achieve particular goals may be available in long-term store or they may be constructed while the interaction is in progress. One would expect frequently used plans to be readily available in memory. Plans that are constructed on-line are most likely derived from other plans; that is, when persons do not have plans for particular goals, they search for similarities between the current situation and their store of plans to find those plans that resemble features of the current situation. From this collection of relevant plans, a new plan is fabricated. A similar process takes place when current plans fail to reach goals; although, evidence from the Berger and Kellermann (1986) study discussed previously suggests that all features of failed plans may not necessarily be discarded. Recall that the thwarted High Seekers did *not* reduce the rate at which they asked questions, even though their partners were being non-responsive. These High Seekers did change other features of their actions in response to failure. This pattern of actions suggests that goal thwarting may force planners to discard some aspects of their plans but maintain others. New tactical variations are then added to those aspects of the plan that are maintained. This *accretive model* of plan modification is considerably different from one that argues for a *discrete-linear* modification process. Under this latter view, failed plans are completely abandoned and new ones instantiated. Evidence from our study favors the accretive model. Apparently, the rule that is applied in the case of plan failure says something like, ''Even though you are failing, keep doing what usually works, but add some new things as well.''

At least two models of plan formation have been suggested by AI researchers. Sacerdoti (1977) has advanced a top-down planner to guide a robot arm. In his system, plans are initially formulated at a high level of abstraction. Successively more concrete levels of action are deduced from more abstract ones. At each level, the deduced sequence is compared with the desired end state through the use of critics to insure that the suggested sequence is one that will actually achieve the goal. In contrast to this top-down approach, Hayes-Roth and Hayes-Roth (1979) have proposed that planning is frequently an event-driven process. They have studied the think-aloud protocols of persons planning a sequence of errands in a hypothetical town. Persons were given a map of the town and a list of errands and and asked to trace the route that would enable them to finish the errands in the least amount of time. Their analyses of the think-aloud protocols revealed that persons frequently make false starts and backtrack as they become aware of various contingencies. Rather than planning in a top-down manner, persons are considerably more opportunistic in their planning.

In the domain of motor control, Newell (1978) has contrasted open-loop and closed-loop control systems. Open-loop systems are those that require detailed initial plans for actions. In such systems, plans are not subject to the vageries of events in the environment. The plan is instantiated on cue and the action sequence runs off ''according to plan.'' In contrast to this more rigid view of motor control is the closed-loop system. In closed-loop systems, initial plans are less detailed and are subject to revision as the action sequence unfolds. Newell argues that the more flexible closed-loop systems are most prevalent in the motor control domain.

In social-interaction situations where social actors and actresses attempt to achieve goals, both top-down, open-loop planning as well as event-driven, closed-loop planning mechanisms may operate. For example, most probably ritualistic interactions are the product of a top-down, open-loop planning process. Consider the following interaction sequence:

Parent: How was school today?
Child: I had a test in Algebra.
Parent: How was it?
Child: Not bad.
Parent: How did you do?
Child: O.K.

When adults are asked about the first thing their parents said to them upon arriving home from school, they frequently give the first line of our example dialogue. In this situation, the responses given by each person are so predictable that relatively little attention is paid to the content of the interaction itself and the parent achieves his or her interaction goal of greeting the child and/or of maintaining a conversation.

Although a considerable number of our daily interactions have a ritualistic character, there are many occasions when we are considerably more sensitive to the feedback our interaction partners provide us. Attempts to persuade, ingratiate, seek information, and so on are likely to be considerably more opportunistic in nature and driven by a closed-loop process that is sensitive to changes in the environment. This planning flexibility comes at a cost. We must expend more time and energy to develop, execute, and modify plans when we employ these planning modes. Top-down, open-loop systems generally require less time and energy for their execution; however, when such processes are used, flexibility is sacrificed.

Meta-Goals.   Wilensky (1981, 1983) has suggested that there are a limited number of meta-goals that guide the planning process. He argues, for example, that plans are developed with reference to their *efficiency*. Within the context of ongoing social interactions that are goal driven, it has been suggested that not only is efficiency one important meta-goal but the goal of *social appropriateness* is also of considerable importance (Berger & Kellermann, 1983; Kellermann & Berger, 1984). In some interaction situations, these two meta-goals may come into conflict with each other; that is, maximizing one will tend to minimize the other. Berger and Kellermann (1983) suggest this possibility in the domain of information seeking. Asking questions as an information-seeking strategy is probably more efficient than simply putting the target person at ease with the hope that the relaxed target will disclose the desired information. However, question-asking is considerably more intrusive than relaxing the target. Persons who ask too many questions in the context of an informal social interaction are likely to be labeled *pushy* or *obnoxious*. By contrast, those using a relaxation strategy by manipulating their verbal and nonverbal behaviors to be as pleasant as possible are likely to be judged more socially appropriate than interrogators.

Kellermann and Berger (1984) reported that persons may compensate for potentially adverse responses in information-seeking situations by trying to be especially positive through their nonverbal behaviors. Thus, persons who tried to be as efficient as possible by asking numerous questions of their partner also tried to increase their output of positive behaviors (smiles, etc.) to offset the potential negative effects of their questionning. Not only can compensation occur in such social-interaction situations, there may be occasions when the goals of efficiency and appropriateness are highly compatible with each other. For example, when persons seek approval (Rosenfeld, 1966) or attempt to ingratiate themselves to others (Jones, 1964; Jones & Wortman, 1973), the most efficient plan may also be the most appropriate one.

Possible and Probable Worlds.   Persons are quite capable of devising plans that they would probably never carry out. At a relatively young age, for example, most persons are capable of planning a variety of crimes; although they would never realize such plans in their actions. Persons may be able to imagine a variety of interaction scenarios with a spouse, boss, or co-worker that they would not actualize in their interactions with these persons. Thus, the number of possible worlds that individuals can imagine is potentially enormous. It is equally clear, however, that for most persons only a small subset of these worlds is translated into action. The critical question is what mechanism acts to select probable from possible worlds.

Certainly, part of the answer is to be found in meta-goals. Some possible worlds are eliminated because they entail actions that are socially inappropriate. Still others are rejected because they are judged to be relatively inefficient in the given situation. There is evidence, however, that when plans fail, actions that were previously suppressed because they were deemed inappropriate will be deployed. For example, two studies (Goodstadt & Kipnis, 1970; Kipnis & Consentino, 1969) reported that persons playing the role of supervisors became progressively more threatening and coersive in their interactions with employees as the employees rejected their influence attempts. When persons attempt to influence others, they generally begin with positive demeanors; however, as the target resists, there is a tendency for those attempting influence to be willing to resort to more negative influence tactics. Casual observation of parents shopping in supermarkets with their young children frequently shows this progression to be the case.

What is happening in these social-influence situations is that plans with an initial low probability of enactment, perhaps because of their low level of social appropriateness, are utilized because the desire to influence the other is so high.

Of course, although persons may drift toward more negative means of influence in the face of failure, the meta-goal of social appropriateness may set an *absolute limit* past which the person will not go. Thus, in the case of a failed influence goal, a given individual may not be willing to employ physical force in order to be influential; whereas, that possible world might become reality for someone whose planning process is either not governed by the meta-goal of social appropriateness or whose conception of social appropriateness differs from the first person's. Goodstadt and Hjelle (1973) found evidence for such individual differences in their study of thwarted influence attempts. Persons with external loci of control were prone to move to coercive influence tactics more quickly in the face of failure than were persons who exhibited internal loci of control.

Interacting Plans.   So far, our discussion of plan formation and its control has focused upon the individual planner. In the context of ongoing social interactions, the relationships between interactants' plans must be considered. Bruce and Newman (1978) have devised a system for representing interacting plans and shown how this system can be used to analyze such stories as *Hansel and Gretel*. In formulating plans for actions, individuals can be differentially sensitive to the possible contingencies that might be produced by the actions of their co-interactants. For example, when faced with the goal of persuading someone else, some persons might devise a single plan that will be followed regardless of the response given by the target of influence. Other persons might approach the same persuasion task with a number of alternative plans that are predicated upon responses of the influence target. Intuitively, it is reasonable to suppose that the latter planner would be more likely to be successful than the former. However, there is the distinct possibility that the person with a single plan may have the plan that is optimal for that particular situation; whereas, the person with a number of alternative plans may not have an optimal planning sequence among his or her options.

Although it is most likely the case that persons with wide-ranging planning repertoires are more able to adjust to the potential action options offered to them by their co-interactants, the sheer number of possibilities available is only a very gross measure of planning competence. Individuals with limited planning repertoires could be "experts" within a narrow domain of interactions. These persons might also be highly sensitive to their limitations so that they avoid interaction situations in which their limited capabilities are likely to be unsuccessful. Knowing one's limitations may be as much a hallmark of a competent social interactor as having a diverse planning repertoire avaliable to guide actions.

The previous discussion raises the thorny issue of defining what an optimal plan is. Certainly, in everyday social life we constantly make judgments about the abilities of family members, friends, and co-workers to reach certain social goals. Persons become known as "good salespersons," "great communicators" or persons who are "easy to talk to." In some cases there is considerable consensus on these social judgments. Similarily, some persons are judged to be relatively less competent at achieving various social goals. These differential judgments suggest the possibility of examining differences in planning capabilities between novices and experts in the same way that differences between novice and expert chess players have been studied (Chase & Simon, 1973). If differences between these groups are found, then it might be possible to determine whether the performances of novices can be improved by making the plans of novices more like those of experts.

While the preceding proposal seems straightforward, it is not without difficulties. It is certainly possible for persons to plan like experts but because of deficits in such areas as communication skills be unable to realize their sophisticated plans in their actions. Persons may be very capable of developing detailed plans concerning what they should say in a job interview but because of voice characteristics and other nonverbal features of their performance they may not be perceived as competent. This possibility suggests that less competent social interactors may have problems at planning and/or skill levels. For both theoretical and practical reasons it is important to separate these two possibilities.

One important measurement implication of the previous discussion is that attempts to develop global measures of social competence or planning competence are likely to be unsuccessful. If persons are differentially sophisticated at achieving different social goals and their performance is dependent on both cognitive and motor skills, it would seem almost futile to invent and attempt to measure general constructs like communicative competence or social competence. Rather, the more productive research strategy is likely to be one that is similar to that employed in the problem-solving literature (Newell & Simon, 1972). Analyses of the social task to be accomplished, the planning capabilities of social interactants, and the strategies used to accomplish social goals are likely to be more productive than the quest for global measures.

Another important implication of the notion of interacting plans is that persons can instantiate plans that are incompatible in some way; even though they are striving toward the same goals. These instances of *plan conflict* may arise because interactants, disagree about the relative efficiency or social appropriateness of their plans. Such disagreements might force interactants into formulating plans that will lessen or eliminate their disagreement. Although plan conflicts can obviously become intense, they are most probably easier to ameliorate than conflicts that arise from goal incompatibility.

One final implication of this discussion of interacting plans for communication researchers is that planning processes yield plans that go beyond the direction of verbal discourse. As we see in a later section of this chapter, plans include both verbal and nonverbal communicative components as well as actions that are not traditionally thought of as communicative in nature. For example, if the goal of an interactant is to acquire information directly from a target person, certain preconditions must be satisfied. The interactants will have to be proximate enough to interact, share a common language, and so on. Thus, plans may include action components that are necessary to satisfy these preconditions, for example, "I'll walk over to him and begin a conversation." Although the action of walking over to another person itself may be seen as less important than the study of the interaction that ensues after the action is performed, the "walking over to" action is a vital precondition that must be met before the interaction can occur. Such preconditions are important elements of plans and need to be considered by those who study social interactions.

Planning and Affect

Earlier, it was noted that planning can be related to both action understanding and action production. For purposes of the present discussion it is convenient to consider separately the relationships between affect and planning in these two domains. It was also pointed out that those interested in the cognitive processes involved in planning have not paid much attention to affect in their discussions. Moreover, Isen (1984) has concluded that relationships between cognition and affect are not very well understood and where such relationships exist, they are relatively complex. Space does not permit an exhaustive examination of the relationships among affect, cognition and action and the reader is referred to Isen's (1984) comprehensive review. What is offered here are some speculations regarding the role that affect plays in the planning process.

Affect, Planning, and Understanding.   Previously it was asserted that persons understand others' actions by inferring the goals that the others are pursuing and the plans they are believed to be using to achieve their goals. When persons achieve goals, their affective responses to success or failure indicate to observers the extent to which they valued the goals. Consider the following two situations:

1. John opened the envelope postmarked "Cambridge, MA." He smiled when he learned of his acceptance to Harvard.
2. John opened the envelope postmarked "Cambridge, MA." He shouted "Wow," and ran into the kitchen, hugged his mother, and cried when he learned of his acceptance to Harvard.

Certainly, most observers of the two Johns' actions would conclude that while both of them must be bright and hard working students, $John_2$ somehow wanted or desired the goal of entering Harvard more than did $John_1$. Similarly, if both had not been admitted to Harvard and $John_1$ simply frowned upon learning of his rejection while $John_2$ threatened suicide, observers would make similar inferences about the relative importance of the goal to the two individuals.

Although this example focuses upon affect that is displayed when persons find out whether or not they have achieved a goal, similar inferences concerning the importance of goals to individuals can be made by observing the conduct they display in the process of trying to reach goals. Thus, if we learned that as a high school student John$_1$ almost never studied and received poor grades, while John$_2$ studied 5 hours every night and received straight As, we would make the obvious inference regarding their relative levels of desire to enter Harvard. Thus, perceptions of energy expended, effort or arousal can guide inferences about goal desirability. This line of reasoning is similar to Heider's (1958) who emphasized the role of effort in his analysis of phenomenal causality.

Not only do affective displays serve as cues for evaluating the importance of goals to persons we observe, affective states may be explained by recourse to plan-goal relationships. Thus, if we ask why John is so happy or why he is so sad, knowledge of his goals and plans enables us to arrive at plausible explanations for the affect he displays. When we know that John wished to go to Harvard very much and spent his entire high school career trying to be a high achiever, we fully understand why he might be ecstatic upon hearing of his acceptance.

Although the present discussion has focused upon observers' understandings of others' actions, the same analysis could be applied to observers' understanding of their own actions and affects. In the spirit of self-perception theory (Bem, 1972), we might infer the importance of our goals from the types and magnitudes of affect we display in response to success or failure. Similarly, our knowledge of our own goals and plans, as well as the levels of effort expended to realize our goals, might serve to explain the direction and magnitude of affects we experience.

Affect, Planning, and Action.   As Isen (1984) notes, there seems to be considerable disagreement over the roles played by affect and cognition in the production of decisions and social judgments. Wilson (1979) and Zajonc (1980) argue for the primacy of affect, while others (Kahneman, Slovic, & Tversky, 1982; Nisbett & Ross, 1980) see judgment and decision making driven by cognitive processes flawed by the limitations of the information-processing system. At this point is time it is difficult to make a choice between these views, if there is one to be made. It is possible that at times, affect does assume a primary role in driving actions whereas at other times cognitive processes are primarily responsible for producing both actions and affect. It is certainly the case, however, that those interested in planning have focused their attention on cold cognitions; although there appear to be a number of different roles their hot counterparts might play in planning-action relationships.

First, persons realize plans with varying degrees of vigor. Thus, individuals may execute actions based upon identical procedural knowledge, but modulate their executions with varying degrees of intensity. Second, this general arousal level may be contrasted with more specific emotions that are part of a plan. For example, an individual might try to gain compliance from another by displaying ·sadness or disappointment as a way of gaining sympathy from the other. These displays might be rendered more or less intense depending on the general level of arousal associated with the execution of the planned emotion. Third, the levels of general activation and the direction of affects may come under the control of the meta-goals of efficiency and social appropriateness discussed earlier. However, under certain conditions, these goals may cease to exert constraints on plans and actions. For example, in instances of rage and extreme euphoria, action may be more driven by affect. Such affects may simply be reactive in nature and not part of any particular action plan. Thus, plans themselves may contain affective components; however, affective displays may not always be the product of plans. Finally, planned actions can be executed along continua of affect. There are usually nice ways to accomplish a particular goal as well as nasty or relatively neutral ways; although some goals almost demand particular affects. For example, ingratiation requires positive affect; by contrast, persuasion or social influence can be accomplished by strategies ranging from friendly persuasion to coersion.

By necessity this discussion has been highly speculative; because the connections among affect, planning, and social action are not well understood. What this discussion has demonstrated, however, is that observations of affective responses to success and failure serve to help persons understand others' actions. Furthermore, there are a number of potential roles that affect may play in the generation of action. Affect may be part of a plan, but not all affective displays are planned-based. Clearly, a critical theoretical and empirical question in need of attention concerns the conditions under which affect exerts a primary influence on action production and the circumstances under which plans that may include affective components are primarily responsible for the generation of action.

PLANNING AND DATE GETTING: WHERE THE ACTION IS

The previous section of this chapter emphasized a number of theoretical issues concerned with the development of a planning theory. Although further theoretical development in this area is essential, it is also important to begin to attack various problems related to the measurement of plans so that research can go forward. This section reports preliminary data that demonstrate the potential utility of a planning approach to the study of action generation. Because the present discussion is based on research that is in progress, there are many unanswered questions left at its conclusion. I hope that some of these unanswered questions are provocative enough to pique the curiosity of others interested action production.

The social goal that has been addressed in this research is that of asking another person for a date. This particular goal was chosen for two principal reasons. First, for many high-school and college students it is an important part of their social life. Research involving college students has been criticized on the grounds that many experimental tasks are irrelevant or uninvolving for the students; thus, their responses to these tasks are often atypical. Such is not the case with the domain of date requesting. Second, informal discussions with students at the beginning of this project revealed that there is considerable variability among students in their abilities to ask for dates. Thus, one might ultimately be able to identify "expert" and "novice" date getters and explore potential differences between these groups with regard to both planning capabilities and communication skills. We have not yet arrived at this point in our line of inquiry.

Planning Protocols.   In the first phase of this research, students were given a short questionnaire that contained the following open-ended item:

> Assume that you are at a party and you have just met a person to whom you are attracted. You decide that you would like to date this person next weekend. How would you go about asking the person for a date? What would you say? What would you do to achieve your objective; that is, what *steps* would you go through to get the date? Please *list* these steps in the space provided below.

In addition, the questionnaire contained a number of items concerned with various aspects of past and current dating behavior. Obviously, asking persons to report about typical action sequences invites potential memory distortion. Furthermore, this procedure does not allow us to determine the kinds of plans that persons can generate in the process of interacting with another. Ericsson and Simon (1984) have strongly advocated the use of think-aloud protocols to investigate cognitive processes during problem solving. However, it is difficult to imagine how such a procedure could be used realistically in the context of a date requesting episode; unless one is willing to place interactants into a rather bizarre set of circumstances.

Responding to the questionnaire during class time were 113 students in various communication courses at Northwestern University. A coding scheme for classifying action units was developed from these data. Because surface language can represent a particular conceptual category in a variety of ways, it was decided to try to develop a small set of conceptual action units (CAUs) to represent various classes of actions. For example, persons can use a variety of actions to make contact with target persons. Asking targets to dance, introducing themselves, or offering them food or drink are some potential ways to achieve this subgoal. All of the actions are subsumed under a more general conceptual category of ESTABLISH CONTACT. This strategy for representing actions at the conceptual level is similar to that employed by Schank (1975, 1982) and Schank and Abelson (1977). Figure 6.1 contains a list of the 15 CAUs isolated in this analysis. The HINT CAU was included because it was found that some persons chose to achieve the date-getting goal by inducing the other person to ask

PRE-INTERACTION ASSESSMENT = Observing, catching eye, etc.

ESTABLISH CONTACT = Introduce self, ask to dance, offer food/drink.

THIRD PARTY REFERENCE = Ask someone who knows person, are they available?

SMALL TALK = Typical initial conversational material.

SEEK SIMILARITIES/INTERESTS = Looking for common ground.

ASSESS INTEREST = Check for approval, ask third party for reaction.

SHOW INTEREST = Dance, offer drink, exchange phone numbers, smile.

FEASIBILITY ASSESSMENT = Find out plans, compare schedules.

INDIVIDUAL PLANNING ACTIVITY = Planning activity covertly for date.

HINT = Using hints to show interest in being asked out.

WAIT = Waiting for other person to ask out.

SEPARATION = Walk person home, get them out of party situation.

DELAY = Call for date later, arrange to bump into person.

ASK OUT = Actual act of requesting date.

FOLLOW-UP = Joint planning for date, assessing reasons for turn down.

FIGURE 6.1. Conceptual action units.

them out. This planning path frequently included hinting as a way of achieving this goal. Not included in the CAU list are actions that were labeled *atmospherics*. These are actions that are continuous in nature and have to do with setting a particular mood for the interaction. Persons mentioned that they would act friendly, use humor, and make eye contact frequently to increase the likelihood that they would be successful in obtaining the date. Presumably, these actions continue throughout the duration of the episode and are not part of the procedural sequence.

The protocols also contained *tests* that persons use to determine whether they should deploy the ASK OUT unit. The ASSESS INTEREST unit represents this kind of test; thus, if the target person appears to be sufficiently interested, ASK OUT is instantiated; however, if the target fails the interest test, the invitation is not extended. This contingency is critical because it hedges against the potential for embarrassment from being turned down. The humor atmospheric may also serve this function; that is, if the ASK OUT unit is deployed in a humorous manner and the target refuses, the asker can claim that he or she was "only kidding" and save face as a result. Thus, the ASSESS INTEREST unit as well as some of the atmospherics serve to lower the potential for negative affect during the date requesting episode.

Certain CAUs shown in Fig. 6.1 refer to highly generalized actions that can be employed in the pursuit of other social goals. For example, the PRE-INTERACTION ASSESSMENT, ESTABLISH CONTACT, SMALL TALK, ASSESS INTEREST, and HINT CAUs could be used in the process of persuading another or attempting to extract information from them. These more generalized subroutines may be action units that subserve the achievement of a wide variety of social goals beyond the one investigated here. How these more general units are organized and integrated with more goal specific actions is an important theoretical question in need of attention. Schank (1982) has sketched the broad outlines of such a theory in which Memory Organization Packets (MOPS) serve to organize scenes which, in turn, are realized in concrete action sequences or scripts. This organization departs considerably from Schank and Abelson's (1977) discussion of scripts and plans and may be a useful way in which to approach the present problem.

As part of the closed-questions at the end of the questionnaire, respondents were asked whether they were: (a) the one who usually asked the other for a date, (b) the one who was usually asked by the other for a date, or (c) asked and were asked with about equal frequency. Comparisons of males and females on this item revealed that females responded that they were asked more frequently than they asked (78% vs. 0%) and males asked more frequently than they were asked (66% vs. 11%). The "equal frequency" alternative was chosen about equally by males (26%) and females(22%). These gender differences are significant ($X^2 = 64.55$ $df = 2, p < .001$). Gender differences were also reflected in the planning units found in the protocols. Females displayed higher frequencies of Hint units

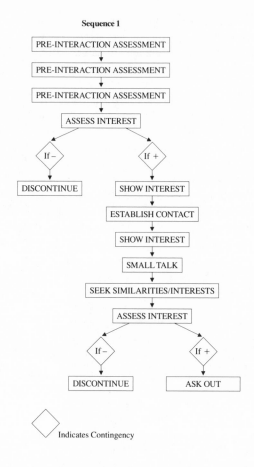

Sequence 1

than did males (females = 23%, males = 2%, $Z = 3.63$, $p < .001$). Thus, females were considerably more indirect in their date getting plans than were males; although a number of females followed the more direct planning paths.

Figure 6.2 displays some sample planning paths employing the CAUs of Fig. 6.1. The sequences displayed in Fig. 6.2 vary along a number of dimensions. Most obvious are the differences in the sheer quantity of action units. Some plans are extremely simple whereas others are quite elaborate. However, one must be careful in interpreting such differences because they may be the product of differential abilities to retrieve planning knowledge from memory rather than differences in the degree of elaboration of the plans themselves. Consistent with this line of reasoning is the fact that several of the example sequences shown in Fig. 6.2 do not explicitly include the ASK OUT unit; Although it is clear that for many of these sequences ASK OUT would be the most probable next step.

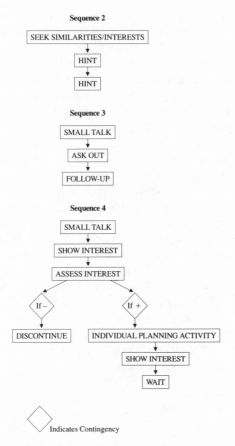

FIGURE 6.2. Example planning sequences.

The sequences in Fig. 6.2 also vary in their degree of sophistication. Although it is the case that longer sequences tend to be more sophisticated than shorter ones, longer sequences may differ with respect to the use of tests and the inclusion of such contingencies as ASSESS INTEREST. Moreover, the use of PRE-INTERACTION ASSESSMENT as well as various contingency paths may bespeak of potentially more effective plans. Again, it should be recalled that relatively simple plans may be more effective than more elaborate ones in a given situation; however, in the event of plan failure, the individuals with the more elaborate plans would most probably have an advantage over their unidimensional counterparts.

Plans and Actions. In order to determine whether there is any relationship between the planning sequences that persons verbally report and their behavior in a date-getting episode, a pilot study was conducted in which naive participants were given the goal of asking an opposite-sex conversational partner, whom they had never met before, for a date during an initial interaction. The conversational partners were confederates who were instructed to have normal initial conversations with their partners. The conversations lasted about 7 minutes. Participants were aware that their conversations were being videotaped from behind a one-way mirror. Three weeks before this session, participants had filled out planning protocols concerned with date getting. Participating in the study were 14 males and 15 females.

The central hypothesis tested in this study was that persons with more sophisticated planning knowledge should show fewer signs of uneasiness and anxiety than persons with less well-developed date-getting plans. The empirical indicator used to index uneasiness was adaptor duration; that is, the amount of time each person spent engaging in such behaviors as scratching themselves, wringing their hands, and playing with objects like keys or pencils. Adaptor duration has been widely used as an index of uneasiness (Knapp, Hart, & Dennis, 1974). The level of sophistication of plans was indexed in three different ways. First, the sheer quantity of actions included in each plan was determined. Second, the number of contingencies included in each plan was counted. Finally, each plan was rated for its overall sophistication by taking into account the use of contingencies and tests. Obviously, plan length correlates with this rating because plans that include contingencies and tests have to be longer than those not including them.

Two coders independently divided each protocol into action units. Action units are sentences or clauses that express a single action. The coders achieved an agreement rate of 80% in this phase of the protocol analysis. Coders then decided into which of the 15 CAU categories of Fig. 6.1 each unit fit. The agreement rate between coders for this phase of coding was 90%. Two coders then independently identified those points on the videotapes where persons showed adaptors. Their agreement rate for identifying these points was 82%. Once these segments were identified, they were independently timed by the coders. The correlation between the two coders' total times for each of the 29 participants was .94. These data lend support to the conclusion that coders were able to code both CAUs and adaptor durations with high levels of reliability. Disagreements that occurred were discussed and resolved.

In order to test the relationships between the three planning indices and total adaptor durations, zero-order correlations were computed between each of the three indices and total adaptor durations. The sheer number of CAUs in the protocols showed a correlation of $-.30$ ($p < .10$) with total adaptor durations. Although this correlation falls short of conventional significance levels, most probably because of the low power of the design, it does give some hint that persons who included more CAUs in their protocols spent less time showing signs of nervousness during their interactions than did persons who included fewer CAUs in their protocols.

Coders agreed on 84% of their contingency judgments. Because the number of contingencies appearing in the protocols is at least partially a function of the lengths of the protocols themselves, the number of contingencies included in each participant's protocol was divided by the number of CAUs contained in the protocol. This contingency ratio was then correlated with total adaptor durations. A correlation of −.22 was obtained in this analysis. Although this correlation is in the predicted direction, it does not approach conventional significance levels.

Three coders judged the overall sophistication of each participant's plan. These judgments were made on 5-point scales ranging from totally unsophisticated to extremely sophisticated. The sophistication judgments were based on the extent to which the planner included ways of testing the potential responses of the target, adapting to the potential responses of the target, and employing such subtle ways of influencing the target as atmospherics. The average correlation among three judges on this index was .91. The relationship between the sophistication index and total adaptor durations was −.34 ($p < .05$). Persons with more sophisticated plans spent less time displaying signs of nervousness during their interactions.

To determine whether there were any significant gender differences in the relationships between the three plan measures and adaptor durations, correlations between the three indices and adaptor durations were computed separately for males and females. The correlations between the number of planning steps and total adaptor durations were virtually identical for males and females (males = −.35; females = −.34). For males, the correlation between the contingency ratio and total adaptor duration was −.17, while the same correlation for females was −.25. Finally, the relationship between the sophistication index and total adaptor durations was −.27 for males and −.42 for females. Neither the contingency ratio nor the sophistication correlations were significantly different between the genders.

In addition to the between-gender correlation comparisons, t-tests were run to determine whether there were any gender differences on the number of steps, contingency ratio, sophistication, and total adaptor duration measures themselves. These tests revealed no significant gender differences for any of these variables; however, it will be recalled that females did include more HINT CAUs in their plans than did males. Thus, gender appears to make little difference in the level of plan complexity, but does make a difference in the specific actions that persons will use in carrying them out.

There are a number of potential explanations for the relatively modest correlations between plan sophistication and performance in interaction situations. First, it has been pointed out that in some instances, a simple plan might be the more optimal one in a given situation. Second, most probably persons can verbally report only parts of plans. Thus, persons whose protocols appear to represent simple plans actually may have considerably more complex plans available to them. The measures used in the present study would misclassify such persons as relatively unsophisticated planners. Third, it was argued previously that levels of communication skills as well as other variables in addition to plans determine social performance. Certainly, the levels of such skills are related to the degree of uneasiness shown in interactions. These skill factors were ignored in the present study. Finally, when persons provide verbal reports of plans, they may not be able to discriminate well between possible and probable worlds. Thus, plans that were actually used in the interactions may have differed from those that were provided on the protocols in terms of their complexity and content.

One way to circumvent this final problem might be to employ recognition measures of plans rather than the recall measure used in the present study. Alternative plans could be embodied in different stories and reading times used to determine which alternative is most prepotent for the individual. Using this approach, one might be able to establish a planning hierarchy for each individual. This kind of measure would help the researcher solve the possible versus probable worlds problem on an individual basis. Of course, the problem would be to provide a sample of plans that is representative of a plan universe. Preliminary work using the story approach has begun and it appears that reading times may provide a useful measure of plan prepotency.

Finally, ways must be developed to assess the extent to which plans are actually realized in social actions. The present study did not compare the structure of plans as articulated in the protocols with the structure of actions shown in the interactions. There are a number of alternative ways in which plan–action congruence might be assessed, but these approaches are likely to require considerable coding effort. What is needed is a relatively quick and easy way to determine structural congruence between plans and actions. In addition, a general theory of planning needs to be developed to guide research in this area. This chapter has presented a number of ideas to be considered in such a theory, but not a formal theory itself. Without such a theory, important aspects of the planning process might be overlooked and we may be left with a set of interesting findings and little else. Planning is critical to the production of human action. On that point many agree. Going beyond that assertion to the task of theory development and theory testing is the next step to be taken.

ACKNOWLEDGMENTS

The author would like to express his deep appreciation to Carol Miller-Tutzauer for her help in data collection. In addition, Martha Mastin and Maria Vignali spent many long hours coding protocols and Nancy Ames typed several versions of the manuscript.

REFERENCES

Abelson, R. P. (1976). Script processing in attitude formation and decision making. In J. S. Carroll & J. W. Payne (Eds.), *Cognition and social behavior* (pp. 33–45). Hillsdale NJ: Lawrence Erlbaum Associates.

Abelson, R. P. (1981). Psychological status of the script concept. *American Psychologist, 36,* 715–729.

Bem, D. J. (1972). Self-perception theory. In L. Berkowitz (Ed.), *Advances in experimental social psychology* (pp. 1–62). New York: Academic Press.

Berger, C. R., & Kellermann, K. A. (1983). To ask or not to ask: Is that a question? In R. N. Bostrom (Ed.), *Communication yearbook 7* (pp. 342–368). Beverly Hills: Sage.

Berger, C. R., & Kellermann, K. A. (1986, May). *Goal incompatibility and social interaction: The best laid plans of mice and men often go astray.* Paper presented at the annual convention of the International Communication Association, Chicago, IL.

Brand, M. (1984). *Intending and acting: Toward a naturalized action theory.* Cambridge, MA: MIT Press.

Bruce, B. C. (1980). Plans and social actions. In R. J. Spiro, B. C. Bruce, & William F. Brewer (Eds.), *Theoretical issues in reading comprehension* (pp. 367–384). Hillsdale, NJ: Lawrence Erlbaum Associates.

Bruce, B., & Newman, D. (1978). Interacting plans. *Cognitive Science, 2,* 195–233.

Chase, W. G., & Simon, H. A. (1973). Perception in chess. *Cognitive Psychology, 4,* 55–81.

Cohen, P. R., & Perrault, C. R. (1979). Elements of a plan-based theory of speech acts. *Cognitive Science, 3,* 177–212.

Ericsson, K. A., & Simon, H. A. (1984). *Protocol analysis.* Cambridge, MA: MIT Press.

Fishbein, M., & Ajzen, I. (1975). *Beliefs, attitudes, intentions, and behaviors.* Reading, MA: Addison-Wesley.

Goodstadt, B. E., & Hjelle, L. A. (1973). Power to the powerless: Locus of control and the use of power. *Journal of Personality and Social Psychology, 27,* 190–196.

Goodstadt, B., & Kipnis, D. (1970). Situational influences in the use of power. *Journal of Applied Psychology, 54,* 201–207.

Hayes-Roth, B., & Hayes-Roth, F. (1979). A cognitive model of planning. *Cognitive Science, 3,* 275–310.

Heider, F. (1958). *The psychology of interpersonal relations.* New York: Wiley.

Hobbs, J. R., & Evans, D. A. (1980). Conversation as planned behavior. *Cognitive Science, 4,* 349–377.

Isen, A. M. (1984). Toward understanding the role of affect in cognition. In R. S. Wyer, Jr. & T. K. Srull (Eds.), *Handbook of social cognition* (pp. 179–236). Hillsdale, NJ: Lawrence Erlbaum Associates.

Jones, E. E. (1964). *Ingratiation: A social psychological analysis.* New York: Appleton-Century-Crofts.

Jones, E. E., & Wortman, C. (1973). *Ingratiation: An attributional approach.* Morristown, NJ: General Learning Press.

Kahneman, D., Slovic, P., & Tversky, A. (Eds.). (1982). *Judgment under uncertainty: Heuristics and biases.* Cambridge: Cambridge University Press.

Kellermann, K. A., & Berger, C. R. (1984). Affect and the acquisition of social information: Sit back, relax and tell me about yourself. In R. N. Bostrom (Ed.), *Communication yearbook 8* (pp. 412–445) Beverly Hills: Sage.

Kipnis, D., & Consentino, J. (1969). Use of leadership powers in industry. *Journal of Applied Psychology, 53,* 460–466.

Knapp, M. L., Hart, R. P., & Dennis, H. S. (1974). An exploration of deception as a communication construct. *Human Communication Research, 1,* 15–29.

Langer, E. J. (1978). Rethinking the role of thought in social interaction. In J. H. Harvey, W. Ickes, & R. F. Kidd (Eds.), *New directions in attribution research* (Vol. 2, pp. 35–58). Hillsdale, NJ: Lawrence Erlbaum Associates.

Langer, E. J., Blank, A., & Chanowitz, B. (1978). The mindlessness of ostensibly thoughtful action: The role of 'placebic' information in interpersonal interaction. *Journal of Personality and Social Psychology, 36,* 635–642.

Langer, E. J., & Weinman, C. (1981). When thinking disrupts performance: Mindlessness on an overlearned task. *Personality and Social Psychology Bulletin, 7,* 240–243.

Miller, G. A., Galanter, E., & Pribram, K. H. (1960). *Plans and the structure of behavior.* New York: Holt, Rinehart & Winston.

Newell, A., & Simon, H. A. (1972). *Human problem solving.* Englewood Cliffs, NJ: Prentice-Hall.

Newell, K. M. (1978). Some issues in action plans. In G. E. Stelmach (Ed.), *Information processing in motor control and learning* (pp. 41–54). New York: Academic Press.

Nisbett, R., & Ross, L. (1980). *Human inference: Strategies and shortcomings of social judgment.* Englewood Cliffs, NJ: Prentice-Hall.

Norman D. A. (1981). Categorization of action slips. *Psychological Review, 88,* 1–15.

Rosenfeld, H. M. (1966). Instrumental affiliative functions of facial and gestural expressions. *Journal of Personality and Social Psychology, 4,* 65–72.

Sacerdoti, E. D. (1977). *A structure for plans and behavior.* New York: Elsevier.

Schank, R. C. (1975). *Conceptual information processing.* New York: American Elsevier.

Schank, R. C. (1982). *Dynamic memory.* New York: Cambridge University Press.

Schank, R. C., & Abelson, R. P. (1977). *Scripts, plans, goals and understanding: An inquiry into human knowledge structures.* Hillsdale, NJ: Lawrence Erlbaum Associates.

Schmidt, C. F. (1976). Understanding human action: Recognizing the plans and motives of other persons. In J. S. Carroll & J. W. Payne (Eds.), *Cognition and social behavior* (pp. 47–67). Hillsdale, NJ: Lawrence Erlbaum Associates.

Taylor, S. E., & Crocker, J. (1981). Schematic bases of social information processing. In E. T. Higgins, C. P. Herman, & M. P. Zanna (Eds.), *Social cognition: The Ontario symposium* (pp. 89–134). Hillsdale, NJ: Lawrence Erlbaum Associates.

Wicker, A. W. (1969). Attitudes versus actions: The relationship of verbal and overt behavioral responses to attitude objects. *Journal of Social Issues, 25,* 41–78.

Wilensky, R. (1981). Meta-planning: Representing and using knowledge about planning in problem solving and natural language understanding. *Cognitive Science, 5,* 197–233.

Wilensky, R. (1983). *Planning and understanding: A computational approach to human reasoning.* Reading, MA: Addison-Wesley.

Wilson, W. R. (1979). Feeling more than we can know: Exposure effects without learning. *Journal of Personality and Social Psychology, 37,* 811–821.

Zajonc, R. B. (1980). Feeling and thinking: Preferences need no inferences. *American Psychologist, 35,* 151–175.

7 The Role of Affect in the Elaboration Likelihood Model of Persuasion

Richard E. Petty
Ohio State University

John T. Cacioppo
University of Iowa

Jeff A. Kasmer
University of Missouri-Columbia

Over the past several decades, researchers have documented a large number of variables that have an impact on persuasion, and a plethora of theories have developed around these variables to account for the underlying processes responsible for attitude change (cf. Kielser, Collins, & Miller, 1969; Petty & Cacioppo, 1981; Smith, 1982). In this chapter, we are concerned primarily with attitude changes that take place as a result of exposure to persuasive communications and we highlight the role of *affect* in the process of attitude change. By *attitudes,* we mean the general evalutaions that people hold of various objects, issues, or other people. These evaluations can be based on a person's assessment of *feelings* (positive or negative affective states), *beliefs* (information and knowledge), *behaviors* (overt movements and action) or some combination of elements (cf. Cacioppo & Petty, 1982a; Petty & Cacioppo, 1986b; Zanna & Rempel, in press).

Our goal in this chapter is to present a general framework for organizing, categorizing, and understanding the basic processes underlying the effectiveness of persuasive communications. This scheme, called the Elaboration Likelihood Model (ELM) of persuasion, describes the specific roles that variables can have in producing attitude change and it specifies the consequences of attitude changes induced by different processes. Before beginning our discussion of the role of affect in persuasion and the ELM, it is necessary to provide a brief overview of the theory.

OVERVIEW OF THE ELABORATION LIKELIHOOD MODEL

In the typical persuasion situation, an individual or group receives a communication from another individual in a particular setting. The communication, which usually presents reasons or arguments in favor of an advocated position, may be delivered in person or via some print, audio, or video medium. Each of the various elements of the persuasion situation (i.e., source, message, recipient, channel, context) has been studied in depth and has been shown to account for some of the variance in attitude change (McGuire, 1969, 1985). Yet, the accumulated literature on the effects of these variables is hardly consistent. For example, although it might seem quite reasonable to propose that by associating a message with an expert source, agreement can be increased (e.g., see Aristotle's *Rhetoric*), contemporary research findings suggest that expertise effects are considerably more complicated than this. Sometimes expert sources have the expected effects (e.g., Kelman & Hovland, 1953), sometimes no effects are obtained (e.g., Rhine & Severance, 1970), and sometimes reverse effects are noted (e.g., Sternthal, Dholakia, & Leavitt, 1978). Unfortunately, no consensus exists as to the conditions under which each of these effects can be obtained and the processes involved in producing them. Similar patterns of contradictory results have been observed for many of the other variables examined by persuasion researchers.

Central and Peripheral Routes to Persuasion

The Elaboration Likelihood Model represents an attempt to integrate the many seemingly conflicting findings regarding source (and other) factors under one conceptual umbrella by specifying a finite number of ways in which source (and other) variables have an impact on persuasion.[1] The ELM is based on the notion that people want to form correct attitudes as a result of exposure to a communication (because these will normally prove most adaptive in functioning in one's environment), but that there are a variety of ways in which a reasonable position may be adopted.

The most effortful procedure for evaluating an advocacy involves carefully scrutinizing and elaborating the issue-relevant arguments in the persuasion situation along the dimensions that are perceived central to the merits of the attitude object. Of course, the dimensions that are perceived central to the merits of any stimulus may vary across attitude objects and across different individuals (cf. Katz, 1960; Snyder & DeBono, 1985). For example, consider three people who

---

[1]Space limitations do not permit a complete explication of the ELM here. Interested readers should consult Petty and Cacioppo (1986a) for a more detailed treatment.

are watching a film extolling the virtues of taking a skiing vacation in Colorado. Person A, who is a sensation seeker (see Zuckerman, this volume), may engage in sports activities primarily because of the feelings of exhilaration that they bring. When Person A watches the film, he is attuned to his bodily responses. An attempt is made to extrapolate the current bodily sensations to those that might be experienced when actually skiing and to compare the present or anticipated feelings to memories of the affect induced by other sports activities, all in an attempt to evaluate the merits of the skiing vacation. Person B, on the other hand, selects sports activities primarily on the basis of the perceived ease or difficulty of engaging in the behavior per se. This person carefully scrutinizes the behavior of the skiers in the film and calls to mind his own behavioral repertoire. During this process he might call to mind his past behaviors that are perceived similar to the target behavior (e.g., water skiing) and his performance on these behaviors. Finally, Person C selects recreational activities primarily on the basis of cost. This person carefully attends to the information presented about the room and meal rates at the resorts, the cost of equipment rentals, and he compares this information to his stored knowledge about the cost of previous vacations.

Importantly, each person in this example is attempting to *elaborate* upon the message in order to determine the true merits of the advocated skiing vacation. That is, each person is attempting to access relevant associations, images, and experiences from memory and to evaluate the appeal in light of this stored information. In short, each person has engaged in considerable cognitive effort in order to evaluate the fundamental merits of the advocated vacation. Of course, this extensive scrutiny provides no guarantee that a subjectively (or objectively) veridical opinion will be formed. For example, all three people may decide to sign up for skiing vacation and discover that it does not meet expectations. Nevertheless, according to the ELM, attitudes formed via this *central route* are expected to be relatively persistent, predictive of behavior, and resistant to change until they are challenged by cogent contrary information along the dimension or dimensions perceived central to the merits of the object.

In the skiing vacation example, each person was diligently processing the communication. However, it is neither adaptive nor possible for people to exert considerable mental effort in processing all of the persuasive communications to which they are exposed (cf. Miller, Maruyama, Beaber, & Valone, 1976). Indeed, people often act as "lazy organisms" (McGuire, 1969) or "cognitive misers" (Taylor, 1981). This does not mean that people never form attitudes when motivation and/or ability to scrutinize a message are low, but rather attitudes may be changed as a result of relatively simple associations or inferences in these situations. For example, consider Person D who also watched the skiing vacation advocacy, but who is not motivated to think about the message in any depth (perhaps because it is perceived as irrelevant). Following the film, this person is asked to give an opinion about a skiing vacation on a questionnaire. The person reports a favorable attitude because the beautiful scenery in the film induced a very positive mood. Unlike Person A for whom the induced affect was central to evaluating the true merits of the vacation (i.e., the affective information served as an argument), for Person D the affect served as a peripheral cue that produced a positive evaluation without extensive thinking about the true merits of the attitude object. Importantly, the film may have produced the same affective response and the same attitudes in Persons A and D, but the affect served very different roles for the two people. Attitude changes that occur via the *peripheral route* are postulated to be less persistent, resistant, and predictive of behavior than attitudes changed via the central route. Figure 7.1 depicts the general antecedents and consequents of the two routes to persuasion.

Possible Effects of a Treatment in the ELM

In the previous discussion we have seen that the ELM holds that variables may have an impact on persuasion by serving as persuasive *arguments,* providing information as to the central merits of an object or issue, or by serving as peripheral *cues,* allowing favorable or unfavorable attitude formation in the absence of a diligent consideration of the true merits of the object or issue. According to the ELM, the third way in which a variable can have an impact on persuasion is by affecting the extent or direction of argument *elaboration.* As shown in Fig. 7.1, persuasion via the central route requires that people have the requisite motivation and ability to personally evaluate the perceived merits of the attitude object or issue. Persuasion via the peripheral route may occur when either motivation or ability to process are low. Thus, the elaboration likelihood, as determined by a person's motivation and ability to process the arguments in the communication, moderates the route to persuasion.

Figure 7.2 summarizes how the possible effects of a variable on persuasion according to the ELM can be uncovered. This depiction assumes that the researcher has identified arguments on the topic of interest that are *strong* (likely to elicit primarily favorable elaborations when scrutinized) and *weak* (likely to elicit primarily unfavorable elaborations when scrutinized) and that the investigator manipulates some "treatment" along with the manipulation of argument quality (the figure also depicts the effects of a message containing a mixture of strong and weak arguments). The top panel of Fig. 7.2. graphs the results of a hypothetical study in which the treatment had no effect on attitudes. In Panel Ia, conditions of low-elaboration likelihood are shown, and in Panel Ib conditions of high-elaboration likelihood are depicted. In neither case does the treatment produce an effect. However, when the elaboration likelihood is very high, the argument quality manipulation exerts a main effect on attitudes. This argument effect is attenuated or eliminated when elaboration likelihood is low.

In Panel II of Fig. 7.2, the effects of a treatment serving as a peripheral cue are diagrammed. In Panel IIa the treatment serves as a positive cue, whereas in Panel IIb the treatment serves as a negative cue. Note that in the pure case of cue

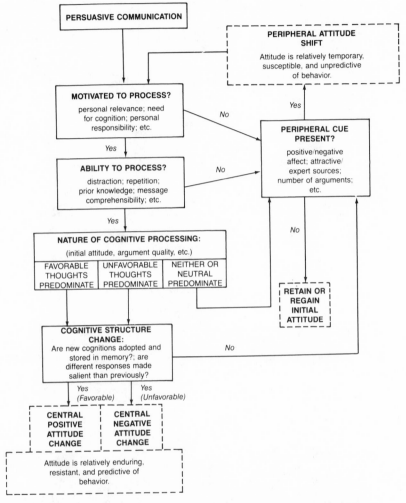

FIGURE 7.1. Schematic depiction of the two routes to persuasion. This diagram depicts the possible endpoints after exposure to a persuasive communication according to the Elaboration Likelihood Model. As shown in the figure, both *motivation* and *ability* to process a message are necessary for the central route to occur (adapted from Petty & Cacioppo, 1981, 1986b).

Effects of a Treatment

I. No Effect:

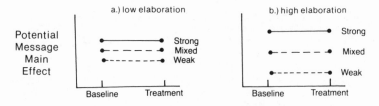

II. Cue Effect:

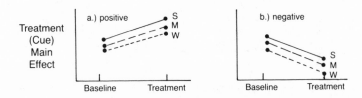

III. Objective Processing:

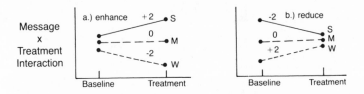

IV. Biased Processing:

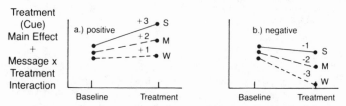

FIGURE 7.2. Impact of variables on attitude change according to the ELM. In Panel I, the treatment has no effect, and argument quality has an impact if the elaboration likelihood is high. In Panel II, the treatment serves as either a positive or negative peripheral cue. In Panel III, the treatment enhances or reduces processing in a relatively objective manner. In Panel IV, the treatment affects processing in a more biased fashion (from Petty & Cacioppo, 1986a).

processing, the cue affects all messages equally. Note also that because cues are postulated to operate mostly when the elaboration likelihood is low, Panel II depicts a large main effect for the cue treatment, but little effect for argument quality.

Panel III in Fig. 7.2 depicts the expected results for variables that affect message elaboration in a relatively objective manner. If the treatment enhances message scrutiny over some baseline condition, then subjects should better realize the cogency of strong arguments but the flaws in weak ones (Panel IIIa); however, if a treatment reduces message scrutiny, then subjects should be less likely to realize the merits of the arguments (Panel IIIb). In short, when a treatment enhances or reduces message elaboration, an interaction between the treatment and argument quality is expected.

In Panel IV of Fig. 7.2, the treatment is also having an impact on message processing, but rather than enhancing or reducing relatively objective processing, the treatment is motivating or enabling processing in a favorable or unfavorable direction. However, unlike the operation of positive and negative peripheral cues (Panel II), the message arguments impose some constraint on the operation of variables that bias processing. For example, consider a person who is motivated to *counterargue* and not simply *discount* a message. Active counterargumentation will be easier (and result in greater resistance) to the extent that the message contains weak rather than strong arguments (see Panel IVb).

Evidence for the Two Routes to Persuasion

Our initial attempts to validate the ELM proceeded in several stages. First, we sought to demonstrate that numerous variables could have an impact on persuasion by affecting the likelihood of message elaboration. Next, we sought to demonstrate that the impact of peripheral cues on persuasion would be greater when the elaboration likelihood was low rather than high. Then, we sought evidence for the postulated consequences of the two routes to persuasion.

Motivation and Ability to Process.   Many variables have been shown to have an impact on persuasion by affecting the likelihood of message elaboration. For example, in Box 1 of Fig. 7.3 the effects of the personal relevance of a message on persuasion are shown. In this study (Petty & Cacioppo, 1979b), college students were exposed to a counterattitudinal message advocating that seniors be required to pass a comprehensive exam in their major area as a prerequisite for graduation. For half of the subjects, the message arguments were strong and compelling (e.g., average starting salaries are higher for graduates of schools with the exams), and for the other half the arguments were weak and specious (e.g., by not administering the exams, a tradition dating back to the ancient Greeks was being violated). To create two levels of personal relevance, half of the subjects were led to believe that the speaker advocated that the exam policy

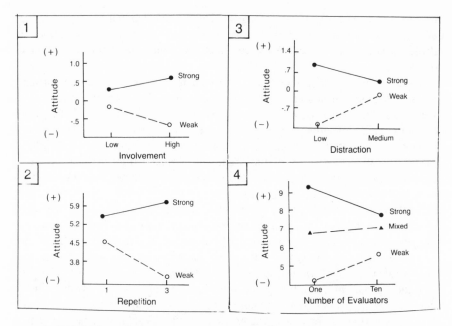

FIGURE 7.3.   Variables that enhance or reduce message processing in a relatively objective manner. In Box 1, the effects of personal relevance (involvement) are depicted (data from Petty & Cacioppo, 1979b). In Box 2, the effects of message repetition are shown (data from Cacioppo & Petty, 1983). In Box 3, the effects of distraction are graphed (data from Petty, Wells, & Brock, 1976). In Box 4, the effects of group responsibility are presented (data from Petty, Harkins, & Williams, 1980).

be instituted at their own university (high relevance), whereas half were led to believe the speaker advocated that the exam policy be instituted at a distant university (low relevance).

Importantly, previous research and theorizing (based on social judgment theory; Sherif & Sherif, 1967) had suggested that increasing the personal relevance of a counterattitudinal appeal would invariably reduce persuasion (e.g., Pallak, Mueller, Dollar, & Pallak, 1972) because increasing relevance (ego involvement) cause subjects to judge a counterattitudinal advocacy as more discrepant thereby making it more likely that the message would fall in a person's "latitude of rejection." Instead of finding increased relevance leading to greater disagreement with the communication, we found that relevance and argument quality interacted. When the arguments were strong, increasing relevance led to more agreement, but when the arguments were weak, increasing relevance led to less agreement (see Box 1, Fig. 7.3). Recall that this is the pattern that would be expected if increasing personal relevance enhances message elaboration (cf.

Panel IIIa in Fig. 7.2). This effect has been replicated by ourselves (e.g., Petty & Cacioppo, 1984) and others (e.g., Leippe & Elkin, 1987).

The remaining boxes in Fig. 7.3 depict the results for other variables we have found to affect message elaboration and thereby persuasion. In Box 2, it can be seen that just as increasing personal relevance motivates additional processing, providing extra opportunities for a person to consider the implications of a message via repetition can also increase argument scrutiny (see Cacioppo & Petty, 1985). On the other hand, if a message is accompanied by external distraction, people have fewer resources to allocate to the message and processing is thereby disrupted (see Box 3; Petty, Wells, & Brock, 1976). Motivation loss can also contribute to reduced message processing such as when it is made salient to a person that he or she is part of a group that is responsible for message evaluation (see Box 4; Petty, Harkins, & Williams, 1980). Other variables that we have found to affect the elaboration likelihood include the number of sources delivering the message (Harkins & Petty, 1981), whether the arguments are summarized in statement form or as rhetorical questions (Petty, Cacioppo, & Heesacker, 1981), the posture of the message recipient (standing or reclining; Petty, Wells, Heesacker, Brock, & Cacioppo, 1983), and whether the individuals show chronic differences in their tendencies to engage in and enjoy thinking (as assessed with the "need for cognition" scale, Cacioppo & Petty, 1982b; Cacioppo, Petty, & Morris, 1983).

In addition to variables affecting motivation and ability to process message arguments in a relatively objective fashion, other variables have an impact on persuasion by *biasing* message elaboration. These variables work by motivating or enabling favorable or unfavorable thoughts in particular. For example, because stored topic-relevant knowledge tends to be biased in favor of peoples' own attitudes (see Crocker, Fiske, & Taylor, 1984), the more issue-relevant knowledge a person has, the more they will tend to be able to counter-argue communications opposed to their opinions and cognitively bolster congruent ones (e.g., Lord, Ross, & Lepper, 1979; Wood, 1982).

In our own research we have uncovered a number of variables that appear to bias message processing. In order to bias processing in the unfavorable direction one can forewarn subjects of the persuasive intent of the speaker on an involving issue (Petty & Cacioppo, 1979a) or repeat the message a tedious number of times (Cacioppo & Petty, 1979). On the other hand, in order to bias processing in the favorable direction one can employ techniques such as presenting arguments that reflect the subjects' self-schemata (Cacioppo, Petty, & Sidera, 1982) or having subjects engage in vertical head movements during message receipt (Wells & Petty, 1980).

Peripheral Cues Versus Message Processing.   Once it was clear that numerous variables could have an impact on persuasion by affecting the extent and/or direction of message processing, it was important to document the postulated tradeoff between message processing and the operation of peripheral cues. Recall that when the elaboration likelihood is high, the ELM holds that persuasion should result primarily from the evaluation of the issue-relevant arguments presented. On the other hand, when the elaboration likelihood is low, persuasion should more likely be a function of the peripheral cues in the persuasion context. Testing this notion requires establishing conditions of high- and low-elaboration likelihood and including manipulations of peripheral cues as well as argument strength in the persuasion context.

In one investigation of the tradeoff between peripheral cues and argument processing, we asked college students to listen to a message over headphones that advocated that seniors be required to pass a comprehensive exam in their major as a requirement for graduation (Petty, Cacioppo, & Goldman, 1981). Three variables were manipulated in the study: personal relevance of the message, argument quality, and the expertise of the source. Relevance was manipulated by having the speaker advocate either that the new exam policy be instituted at the students' own university next year (high relevance) or 10 years in the future (low relevance). The eight strong or eight weak arguments comprising the message were attributed to either a report prepared by a local high-school class (low expertise) or to a paper prepared by the Carnegie Commission on Higher Education that was chaired by a Princeton University professor (high expertise).

Following message exposure, subjects rated their attitudes toward the exams. Main effects for the source and arguments manipulations were qualified by two significant interactions. First, a relevance × argument quality interaction replicated the finding reported previously (Box 1, Fig. 7.3) that as personal relevance increased, argument quality became a more important determinant of persuasion. In addition, however, a Relevance × Source expertise interaction indicated that source expertise became a more important determinant of persuasion as relevance *decreased*. The results for all cells in this study are graphed in Fig. 7.4. In the top panel it can be seen that under low-relevance conditions, increasing source expertise enhanced agreement regardless of argument quality (a peripheral cue effect as depicted in Panel IIa in Fig. 7.2). In the bottom panel it can be seen that under high-relevance conditions, source expertise had no significant effect on attitudes, only argument quality was important.

Several conceptual replications of this research have been reported. For example, in one study we presented print advertisements to students and led them to believe that they either would (high relevance) or would not (low relevance) soon make a decision about the product class featured in the target advertisement (Petty, Cacioppo, & Schumann, 1983). The target ad depicted either a pair of liked (celebrity athletes) or neutral (average citizen) endorsers and presented either strong or weak arguments for the product. As in the previous study, argument quality was a more important determinant of persuasion when the relevance of the ad was high rather than low, but the celebrity status of the endorsers was a more important determinant of influence when the relevance of

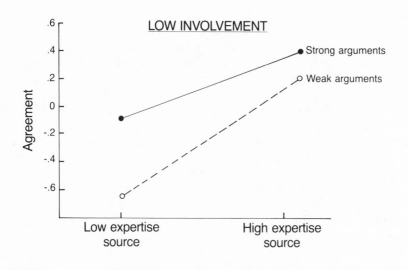

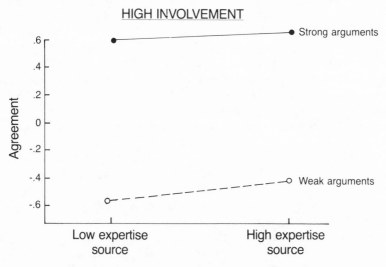

FIGURE 7.4. Issue involvement moderates the route to persuasion. The top panel shows that source expertise serves as a peripheral cue under low-relevance (involvement) conditions, and the bottom panel shows that argument quality exerts a greater impact on attitudes under high-relevance conditions (data from Petty, Cacioppo, & Goldman, 1981).

the ad was low rather than high (see also, Chaiken, 1980; Rhine & Severance, 1970).

The accumulated research on persuasion not only supports the view that source expertise and attractiveness are more important as peripheral cues when the personal relevance of a message is low rather than high, but so too are other simple cues such as the mere number of arguments in a message (Petty & Cacioppo, 1984), the visual salience of the message source (Borgida & Howard-Pitney, 1983), and the nonverbal behavior of the source (Huddleston, 1985). In addition, variables other than personal relevance that have proven to be effective moderators of the extent of argument processing have also proven to be effective moderators of peripheral cues. Thus, high distraction disrupts argument processing (Petty et al., 1976) but enhances reliance on peripheral cues such as source expertise (Kiesler & Mathog, 1968); people low in need for cognition show less reliance on argument quality than do people high in need for cognition (Cacioppo et al., 1983), but more reliance on peripheral cues such as the mere number of others who endorse a position (Chaiken, in press; Haugtvedt, Petty, & Cacioppo, 1986, Experiment 1); high prior knowledge enhances argument processing but reduces the impact of peripheral cues such as the simple length of a message (Wood, Kallgren, & Priesler, 1985) or the mere number of arguments presented (Alba & Marmorstein, in press).

Consequences of the Route to Persuasion.   As we noted previously, the existing literature is quite consistent with our view that there are two fundamentally different routes to persuasion. One is based on a careful and deliberate consideration of arguments central to the merits of the advocacy, whereas the other is based on peripheral cues in the persuasion context that induce change in the absence of argument scrutiny. Importantly, changes induced via these different routes may appear quite similar immediately after message exposure, but are postulated to have quite different properties. For example, reconsider the data presented in Fig. 7.4. Two groups of subjects in this study (Petty, Cacioppo, & Goldman, 1981) received a message from an expert source that contained strong arguments. For one of these groups the message was on a topic of high personal relevance, but for the other group the message was of low relevance. As indicated in Fig. 7.4, both of these groups showed *equally favorable* attitudes toward the issue after message exposure. However, according to the ELM, these two groups of subjects supposedly followed two very different routes to persuasion. Similarly, two groups of subjects in this study received a message from a low expertise source that contained weak arguments. Again, one group received the message under conditions of high relevance and the other received the message under conditions of low relevance. Both groups of subjects showed *equally unfavorable* attitudes toward the issue following message exposure. Again, however, the ELM postulates that even though the two groups adopted similar attitudes, the processes underlying persuasion were very different.

Although the attitudes in this study that were presumably induced by different processes do not appear any different upon immediate measurement, it should be possible to document the postulated consequences of the different routes to persuasion. In one study, for example, we validated the hypothesized difference in temporal persistence of attitudes induced via the two routes. Specifically, in this study (Petty, Cacioppo, Haugtvedt, & Heesacker, 1986, Experiment 1) experimental subjects were exposed to the strong or weak senior comprehensive exam message under conditions of either high or low personal relevance. The strong message was always attributed to a prestigious and expert source, whereas the weak message was always attributed to a low prestige and inexpert source. Attitudes were measured immediately after message exposure and again 10 to 14 days later under the guise of a phone opinion survey. The control subjects were not exposed to either of the comprehensive exam messages but had their attitudes measured at the same times as the experimental subjects.

The results of this study are presented in Fig. 7.5. As expected, on the initial measure of attitudes, both the high- and low-relevance groups exposed to the positive communication (i.e., strong message from an expert source) did not differ from each other, but were more favorable than controls. Also, both the high- and low-relevance groups exposed to the negative communication (i.e., weak arguments from an inexpert source) did not differ from each other, but were less favorable than controls. More interestingly, the degree of personal relevance had an impact on whether or not these initial attitudes persisted. An analysis of attitudes of subjects in the high-relevance group showed only a main effect for message indicating that the attitudes of these subjects persisted over time. However, an analysis of attitudes of subjects in the low-relevance group revealed a Message × Time interaction. For these subjects, the initial difference between the two message conditions was no longer apparent at the delayed testing. In short, those subjects who formed their initial attitudes based on a careful consideration of issue-relevant arguments (high relevance) showed greater persistence of attitude change than those subjects whose attitudes were based primarily on the peripheral source cue (low relevance).[2]

Importantly, other persuasion studies also support the view that conditions that foster people's motivation or ability to engage in issue-relevant cognitive activity enhance the persistence of persuasion (see Cook & Flay, 1978; Petty, 1977, for reviews). In addition, the available literature is generally congenial to

---

[2]In general, attitudes based on issue-relevant thinking should persist longer than attitudes based on relatively simple cues. Two factors may produce exceptions to this principle, however. First, relative persistence may result from the *repeated* pairing of a peripheral cue with an advocacy. These attitudes, although persistent in a vacuum, would likely be highly susceptible to counterpropaganda because people would have great difficulty defending their positions if attacked with strong arguments. Second, enduring attitudes may be classically conditioned with *one* exposure if the cue (i.e., CS) is sufficiently intense. Persuasive communications are rarely associated with such powerful cues, however.

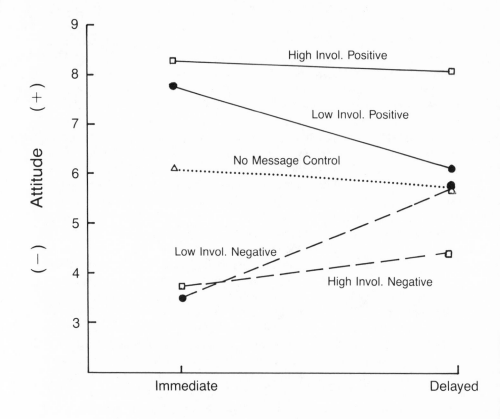

Time of Attitude Measurement

FIGURE 7.5. Temporal persistence of attitude changes induced under the central and peripheral routes. The figure shows that attitude changes, whether induced by a positive (strong arguments, expert source) or negative (weak arguments, inexpert source) communication, persist longer when initially processed under high rather than low-involvement conditions (data from Petty, Cacioppo, Haugtvedt, & Heesacker, 1986).

the view that when the experimental conditions or dispositional factors enhance people's motivation or ability to process issue-relevant information, the resulting attitudes are more resistant to counterpersuasion and predictive of behavior (see McGuire, 1964; Petty & Cacioppo, 1986a, for reviews). For example, in one study we found that people who differed dispositionally in their enjoyment of thinking also differed in the extent to which their attitudes predicted their behavior (Cacioppo, Petty, Kao, & Rodriguez, 1986). Specifically, the pre-election attitudes toward the candidates in the 1984 Presidential campaign were more predictive of subsequent voting behavior for people who were high rather than low in need for cognition.

MULTIPLE ROLES FOR VARIABLES IN THE ELM

We have now seen that there are two fundamentally different routes to persuasion that have different antecedents and consequences. When the elaboration likelihood is high, argument processing dominates. When the elaboration likelihood is low, cue processing is more likely. One of the intriguing, but complicating aspects of the ELM, is that it holds that any one variable can serve in multiple roles. Thus, any variable may serve as a persuasive argument in some situations, act as a peripheral cue in others, and affect the extent or direction of argument elaboration in still other contexts. Importantly, the ELM specifies the general conditions under which variables operate in these different roles.

Multiple Effects of Source Attractiveness

Some examples should help to clarify the multiple roles that variables can play in persuasion according to the ELM. In our own research, for instance, we have observed that source attractiveness can affect attitudes in different ways. Based on the research presented thus far, it might seem reasonable to propose that source attractiveness serves as a peripheral cue, inducing attitude change in the absence of argument scrutiny (cf. Mills & Harvey, 1972). Indeed, we have found that the physical attractiveness of a message source can serve as a simple positive cue for people who characteristically tend to dislike thinking. In one study, for instance, people who were high and low in their need for cognition (NC) were exposed to an advertisement for an electric typewriter (Haugtvedt et al., 1986, Experiment 2). One version of the ad featured two very attractive endorsers of the product and the other ad featured two unattractive endorsers. As expected, the results of this study showed that subjects who were low in NC were influenced by the attractiveness of the endorsers, but that subjects who were high in NC were not (see also, Cacioppo & Petty, 1984).

Importantly, we have also observed other effects for source attractiveness. In the study just described, the attractiveness of the endorsers was completely peripheral to the merits of the product (a typewriter). For some products, however, endorser attractiveness may provide information that is central to an evaluation of merit. For example, what if the product was shampoo rather than a typewriter? Now the physical appearance of the endorsers may provide visual testimony about the effectiveness of the product. In a study that was conceptually similar to the typewriter study, we exposed students to an advertisement for a new shampoo product that featured either two very attractive endorsers or two unattractive endorsers (Petty & Cacioppo, 1980). To manipulate the students' motivation to elaborate the ads, some were told that the shampoo would be marketed only in Europe (low relevance), whereas others were told that the product would soon be marketed in the local area. In addition, the ads employed either strong verbal arguments or weak ones for the shampoo. First, this study replicated the Relevance × Argument quality interaction that we have observed in previous research—the verbal arguments had a greater impact on attitudes toward the product under high- than low-relevance conditions, providing some evidence for the view that the relevance manipulation was successful in varying motivation to elaborate the message. However, unlike the study with the typewriter product just described (Haugtvedt et al., 1986), the attractiveness of the endorsers in this study was an equally potent determinant of product attitudes under both high- and low-elaboration likelihood conditions. This is just what would be expected if attractiveness served as a peripheral cue under low-relevance conditions, but served as pertinent product evider .e under high relevance.

Finally, we have observed a third effect for source attractiveness. In this study, the subjects were led to believe that they were evaluating the essays produced by students in an evening continuing education course (Puckett, Petty, Cacioppo, & Fisher, 1983). Each subject was given a folder containing a typed essay along with a card containing a picture and a brief description of the author of the essay. Two major variables were manipulated in the study: the social attractiveness of the essay author (attractive authors were more physically attractive and had more prestigious hobbies and backgrounds than unattractive authors) and the quality of the arguments in the essay (strong or weak). All essays argued that seniors should be required to pass a comprehensive exam in their major as a requirement for graduation. After examining the appropriate folder, subjects provided their own opinions about the topic of the essay. The major result was an Attractiveness × Argument quality interaction indicating that the arguments were more carefully processed when they were associated with the attractive than the unattractive sources.

In summary, in separate studies we have observed that source attractiveness, when irrelevant to the central merits of the issue or object under consideration, could serve as a simple peripheral cue (Haugtvedt et al., 1986) or it could affect argument processing (Puckett et al., 1983). When attractiveness was relevant to the central merits of an issue or object, however, it could serve as a persuasive argument (Petty & Cacioppo, 1980). Given this complication, it is crucial to specify the general conditions under which variables act in each of these distinct roles postulated for variables by the ELM. For source attractiveness, the results can be summarized as follows: Under conditions of *low-elaboration likelihood,* source attractiveness, if it has any impact at all, will serve as a peripheral cue. Under conditions of *high-elaboration likelihood,* source attractiveness will not serve as a simple cue but may instead serve as a persuasive argument if it provides information central to the merits of the attitude object. Finally, under conditions of *moderate-elaboration likelihood,* source attractiveness may affect the extent of argument elaboration.

When the elaboration likelihood is high (e.g., high personal relevance, high knowledge, simple message, no distractions, etc.), people typically know that they want and are able to evaluate the merits of the arguments presented, and they do so. Simple peripheral cues have relatively little impact on evaluations.

When the elaboration likelihood is low (e.g., low personal relevance, low knowledge, complex message, many distractions), people know that they do not want and/or are not able to evaluate the merits of the arguments presented (or they do not even consider exerting effort to process the message). Thus, if any evaluation is formed, it is likely to be the result of relatively simple associations or inferences. When the elaboration likelihood is moderate (e.g., uncertain personal relevance, moderate knowledge, moderately complex message, a few distractions, etc.), however, people may be uncertain as to whether or not the message warrants or needs scrutiny and whether they are capable of providing this analysis. In these situations they may examine the persuasion context for indications of whether or not they should attempt to process the message.

The left side of Fig. 7.6 depicts the hypothesized effects of variables serving in multiple roles under conditions of low-, moderate-, and high-elaboration likelihood. Importantly, the ELM holds that many of the traditionally studied variables known to affect persuasion are capable of operating in multiple roles as depicted in the figure. Thus, a whole list of source (e.g., expertise), message (e.g., discrepancy), audience (e.g., presence of hecklers), and other variables may affect attitudes by modifying information processing under certain conditions, serving as peripheral cues in others, and acting as persuasive arguments in still other contexts. Importantly, even though the ELM holds open the possibility that variables can affect attitudes in multiple ways, the ELM specifies, in a general manner at least, the conditions under which each process is likely to operate.

Multiple Effects for Source Expertise

We are aware of only one experiment that has examined the multiple effects of a variable across three distinct levels of elaboration likelihood and has also included a manipulation of argument quality so that the predictions of the ELM could be examined. In this study (Moore, Hausknecht, & Thamodaran, 1986), the elaboration likelihood was manipulated by varying the speed of speech in radio commercials for two products. The overall design of the study was a 2 (Product class: disposable razor or calculator) × 2 (Argument quality: strong or weak) × 2 (Source credibility: high or low) × 3 (Message exposure rate: normal, fast, very fast) factorial. Subjects listened to one of the 24 target advertisements generated by this design and the critical ad was always embedded in the third position in a tape containing five commercials.

The target ads were initially recorded at an average speaking rate (145 words per minute) and then either presented at this rate (high-elaboration likelihood), compressed to 130% of normal (moderate-elaboration likelihood), or compressed to 160% of normal (low-elaboration likelihood). For the disposable razor, the high-credibility commercial associated the product with professional athletes, whereas the low-credibility commercial associated it with citizens from

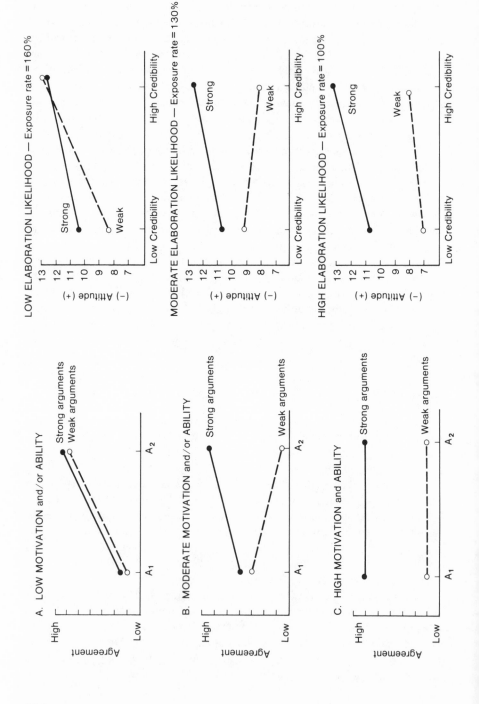

134

Miami, Florida. Previous research had shown this manipulation (although conceptualized as attractiveness rather than credibility) to be effective as a peripheral cue for this product under conditions of low-elaboration likelihood (Petty, Cacioppo, & Schumann, 1983). For the calculator, the high-credibility commercial associated the information about the product with a professor of mathematics at Princeton University, whereas the low-credibility commercial associated it with a New Jersey high-school student. Finally, each commercial presented either strong or weak arguments for the product, which had been validated in pilot testing. Following exposure to one of the target ads, subjects listed their thoughts, provided their attitudes about the advertised brand, and answered a number of ancillary items.

Manipulation checks revealed that subjects viewed the athletes and the Princeton professor as both more expert and more attractive than the Miami citizens and the New Jersey high-school student. In addition, subjects rated the strong arguments as more persuasive than the weak ones. Of most interest, however, are the effects of the manipulations on attitudes toward the brand advertised in the commercial. In addition to significant main effects for credibility and argument strength (more favorable attitudes with greater credibility and argument strength), two interactions were obtained. The first interaction between argument strength and exposure rate indicated that argument quality was a less important determinant of attitudes as exposure rate increased (i.e., as the elaboration likelihood declined). In the right half of Fig. 7.6, the second three-way interaction between argument strength, exposure rate, and source credibility is depicted. To better understand this interaction, the authors conducted separate analyses at each exposure level. Under the fastest exposure conditions (lowest elaboration likelihood; top panel of graph), only a main effect for source credibility emerged, $F = 15.32, p < .0001$ (all Fs are based on 1 and 218 degrees of freedom). At the other extreme, under the normal exposure conditions (highest elaboration likelihood;

FIGURE 7.6. LEFT PANEL—Depiction of hypothesized multiple effects of a treatment under different elaboration likelihood conditions. Top panel shows the treatment serving as a cue under conditions of low elaboration likelihood. Middle panel shows the treatment affecting message processing under conditions of moderate elaboration likelihood. Bottom panel shows that the treatment has no effect under conditions of high elaboration likelihood. Instead, argument processing dominates (adapted from Petty & Cacioppo, 1984b). RIGHT PANEL —Effects of source credibility under different elaboration likelihood conditions. Top panel shows that credibility serves as a cue under conditions of low elaboration likelihood. Middle panel shows that credibility affects argument processing under conditions of moderate elaboration likelihood. Bottom panel shows that argument processing dominates under conditions of high elaboration likelihood and credibility effects are attenuated (data from Moore, Hausknecht, & Thamodaran, 1986).

bottom panel of graph), the effect of source credibility was considerably weaker, F = 6.78, p < .01; however, a very large main effect for argument quality emerged, F = 29.88, p < .0001. Finally, when the speed of speech was intermediate (moderate-elaboration likelihood; middle panel of graph), a main effect for argument quality was observed, F = 12.11, p < .0001, as well as a Source credibility × Argument strength interaction, F = 3.62, p < .04.

In summary, these results indicated that: (a) argument quality was the most important determinant of attitudes when the elaboration likelihood was highest; (b) source credibility was the most important determinant of attitudes when the elaboration likelihood was lowest; and (c) source credibility and argument quality interacted when the elbaoration likelihood was moderate. Thus, just as anticipated by the ELM, subjects processed the arguments when it was easy to do so, but used the message source as a peripheral cue when message processing was very difficult. When message processing was just somewhat difficult, subjects appeared to decide to exert the effort necessary to process the arguments mostly when they deemed it worthwhile to do so—when the source was of high credibility.

AFFECTIVE PROCESSES IN THE ELM

Now that we have outlined the major principles of the ELM in some detail, we can turn to an analysis of the role of affect in persuasion. The existing literature on attitude formation and change clearly indicates that affect can be instrumental in producing positive and negative evaluations. Many of the early studies were based on classical conditioning and reinforcement notions and demonstrated that the evaluations of individual words, slogans, and hypothetical people could be modified by pairing the attitude object with such affect producing stimuli as unpleasant odors (Razran, 1940) and temperatures (Griffit, 1970), the onset and offset of electric shock (Zanna, Kiesler, & Pilkonis, 1970), harsh sounds (Staats, Staats, & Crawford, 1962), and elating and depressing films (Gouaux, 1971).

The literature also suggested that reactions to a persuasive communication could be modified by pairing the message with an affect eliciting stimulus. For example, in an often cited study, Janis, Kaye, and Kirschner (1965) found that providing food (Pepsi and peanuts) to subjects while they read persuasive communications on various topics (e.g., the United States armed forces can be reduced to less than 85% of its present strength) increased attitude change over that found for a control group that received the message only; however, exposing subjects to a noxious odor did not significantly reduce persuasion. Although this study, and some others (e.g., Galizio & Hendrick, 1972), are open to the possibility that the manipulation worked because it *distracted* subjects from processing the cogent message arguments, and not because of any affective properties of the manipulation (cf. Petty & Brock, 1981), other studies have used manipulations that are more clearly affective and have achieved similar results. For example, Dribben and Brabender (1979) used the Velten (1968) mood induction procedure to create a positive mood prior to exposing subjects to a taped message either favoring or opposing motorcycle helmet laws. Only subjects who strongly favored the helmet laws were included in the study. The major result of this research was that the counterattitudinal (anti-helmet) message produced more attitude change in the direction advocated when subjects had previously read positive mood-inducing statements rather than neutral ones. Although this study appears to indicate that positive mood was associated with enhanced agreement with a counterattitudinal appeal, it is not clear *why* this effect occurred (see also, Biggers & Pryor, 1982).

Based on our presentation of the ELM earlier in this chapter, it should be quite clear what roles the model reserves for affect—the same as that accorded to other variables. Specifically, the ELM holds that affect may serve as a persuasive argument, it may serve as a peripheral cue, or it may affect the extent or direction of argument processing. In the remainder of this chapter we comment briefly on how affect might serve in each of these roles.

Affect Under Conditions of High-Elaboration Likelihood

Earlier in this chapter we noted that for some people or in some situations, a determination of the central merits of an attitude object might entail an analysis of one's *feelings* rather than one's beliefs or behaviors. Thus, attitudes toward a roller coaster might be based on the extent to which it makes one feel excited rather than nauseous or fearful; attitudes toward a potential spouse might be based on the extent to which one feels love and warmth in his or her presence. Importantly, the fact that attitudes are based on the affective properties of the attitude object does not mean that people carry this affect with them at all times. Rather, it means that attitude *change* will be based largely on a reconsideration of the affective properties of the stimulus (e.g., Do I still *love* you? Am I still *afraid* of roller coasters?; Cacioppo & Petty, 1982a). This consideration of affect as it relates to the central merits of the object should become more consuming, for example, as the object increases in personal relevance or consequences (e.g., as the date for the marriage comes closer; as approaching the waiting line for the roller coaster).

Research is consistent with the view that when affect is relevant to an evaluation of the central merits of an involving issue, it can serve an informational function. For example, Schwartz and Clore (1983) demonstrated that people's assessments of their current life satisfaction could be influenced by their present affective states. Clearly, a consideration of personal feelings can be directly relevant to determining how satisfied people are with their lives.

Fear as Information. Perhaps the most abundant literature dealing with affect and persuasion is that dedicated to the study of fear-arousing communications. The typical fear communication employed in social psychological research presents the noxious (fear-arousing) consequences resulting from specific behaviors (e.g., smoking, failure to wear seatbelts, etc.; see Beck & Frankel, 1981; Janis, 1967). Interestingly, recent reviews of this literature have concluded that the arousal of fear has no direct effect on attitude change, "but only an indirect effect via the cognitive appraisal of the severity of the threat" (Rogers, 1983, p. 165; see also, Leventhal, 1970). In short, the fear experienced by the message recipient is used to judge the validity of some of the information presented in the message.

The informational value of the fear induced by a persuasive message is shown in a study by Schwarz, Servay, and Kumpf (1985). The subjects in this study were male students who reported smoking more than 10 cigarettes per day. Thus, a message on smoking would have high personal relevance. In three experimental conditions, subjects were exposed to a moderately fear-arousing anti-smoking movie that included interviews with patients suffering or dying from lung cancer and other smoking-related diseases. The movie also included statistics and interviews with scientists on the dangers of smoking, as well as available therapies and methods for changing one's smoking behavior. Following a misattribution procedure developed by Zanna and Cooper (1974), some subjects were provided the possibility of attributing their fear arousal to a source other than the persuasive message (and the danger of smoking). Specifically, they were administered a placebo pill that was said to have arousing side effects. In the other experimental conditions, subjects were either informed that the pill had no side effects or that it was tranquilizing. A group of control subjects did not take a pill or see the movie but did complete the dependent measures.

If fear can help people evaluate the danger of smoking when the experienced affect is attributed to the noxious consequences depicted in the film, then those people who can misattribute their fear to a presumably arousing pill should evaluate the danger of smoking as less severe than when no side effects are expected. In addition, subjects who expect the pill to have a tranquilizing effect, should evaluate the danger of smoking to be even more severe. The results of the study by Schwarz and colleagues indicated that the group viewing the movie under the expectation of no side effects from the pill reported reduced intentions to smoke cigarettes in the future compared to control subjects, attesting to the effectiveness of the film under "normal" conditions. However, when the subjects could misattribute their feelings to the arousing pill, intentions to stop smoking were not different from controls. As expected, the film was most effective for the group that was led to believe that the pill would produce a tranquilizing effect. As Schwarz et al. (1985) conclude, "the results suggest that subjects utilized their perceived arousal symptoms along with their explanations of them in evaluating the severity of the dangers described in the message

. . . and support the notion that affective states may serve informational functions" (pp. 184–185).[3]

Biased Information Processing.   In the research on fear communications, the fear experienced by message recipients was directly *relevant* to evaluating the merits of some of the arguments in the message (e.g., the aversive consequences of smoking). However, *irrelevant* affective states may also be introduced under conditions of high-elaboration likelihood. Under these conditions, affect is expected to color or bias the ongoing information-processing activity. That is, when people are actively processing a message, affect can serve as a retrieval cue for material in memory influencing what comes to mind. In general, positive affect should enhance the accessibility of positive associations and negative affect should enhance the accessibility of negative associations (Bower, 1981; Clark & Isen, 1982; see Bargh, this volume; Crockett, this volume).

As an example of the rather general biasing properties of affect, consider a series of studies by Johnson and Tversky (1983). In this research, affect was manipulated by having subjects read newspaper stories (e.g., describing tragic or happy events) that produced either positive or negative affect. Following exposure to the stories, subjects were asked to provide frequency estimates of a number of negative occurrences (e.g., fatalities due to heart disease, floods) that were either related or unrelated to the newspaper accounts. The induction of negative affect produced a global increase in the estimated frequency of the negative events, but positive affect produced a global decrease in estimates of these events. In short, the induced affect colored subjects judgments (see Isen, 1984, for a review of the biasing effects of affect on cognition).

Evidence for irrelevant affect biasing information processing in a persuasion situation was obtained in a recent experiment by Schumann (1986). In this study, subjects were exposed to a commercial for a new pen in the context of either a liked or a disliked television show. The liked show induced a positive mood in subjects, whereas the negative show induced a negative mood. The likelihood of elaboration of the pen ad was manipulated by varying whether subjects were expecting to make a choice after the experiment about which brand of pen to select as a free gift (high-elaboration likelihood) or which brand of coffee (low-elaboration likelihood). Following exposure to the ads in the context of the television program, subjects listed their thoughts about the product and commercial. Although the nature of the program tended to modify evaluations of the pen under both low- and high-relevance conditions, the program had an impact on subjects' *thoughts* only when the elaboration likelihood was high. For example,

---

[3]Importantly, fear should serve in this informational role primarily when the elaboration likelihood is high and the fear is relevant to an evaluation of the arguments presented. When the elaboration likelihood is low and/or the fear is irrelevant, it should serve in the other roles postulated for variables by the ELM.

under high-relevance conditions, subjects generated more favorable thoughts about the brand and fewer negative thoughts about the commercial when the program induced mood was positive rather than negative. Under low relevance, thoughts were unaffected by the program.

Affect Under Conditions of Moderate-Elaboration Likelihood

When the elaboration likelihood is moderate, affect is expected to have an impact on the extent of elaboration and thus moderate the route to persuasion. In this regard, it is important to realize that affective experiences may differ in both *valence* (e.g., happiness vs. sadness) and *intensity* (e.g., sadness vs. anger). A common assumption of arousal theories is that moderate arousal is most conducive to optimal performance (cf. Yerkes & Dodson, 1908). Thus, both low and high intensity affective experiences could hinder or disrupt information processing (or any ongoing behavior; Easterbrook, 1959; Young, 1961) and thereby increase the likelihood of the peripheral over the central route to persuasion (see Cacioppo & Petty, in press, for further discussion).

According to the ELM, the valence of affective experiences may also moderate the route to persuasion. At present, however, research is somewhat inconsistent with regard to the effects of affect on the extent of thinking (Isen, 1984). More studies have examined positive than negative affect with some research indicating that positive affect leads to attempts to reduce the load on working memory and the complexity of decisions; other studies, however, have suggested that positive affect is associated with more creative problem solving and unique responses (Isen, Means, Patrick, & Nowicki, 1982). In one directly relevant investigation modeled after the Petty, Cacioppo, and Goldman (1981) study on persuasion described previously (Fig. 7.4), Worth and Mackie (in press) manipulated argument quality (strong or weak), source expertise (high or low), and whether subjects were exposed to a communication on "acid rain" while in a positive or neutral affective state. Subjects who experienced positive affect (winning $1) prior to the communication reported attitudes that were based less on argument quality and somewhat more on source expertise than subjects who were in a more neutral mood. This research, of course, is consistent with the view that affective states may moderate the route to persuasion.

Affect Under Conditions of Low-Elaboration Likelihood

According to the ELM, if people have relatively low motivation and ability to process a persuasive communication, then affect, to the extent that it has any effect on persuasion, should serve as a simple peripheral cue. As a cue, affect would induce change that was consistent with its direction—the presence of positive affect would lead to more favorable attitudes than if no affect was present, but the induction of negative affect would lead to more unfavorable attitudes than if no affect was present.

In addition to the studies on classical conditioning of attitudes noted previously, a number of other studies are also consistent with the view that affect can serve as a relatively simple cue in a persuasion context when the elaboration likelihood is low. For example, Gorn (1982) manipulated the relevance of an advertisement for a pen by telling some subjects that they were serving as consultants to an advertising agency and that they would later get to choose a pack of pens as a gift (high relevance), whereas other subjects were given little reason to process the target pen ad (low relevance). All subjects were exposed to two different ads for a pen. One ad was attribute-oriented and provided information relevant to evaluating the product (e.g., never smudges), whereas the other ad featured pleasant music rather than information. About 1 hour after ad exposure, subjects were given a choice between the two brands of advertised pens. When conditions were of low relevance, subjects favored the pen advertised with the pleasant music; however, under high-relevance conditions they favored the pen advertised with the informational campaign. In a conceptually similar study, Srull (1983) found that manipulated mood had a significant impact on the product evaluations of people who reported having little product-relevant knowledge, but did not have an impact on the evaluations of high-knowledge subjects. Thus, just as issue-irrelevant affect appears to operate as a simple cue when motivation to process is low (e.g., Gorn, 1982), it appears to operate similarly when ability (knowledge) is low (see also Batra & Ray, 1985).

SUMMARY

In this chapter we have presented a general conceptualization of the processes by which persuasive communications induce attitude change, called the Elaboration Likelihood Model, and we have highlighted the role of affect in this framework. In particular, we have seen that affect may have much in common with other variables known to modify attitudes. That is, we have argued that affect may change attitudes by the same processes as other more commonly studied variables such as source expertise or attractiveness.

We began this chapter by noting that the literature on attitude change is characterized by many seemingly conflicting results. The ELM attempts to place these many conflicting results under one conceptual umbrella by specifying the major processes underlying persuasion and indicating how many of the traditionally studied variables relate to these basic processes. We have argued that manipulations of affect are capable of modifying attitudes in rather complex ways. The ELM elucidates, in a general manner at least, the conditions under which these different effects and processes are likely to occur. In brief, we have argued that when people are highly motivated and able to process issue-relevant arguments, affect will either serve as an argument if it is relevant to a determination of the central merits of the issue, or it will bias the ongoing information processing. When people lack the requisite motivation and/or ability to process issue-relevant arguments, affect may serve as a simple peripheral cue. Finally, when people are uncertain as to whether the message warrants or needs scrutiny, affect may influence the intensity of information processing. Research on the role of affect in persuasion is very sparse at present and it is not surprising that there are insufficient studies containing the appropriate conditions to truly test the ELM hypotheses regarding affect. Nevertheless, current research suggests that affect may be capable of modifying attitudes in the multiple ways postulated by the ELM.

ACKNOWLEDGMENT

Preparation of this chapter was supported by National Science Foundation Grant BNS 8418038.

REFERENCES

Alba, J. W., & Marmorstein, H. (in press). The effects of frequency knowledge on consumer decision making. *Journal of Consumer Research.*

Batra, R., & Ray, M. (1985). How advertising works at contact. In L. Alwitt & A. Mitchell (Eds.), *Psychological processes and advertising effects: Theory, research and application* (pp. 13–44). Hillsdale, NJ:Lawrence Erlbaum Associates.

Beck, K. H., & Frankel, A. (1981). A conceptualization of threat communications and preventive health behavior. *Social Psychology Quarterly, 44,* 204–217.

Biggers, T., & Pryor, B. (1982). Attitude change: A function of emotion-eliciting qualities of environment. *Personality and Social Psychology Bulletin, 8,* 94–99.

Borgida, E., & Howard-Pitney, B. (1983). Personal involvement and the robustness of perceptual salience effects. *Journal of Personality and Social Psychology, 45,* 560–570.

Bower, G. H. (1981). Mood and memory. *American Psychologist, 36,* 129–148.

Cacioppo, J. T., & Petty, R. E., (1979). Effects of message repetition and position on cognitive responses, recall, and persuasion. *Journal of Personality and Social Psychology, 37,* 97–109.

Cacioppo, J. T., & Petty, R. E. (1982a). A biosocial model of attitude change. In J. T. Cacioppo & R. E. Petty (Eds.), *Perspectives in cardiovascular psychophysiology* (pp. 151–188). New York: Guilford.

Cacioppo, J. T., Petty, R. E., Kao, C., & Rodriguez, R. (1986). *Journal of Personality and Social Psychology, 42,* 116–131.

Cacioppo, J. T., & Petty, R. E., (1984). The need for cognition: Relationship to attitudinal proceses. In R. McGlynn, J. Maddux, C. Stotlenberg, & J. Harvey (Eds.), *Social perception in clinical and counseling psychology* (pp. 113–139). Lubbock: Texas Tech University Press.

Cacioppo, J. T., & Petty, R.E., (1985). Central and peripheral routes to persuasion: The role of message repetition. In L. Alwitt & A. Mitchell (Eds.) *Psychological processes and advertising effects* (pp. 91–111). Hillsdale, NJ: Lawrence Erlbaum Associates.

Cacioppo, J. T., & Petty, R. E. (in press). The Elaboration Likelihood Model: The role of affect and affect-laden information processing on persuasion. In A. Tybout & P. Cafferata (Eds.). *Advertising and consumer psychology.* Hillsdale, NJ: Lawrence Erlbaum Associates.

Cacioppo, J. T., Petty, R. E., Kao, C., & Rodriguez, R. (1986). *Journal of Personality and Social Psychology, 51,* 1032–1043.

Cacioppo, J. T., Petty, R. E., & Morris, K. (1983). Effects of need for cognition on message evaluation, recall, and persuasion. *Journal of Personality and Social Psychology, 45,* 805–818.

Cacioppo, J. T., Petty, R. E., & Sidera, J. (1982). The effects of salient self-schema on the evaluation of proattitudinal editorials: Top-down versus bottom-up message processing. *Journal of Experimental Social Psychology, 18,* 324–338.

Chaiken, S. (1980). Heuristic versus systematic information processing and the use of source versus message cues in persuasion. *Journal of Personality and Social Psychology, 39,* 752–756.

Chaiken, S. (in press). The heuristic model of persuasion. In M. Zanna, J. Olson, & C. Herman (Eds.), *Social influence: The Ontario symposium* (Vol. 5). Hillsdale, NJ: Lawrence Erlbaum Associates.

Clark, M. S., & Isen, A. M. (1982). Toward understanding the relationship between feeling states and social behavior. In A. H. Hastorf & A. M. Isen (Eds.), *Cognitive social psychology* (pp. 73–108). New York: Elsevier / North Holland.

Cook, T. D., & Flay, B. (1978). The temporal persistance of experimentally induced attitude change: An evaluative review. In L. Berkowitz (Ed.), *Advances in experimental social psychology* (Vol. 11, pp. 1–57). New York: Academic Press.

Crocker, J., Fiske, S. T., & Taylor, S. E. (1984). Schematic bases of belief change. In R. Eiser (Ed.), *Attitudinal judgment* (pp. 197–226). New York: Springer-Verlag.

Dribben, E., & Brabender, V. (1979). The effect of mood inducement upon audience receptiveness. *The Journal of Social Psychology, 107,* 135–136.

Easterbrook, J. A. (1959). The effect of emotion on cue utilization and the organization of behavior. *Psychological Review, 66,* 183–201.

Galizio, M., & Hendrick, C. (1972). Effect of musical accompaniment on attitude: The guitar as a prop for persuasion. *Journal of Applied Social Psychology, 2,* 350–359.

Gorn, G. (1982). The effects of music in advertising on choice behavior: A classical conditioning approach. *Journal of Marketing Research, 46,* 94–101.

Gouaux, C. (1971). Induced affective states and interpersonal attraction. *Journal of Personality and Social Psychology, 20,* 37–43.

Griffit, W. B. (1970). Environmental effects on interpersonal behavior: Ambient effective temperature and attraction. *Journal of Personality and Social Psychology, 15,* 240–244.

Harkins, S. G., & Petty, R. E. (1981). The multiple source effect in persuasion: The effects of distraction. *Personality and Social Psychology Bulletin, 7,* 627–635.

Haugtvedt, C., Petty, R. E., Cacioppo, J. T. (1986). *Need for cognition and the use of peripheral cues.* Unpublished manuscript, Department of psychology, University of Missouri, Columbia, MO.

Huddleston, B. M. (1985). *An experimental investigation of the influence deceptive nonverbal cues exert on persuasive processes.* Unpublished doctoral dissertation, Department of Communication, University of Missouri, Columbia, MO.

Isen, A. M. (1984). Toward understanding the role of affect in cognition. In R. Wyer & T. Srull (Eds.) *Handbook of social cognition* (Vol. 3, pp. 174–236). Hillsdale, NJ: Lawrence Erlbaum Associates.

Isen, A. M., Means, B., Patrick, R., & Nowicki, G. (1982). Some factors influencing decision making strategy and risk taking. In M. S. Clark & S. T. Fiske (Eds.), *Affect and cognition* (pp. 243–262). Hillsdale, NJ: Lawrence Erlbaum Associates.

Janis, I. L. (1967). Effects of fear arousal on attitude change: Recent developments in theory and experimental research. In L. Berkowitz (Ed.), *Advances in experimental social psychology* (Vol. 3, pp. 166–224). New York: Academic Press.

Janis, I. L., Kaye, D., & Kirschner, P. (1965). Facilitating effects of "eating while reading" on responsiveness to persuasive communications. *Journal of Personality and Social Psychology, 1,* 181–186.

Johnson, E., & Tversky, A. (1983). Affect, generalization, and the perception of risk. *Journal of Personality and Social Psychology, 45,* 20–31.

Katz, D. (1960). The functional approach to the study of attitudes. *Public Opinion Quarterly, 24,* 163–204.

Kelman, H. C., & Hovland, C. I. (1953). Reinstatement of the communicator in delayed measurement of opinion change. *Journal of Abnormal and Social Psychology, 48,* 327–335.

Kiesler, C. A., Collins, B., & Miller, N. (1969). *Attitude change: A critical analysis of theoretical approaches.* New York: Wiley.

Kiesler, C. A., & Mathog, R. (1968). The distraction hypothesis in attitude change. *Psychological Reports, 23,* 1123–1133.

Leippe, M. R., & Elkin, R. A. (1987). When motives clash: Issue involvement and response involvement as determinants of persuasion. *Journal of Personality and Social Psychology, 52,* 269–278.

Leventhal, H. (1970). Findings and theory in the study of fear communications. In L. Berkowitz (Ed.), *Advances in Experimental Social Psychology* (Vol. 5, pp. 119–186). New York: Academic Press.

Lord, C. G., Ross, L., & Lepper, M. R. (1979). Biased assimilation and attitude polarization: The effects of prior theories on subsequently considered evidence. *Journal of Personality and Social Psychology, 42,* 193–210.

McGuire, W. J. (1964). Inducing resistance to persuasion: Some contemporary approaches. In L. Berkowitz (Ed.), *Advances in Experimental Social Psychology* (Vol. 1, pp. 191–229). New York: Academic Press.

McGuire, W. J. (1969). The nature of attitudes and attitude change. In G. Lindzey & E. Aronson (Eds.), *The handbook of social psychology* (2nd ed., Vol. 3, pp. 136–314). Reading, MA: Addison-Wesley.

McGuire, W. J. (1985). Attitudes and attitude change. In G. Lindzey & E. Aronson (Eds.), *The handbook of social psychology* (3rd ed., Vol. 2, pp. 233–346). New York: Random House.

Miller, N., Maruyama, G., Beaber, R., & Valone, K. (1976). Speed of speech and persuasion. *Journal of Personality and Social Psychology, 34,* 615–625.

Mills, J., & Harvey, J. H. (1972). Opinion change as a function of when information about the communicator is received and whether he is attractive or expert. *Journal of Personality and Social Psychology, 21,* 52–55.

Moore, D. L., Hausknecht, D., & Thamodaran, K. (1986). Time compression, response opportunity, and persuasion. *Journal of Consumer Research, 13,* 85–99.

Pallak, M. S., Mueller, M., Dollar, K., & Pallak, J. (1972). Effect of commitment on responsiveness to an extreme consonant communication. *Journal of Personality and Social Psychology, 23,* 429–436.

Petty, R. E. (1977). *A cognitive response analysis of the temporal persistence of attitude changes induced by persuasive communications.* Unpublished doctoral dissertation, Department of Psychology, Ohio State University, Columbus, OH.

Petty, R. E., & Brock, T. C. (1981). Thought disruption and persuasion: Assessing the validity of attitude change experiments. In R. Petty, T. Ostrom, & T. Brock (Eds.), *Cognitive responses in persuasion* (pp. 55–79). Hillsdale, NJ: Lawrence Erlbaum Associates.

Petty, R. E., & Cacioppo, J. T. (1979a). Effects of forewarning of persuasive intent and involvement on cognitive responses and persuasion. *Personality and Social Psychology Bulletin, 5,* 173–176.

Petty, R. E., & Cacioppo, J. T. (1979b). Issue-involvement can increase or decrease persuasion by enhancing message-relevant cognitive responses. *Journal of Personality and Social Psychology, 37,* 1915–1926.

Petty, R. E., & Cacioppo, J. T. (1980). Effects of issue involvement on attitudes in an advertising context. In G. Gorn & M. Goldberg (Eds.), *Proceedings of the Division 23 program* (pp. 75–79). Montreal: Division 23 of the American Psychological Association.

Petty, R. E., & Cacioppo, J. T. (1981). *Attitudes and persuasion: Classic and contemporary approaches*. Dubuque, IA: Wm. C. Brown.

Petty, R. E., & Cacioppo, J. T. (1984). The effects of involvement on responses to argument quantity and quality: Central and peripheral routes to persuasion. *Journal of Personality and Social Psychology, 46*, 69–81.

Petty, R. E., & Cacioppo, J. T. (1986a). *Communication and persuasion: Central and peripheral routes to attitude change*. New York: Springer/Verlag.

Petty, R. E., & Cacioppo, J. T. (1986b). The Elaboration Likelihood Model of persuasion. In. L. Berkowitz (Ed.), *Advances in Experimental social psychology* (Vol. 19, pp. 123–205). New York: Academic Press.

Petty, R. E., Cacioppo, J. T., & Goldman, R. (1981). Personal involvement as a determinant of argument-based persuasion. *Journal of Personality and Social Psychology, 41*, 847–855.

Petty, R. E., Cacioppo, J. T., Haugtvedt, C., & Heesacker, M. (1986). *Consequences of the route to persuasion: Persistence and resistance of attitude changes*. Unpublished manuscript, University of Missouri, Columbia, MO.

Petty, R. E., Cacioppo, J. T., & Heesacker, M. (1981). The use of rhetorical questions in persuasion: A cognitive response analysis. *Journal of Personality and Social Psychology, 40*, 432–440.

Petty, R. E., Cacioppo, J. T., Schumann, D. (1983). Central and peripheral routes to advertising: The moderating role of involvement. *Journal of Consumer Research, 10*, 134–148.

Petty, R. E., Harkins, S. G., & Williams, K. D. (1980). The effects of group diffusion of cognitive effort on attitudes: An information processing view. *Journal of Personality and Social Psychology, 38*, 81–92.

Petty, R. E., Wells, G. L., & Brock, T. C. (1976). Distraction can enhance or reduce yielding to propaganda: Thought disruption versus effort justification. *Journal of Personality and Social Psychology, 34*, 874–884.

Petty, R. E., Wells, G. L., Heesacker, M., Brock, T., & Cacioppo, J. T. (1983). The effects of recipient posture on persuasion: A cognitive response analysis. *Personality and Social Psychology Bulletin, 9*, 209–222.

Puckett, J., Petty, R. E., Cacioppo, J. T., & Fisher, D. (1983). The relative impact of age and attractiveness stereotypes on persuasion. *Journal of Gerontology, 38*, 340–343.

Razran, G. H. S. (1940). Conditioned response changes in rating and appraising sociopolitical slogans. *Psychological Bulletin, 37*, 481.

Rhine, R., & Severance, L. (1970). Ego-involvement, discrepancy, source credibility, and attitude change. *Journal of Personality and Social Psychology, 16*, 175–190.

Rogers, R. (1983). Cognitive and physiological processes in fear appeals and attitude change: A revised theory of protection motivation. In Cacioppo, J. T. & Petty, R. E. (Eds.), *Social psychophysiology: A sourcebook* (pp. 153–176). New York: Guilford Press.

Schumann, D. (1986). *Effects of attitude toward the program on attitudes toward commercials*. Unpublished doctoral dissertation, Department of psychology, University of Missouri, Columbia, MO.

Schwarz, N., & Clore, G. L. (1983). Mood, misattribution, and judgments of well-being: informative and directive functions of affective states. *Journal of Personality and Social Psychology, 45*, 513–523.

Schwarz, N., Servay, W., & Kumpf, M. (1985). Attribution of arousal as a mediator of fear-arousing communications. *Journal of Applied Social Psychology, 15*, 178–188.

Sherif, M., & Sherif, C. W. (1967). Attitude as the individual's own categories: The social judgment-involvement approach to attitude and attitude change. In C. W. Sherif & M. Sherif (Eds.), *Attitude, ego-involvement, and change* (pp. 105–139). New York: Wiley.

Smith, M. J. (1982). *Persuasion and human action*. Belmont, CA: Wadsworth.

Snyder, M., & DeBono, K. G. (1985). Appeals to image and claims about quality: Understanding the psychology of advertising. *Journal of Personality and Social Psychology, 49,* 586–597.

Srull, T. K. (1983). The role of prior knowledge in the acquisition, retention, and use of new information. *Advances in Consumer Research, 10,* 572–576.

Staats, A. W., Staats, C. K., & Crawford, H. L. (1962). First-order conditioning of meaning and the parallel conditioning of a GSR. *Journal of General Psychology, 67,* 159–167.

Sternthal, B., Dholakia, R., & Leavitt, C. (1978). The persuasive effect of source credibility: A test of cognitive response analysis. *Journal of Consumer Research, 4,* 252–260.

Taylor, S. E. (1981). The interface of cognitive and social psychology. In J. H. Harvey (Ed.), *Cognition, social behavior, and the environment*. Hillsdale, NJ: Lawrence Erlbaum Associates.

Velten, E. (1968). A laboratory task for induction of mood states. *Behavior Research and Therapy, 6,* 473–482.

Wells, G. L., & Petty, R. E. (1980). The effects of overt head movements on persuasion: Compatibility and incompatibility of responses. *Basic and Applied Social Psychology, 1,* 219–230.

Wood, W. (1982). Retrieval of attitude-relevant information from memory: Effects on susceptibility to persuasion and on intrinsic motivation. *Journal of Personality and Social Psychology, 42,* 798–810.

Wood, W., Kallgren, C. & Priesler, R. (1985). Access to attitude relevant information in memory as a determinant of persuasion. *Journal of Experimental Social Psychology, 21,* 73–85.

Worth, L. T., & Mackie, D. M. (in press). Cognitive mediation of positive affect in persuasion. *Social Cognition*.

Yerkes, R. M., & Dodson, J. D. (1908). The relation of strength of stimulus to rapidity of habit formation. *Journal of Comparative and Neurological Psychology, 18,* 459–482.

Young, P. T. (1961). *Motivation and emotion*. New York: Wiley.

Zanna, M. P., & Cooper, J. (1974). Dissonance and the pill: An attribution approach to studying the arousal properties of dissonance. *Journal of Personality and Social Psychology, 29,* 703–709.

Zanna, M. P., Kiesler, C. A., & Pilkonis, P. A. (1970). Positive and negative attitudinal affect established by classical conditioning. *Journal of Personality and Social Psychology, 14,* 321–328.

Zanna, M. P., & Rempel, J. K. (in press). Attitudes: A new look at an old concept. In D. Bar-Tal & A. Kruglanski (Eds.), *The social psychology of knowledge*. New York: Cambridge University Press.

8 Mood Management: Using Entertainment to Full Advantage

Dolf Zillmann
Indiana University

This chapter presents a theory of stimulus arrangement that projects, among other things, that individuals consume media entertainment purposively in efforts to manage moods. More specifically, the theory posits that individuals are capable of choosing materials for exposure that modify and regulate affective experiences and mood states in desirable ways, and that these individuals frequently and habitually make choices that actually serve the specified ends. The mechanics of the proposed purposive behavior are discussed in some detail. This discussion is followed by a brief summary of research showing that exposure to a variety of entertaining messages impacts affect and mood in a consistent and therefore predictable manner. Focus is on isolating some of the principal variables that mediate this impact. Thereafter, recent research evidence is aggregated to support the initially developed theoretical proposals that project mood management via specific message choices.

MOOD MANAGEMENT BY STIMULUS ARRANGEMENTS GENERALLY

A general theory of affect-dependent stimulus arrangements has been presented elsewhere (Zillmann & Bryant, 1985). Its main premises and propositions are outlined here only to make the subsequent discussion of entertainment choices as mood management more meaningful. The objective is to show that affect and mood are strongly influenced by stimulus environments, that these environments can be controlled, and that media presentations of any kind constitute artificial stimulus environments that are (a) easily controlled by individuals and (b) more readily manipulated for purposes of mood management than alternative environments.

In brief, the theory is as follows:

Premise 1: Individuals are motivated to terminate noxious, aversive stimulation of any kind and to reduce the intensity of such stimulation at any time.

Premise 2: Individuals are similarly motivated to perpetuate and increase the intensity of gratifying, pleasurable experiential states.

Proposition 1: To the extent possible, individuals arrange internal and external stimulus conditions so as to minimize aversion and maximize gratification. Both minimization and maximization are in terms of time and intensity.

Proposition 2: To the extent that the control of stimulation is limited to environmental stimuli, individuals arrange and rearrange their environment so as to best accomplish the ends stipulated in Proposition 1.

These hedonistic propositions are based on the assumption that individuals are capable of selecting environmental stimulation that serves either the minimization of aversion or the maximization of gratification. This capability is presumed to develop in the following fashion:

1. Initially, individuals in states of aversion or gratification arrange stimulus environments in a random fashion.

2. Arrangements that are incidentally made during states of aversion and that terminate or reduce the hedonically negative experience leave a memory trace that increases the likelihood for making similar arrangements under similar circumstances. In Thorndikean (1911, 1932) terms, *relief stamps in preference;* or in more contemporary language, stimulus arrangements that provide relief from aversion are negatively reinforced (e.g., Nevin, 1973; Skinner, 1969) and thus placed in a superior position for reenactment under similar conditions of aversion.

3. Arrangements that are incidentally made during states of gratification and that extend or enhance the hedonically positive experience analogously leave a memory trace that increases the likelihood for making similar stimulus arrangements under similar circumstances. In this case, the reinforcement is positive, and pleasure stamps in the preference.

The general theory, then, projects the development of affect- or mood-specific preferences for environmental stimulation; and it posits that individuals, given the opportunity, seek to arrange their environment in particular ways. As the preferences in question are assumed to be controlled by operant learning, individuals may or may not be aware of their motivation. It should also be noticed that stimulus arrangements may require considerable activity or be entirely passive. Climbing mountains, playing tennis, or jogging, for example, are highly energy-consuming choices that control external stimulation and that thereby can impact mood. The proverbial "change of scenery" accomplished with traveling, usually undertaken in hopes for beneficial effects on moody slumps, is less demanding of energy. However, it is similarly achieved by locomotion, although this locomotion is aided by technical means of transportation. Even fishing or bird watching qualify as active stimulus arrangements. The common element in these examples is that individuals move themselves to locales that constitute alternative environments and that provide opportunities for mood-altering experiences. But individuals need not abandon their immediate environment in order to have experiences of this kind. They can resort to playing cards with friends, relax at the pool side, or indulge in gourmet cooking. The extent to which individuals can exert control over their environment in such a rather passive fashion is quite limited. This situation changes drastically, however, with the involvement of *representations* of environments. Representations move environments to individuals. Books and a bit of imagination bring uncounted physical and social environments to readers. Motion pictures do so more directly, bypassing comparatively high demands on imagination and experience. In a fashion that can be described as total inactivity (we consider the pushing of buttons on remote controls and on similar apparati activity of trivial magnitude and neglect it), consumers of modern electronic media can access a wealth of iconic representations of extreme fidelity. They can select, whether on impulse or on reflection, from a potentially large number of stimulus events. They can abandon their choices instantly in the same manner. They can fluctuate between stimulus environments and finally elect to stay with a particular one for some time. Given such vast control over auditory, visual, and audiovisual stimuli in the environment, can it be assumed that entertainment choices will serve the management of moods?

MOOD MANAGEMENT THROUGH ENTERTAINMENT

The theory of affect-dependent stimulus arrangements directly applies to entertainment choices. It is only necessary to restrict Proposition 2 to the selection of entertaining events: music, comedy, drama, sports, and the like.

Proposition 3: To the extent that the control of external stimulation is limited to entertainment offerings, individuals arrange and rearrange their exposure so as to minimize aversion and maximize gratification—both minimization and maximization being in terms of time and intensity.

The theory, at this point, is specific to affective state and mood, but not to entertainment stimuli. It projects that individuals who experienced relief from aversion during or following exposure to a particular form of entertainment will revert to consuming this form in future aversions. Analogously, it projects that individuals who experienced enhanced gratification during or following exposure to a particular form of entertainment will revert to this form in future mood states that allow the enhancement in question. Relief from a bad mood or enhancement of a good mood might, for example, be achieved by consuming a comedy. It might also be achieved by rock music, a romantic novel, or a horror movie. Whatever happened to be associated with relief or with gratification in initial chance encounters with entertaining stimuli should come to be preferred over alternatives. By the same token, in combating aversion, one individual might resort to classical music, another to thrillers, and yet another to game shows. Similar choices might be made in efforts to enhance positive moods.

It should be noticed that it has not been stipulated that the consumption of the entertainment stimuli themselves must relieve or gratify to impact the formation of preferences. Relief and gratification may be achieved by conditions other than exposure to the entertaining material proper. For example, a person experiencing relief during and after seeing a comedy might have undergone excitatory recovery that occurred mainly for reasons of autonomic homeostasis and that would have occurred in the absence of diversionary, entertaining stimulation. The person is nonetheless likely to attribute his or her improved mood state to the comedy. Similarly, the experience of watching a movie may be gratifying in part because of holding hands with a date, and the film is likely to be credited with more than it accomplished. Complications such as these are of little consequence for the theory under consideration, however. As the theory relies on operant learning, a contiguity between mood before consumption of entertaining stimuli, on the one hand, and mood during and after consumption of these stimuli, on the other hand, suffices to predict the formation and alteration of mood-specific preferences. The reliance of operant learning also means that individuals need not be cognizant of the reasons for their preference. This does not rule out, however, that some individuals may comprehend some of the circumstances and arrive at causal attributions about their choices. These attributions may well be correct. But they also may be erroneous. Whether veridical or in error, they tend to stabilize the preferences that were acquired by operant learning. The difference is that they are genuine insight in the former case and "rationalization" in the latter.

The point to be made is that the theoretical treatment of preference formation and preference modification is insufficiently sensitive as long as all entertainment stimuli are considered equally capable of achieving relief from bad moods and enhancement of good moods. Under such an assumption, preferences would be entirely idiosyncratic because of idiosyncratic individual histories. Surely, individual histories are likely to produce considerable variation in entertainment preference. They cannot produce overly esoteric choice patterns, however, because entertainment stimuli allow groupings that are associated with the consistent evocation of specific affects—in short, with predictable effects on particular moods.

In the following, some of the emerging consistencies in the impact of entertaining stimuli on mood states are enumerated and theoretically integrated in order to obtain predictions that are both mood- and message-specific. They are expressed in propositional form and then explained.

Proposition 4: Persons in states of extreme understimulation that are construed as aversive select highly varied, potentially arousing stimuli over poorly varied, potentially calming ones.

Proposition 5: Analogously, persons in states of extreme overstimulation that are construed as aversive select poorly varied, potentially calming stimuli over highly varied, potentially arousing ones.

The stipulated selections serve the normalization of excitatory activity. As normalizing choices are reinforced (with relief stamping in the preference), the mood-specific preference that is being formed can be said to serve excitatory homeostasis.

Proposition 6: In seeking alleviation, persons in acutely aversive states select the most engaging and most absorbing types of stimulation available.

Proposition 7: In seeking to perpetuate their affective state, persons experiencing gratification select the least engaging and least absorbing types of stimulation available.

Both propositions are based on the fact that the cognitive accompaniment of acute affect tends to facilitate and extend the affective experience, and that any stimulus intervention tends to disrupt and impair the affect-maintaining rehearsal of cognitions pertaining to the particular affective experience (cf. Kendall & Hollon, 1979). The more engaging and absorbing any intervening stimulation, the more likely it becomes that the affective state in which it intervenes will diminish in intensity and terminate rapidly. This potential effect (i.e., relief from aversion) should stamp in the preference specific to negative moods. Persons in positive mood states, in contrast, should want to revel in the cognitions pertaining to their experience of gratification and avoid or minimize intervening stimulation. The inclination to avoid potentially distracting stimulation altogether should be strongest in extreme states of positive affect, such as elation and triumph.

Proposition 8: Persons in acutely aversive states select stimuli that have minimal, if any, behavioral affinity with their experiential state over stimuli that exhibit strong affinity.

Proposition 9: In contrast, persons experiencing gratification prefer stimuli of high behavioral affinity—should they elect to expose themselves to distracting stimulation at all.

These propositions derive from the observation that behavioral affinity between an experiential state, on the one hand, and intervening stimuli, on the other, tends to impair or remove the experience-diminishing or experience-terminating effect of stimulus intervention. Intervening stimulation of high behavioral affinity is likely to perpetuate prior affect because it revives affect-maintaining cognitions (Zillmann, 1979). Such revival is due to the fact that behaviorally related affective reactions share associative networks (Anderson & Bower, 1973; Landman & Manis, 1983; Lang, 1979) and that cortical excitation is capable of spreading so as to bridge minor associative discrepancies (Collins & Loftus, 1975). Only engaging and absorbing intervening stimulation that is devoid of any affinity with the experience in which it intervenes, or whose affinity is minimal, can manifest its full impact in disrupting and thus diminishing an emotional experience.

Proposition 10: Persons in acutely aversive states select hedonically positive stimuli over hedonically negative stimuli.

Proposition 11: Persons experiencing gratification display this preference to a lesser degree, if at all.

These two propositions are based on the expectation that the hedonic valence of intervening stimulation eventually will come to dominate affect and supersede earlier affective experience. At the very least, hedonically positive stimulation is expected to impair the maintenance of hedonically negative affect and to reduce the intensity of negative affect that might persist (Baron, 1977).

EFFECTS OF ENTERTAINMENT ON MOODS

Before turning to the research designed to test several of the outlined propositions regarding the selection of specific entertaining stimuli as a function of specific moods, it is necessary to establish that particular forms of entertaining stimulation have particular mood-altering effects, and that they have these effects with regularity. Clearly, the projected preferences can be formed and maintained—or altered—only to the extent that consistent effect patterns exist. The brief summary of research here is obviously not exhaustive and should be viewed as illustrative only. (For a more complete account, see Zillmann, 1982; Zillmann & Bryant, 1985.)

Effects on Excitation

In this realm of inquiry, excitatory reactions are usually conceptualized as sympathetic dominance in the autonomic nervous system. Such reactions have been measured in peripheral manifestations (mainly in increased cardiovascular activity) and endocrine concomitants (mainly in traces of catecholamine release). The assessment of excitatory responses to entertaining messages has led to the emergence of stimulus categories and stimulus hierarchies from nonarousing to arousing. Nonvaried, monotonous stimuli form the bottom of the implicit continuum (Bryant & Zillmann, 1977). Nature films that emphasize the grandeur of creation (without showing predation and the like) are to be placed similarly. These films have been found to be utterly nonarousing. In fact, they have been found to reduce excitedness in respondents who were minimally aroused prior to exposure (Levi, 1965; Wadeson, Mason, Hamburg, & Handlon, 1963). Action drama, comedy, and game shows tend to be moderately arousing. Dependent on the respondents' affective dispositions toward the interacting parties (cf. Zillmann, 1980), such fare can become highly arousing, however (Bryant & Zillmann, 1977; Carruthers & Taggart, 1973; Levi, 1965). Highly violent and potentially fear-evoking drama assumes a position close to the top of the continuum (e.g., Zillmann, Hoyt, & Day, 1974). Nonfictional material of this kind (as in sports, documentaries, and newscasts) tends to produce even stronger excitatory reactions (Bryant & Zillmann, 1977; Geen, 1975; Geen & Rakosky, 1973). Materials need not feature threats to well-being and destructiveness, however. Sexual themes rank among the strongest arousers available (e.g., Donnerstein & Hallam, 1978; Levi, 1969; Zillmann, 1971; Zillmann, Hoyt, & Day, 1974). There can be no doubt, then, that excitatory reactions to specific classes of entertaining stimuli are consistent within classes and greatly variable across classes.

Effects of Differently Engaging Messages

Research on the mood-altering effects of entertainment stimuli that differ in their capacity to engage and absorb respondents, in their semantic affinity with preexposure moods, and in their hedonic valence is less abundant, but sufficient to consider characteristic response patterns established.

The effects of stimuli differing in involvement potential on mood have been explored in an investigation by Bryant and Zillmann (1977). Subjects were placed in a state of annoyance and anger. They were then exposed to messages that differed sharply in their capacity to engage and absorb the respondents. This capacity had been predetermined with nonannoyed subjects. In the main experiment, after exposure to the entertainment stimuli, the subjects were provided with an opportunity to express their remaining anger in aggressive actions against

153

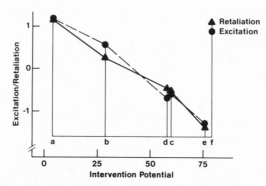

FIGURE 8.1.   Level of excitation and retaliatory behavior as a function of the intervention potential of entertaining television programs. The greater the capacity of contents to absorb respondents (points connected by gradients), the greater the recovery from annoyance-produced excitation (circles) and the less severe the postexposure retaliation against the annoyer (triangles). Contents featuring hostilities were absorbing to nonannoyed subjects but failed to induce efficient recovery from excitation and failed to lower the level of retaliatory behavior in annoyed subjects (isolated points on coordinate f). The programs were: (a) a monotonous stimulus, (b) a nature film, (c) a comedy show, (d) nonaggressive sport, (e) a quiz show, and (f) contact sport entailing aggressive actions beyond the legitimate sport activity. Excitation and retaliation are expressed in z scores for ease of comparison (from Zillmann, 1979).

their annoyer. As was expected, minimally engaging messages, presumably because of their inability to disrupt the subjects' cognitive preoccupation with the experience of annoyance and anger, proved minimally effective in altering mood state and dependent behaviors. The more engaging messages, in contrast, led to diminished anger and aggression. Apparently, subjects were less able to maintain mood-perpetuating cognitions. The most engaging message of those devoid of contents pertaining to provocation, anger, and retaliation (i.e., the behavioral components of the subjects' affect) produced the strongest intervention effect. The pronounced involvement with the entertaining message diminished the experience of anger and reduced aggression. The linear relationship between the capacity of messages to engage and absorb respondents and the mood-diminishing effect of intervening exposure is summarized in Fig. 8.1.

Effects of Mood-Message Affinity

The investigation by Bryant and Zillmann (1977) also provided a test of the proposal that messages that feature behaviors of great affinity to the mood state during which they are received have limited mood-diminishing strength. The angry subjects' exposure to violent sports (specifically, rough ice hockey with extracurricular aggressive activities) failed to reduce arousal, anger, or aggressiveness, and this despite the fact that nonannoyed persons had found the program to be highly absorbing. The effect of mood-message affinity is obtrusive in Fig. 8.1 (Point f). Similar findings have been reported for fictional violence by Zillmann and Johnson (1973).

Further corroboration of the proposal that behavioral affinity between message and mood prior to message consumption removes much of the intervention capacity of messages comes from research on the effects of humor and comedy. In an investigation conducted by Berkowitz (1970) subjects were or were not provoked by a peer, exposed to hostile or nonhostile comedy, and then allowed to express their mood by directing hostilities toward their peer. After hostile comedy, provoked subjects retaliated more strongly than their counterparts who had been exposed to nonhostile comedy. No such effect was found in unprovoked subjects. The materials that featured actions closely related to the subjects' state (i.e., belittlement, degradation) apparently failed to let them forget about their own mistreatment. But materials devoid of such relatedness (that were similarly funny and similarly absorbing in the absence of anger) accomplished the intervention necessary for anger to dissipate.

Effects of Hedonic Valence

The effects of the hedonic valence of entertaining messages on mood prior to and during reception have been explored with different types of stimuli: humor, music, and erotica.

Baron and Ball (1974) conducted an investigation in which subjects were or were not provoked, exposed to entirely nonhostile cartoons or pictures of scenery, furniture, and abstract paintings in a control condition, and then provided with an opportunity to express their moods in actions against their provoker or nonprovoker. Amusement from exposure to humor, compared against the lack of amusement in the control condition, led to diminished retaliatory inclinations of provoked subjects. Amusement was of no consequence for unprovoked subjects, however. For persons in an acutely negative mood state, then, exposure to material that triggers a positive mood state, if only temporarily, appears to cut into the initial negative mood state, reducing its intensity.

Day (1980) demonstrated that exposure to pleasant music is similarly capable of reducing negative moods.

Moreover, exposure to pleasant but nonarousing erotic materials has been shown to accomplish alleviation from negative mood states. Baron (1974) reported an experiment in which males were or were not provoked by a male peer, exposed to photographs of beautiful female nudes or to innocuous nonerotic control stimuli, and then given an opportunity to behave aggressively toward their peer. Paralleling Baron's findings on the effect of amusement from humor, the pleasant erotic stimulation, compared against the less pleasant control stimulation, led to decreased anger and aggressiveness in provoked subjects but was of no consequence for unprovoked subjects. This finding has been replicated repeatedly (e.g., Ramirez, Bryant, & Zillmann, 1982).

Exposure to pleasant erotica does not necessarily reduce prevailing bad moods, however. In fact, such exposure may facilitate negative affect that recurs after exposure. If erotic materials are both pleasant and arousing, the aversion-alleviating effect of positive hedonic valence tends to be counteracted by the emotion-enhancing effect of residual excitation from exposure (cf. Zillmann, 1983). Strongly arousing stimuli are likely to intensify negative affect in the postexposure period despite the positive valence of the erotica. Moderately arousing stimuli, in contrast, may have no particular effect on prevailing moods, as positive and negative influences tend to neutralize each other. It should also be clear that exposure to displeasing stimuli, whether erotic or not, is likely to annoy angry persons further. Annoyance from exposure should combine with pre-exposure anger, and post-exposure anger should consequently be more intense. In short, negative affect is expected to sum. Positive affect of stimulus intervention is expected to sum similarly with prevailing negative affect. In this case, positive affect is subtracted from the initial negative affect.

Zillmann, Bryant, Comisky, and Medoff (1981) explored all these expectations in an investigation that varied both the hedonic valence of intervening stimuli and their excitatory potential. Additionally, erotica were matched with nonerotic stimuli in terms of both hedonic and excitatory properties. As in other investigations of this kind, subjects were annoyed, exposed to communication, and then allowed to vent their remaining annoyance by retaliating against their annoyer. It was found that both the hedonic valence and the excitatory potential of intervening messages exerted a degree of control over aggressive behavior and, apparently, over the affective experience, anger, that mediates this behavior. The findings, presented in Fig. 8.2, led to the proposal of a two-component model of stimulus intervention. This model projects, essentially, that intervention in negative mood states is likely to be effective if the intervening stimuli have positive valence and/or low excitatory potential, and that it is likely to be

FIGURE 8.2. Effects of stimulus intervention in acute anger. The horizontal line defines retaliation without intervention. The zero-valence gradient indicates the hypothetical effect of hedonically neutral materials as a function of residual excitation. The heavy lines specify the joint operation of excitatory and hedonic properties of messages in the modification of retaliatory behavior. Triangles denote erotic materials, squares nonerotic fare. Retaliation was measured in the frequency of noxious noise delivered to punish the tormentor (adapted from Zillmann, Bryant, Comisky, & Medoff, 1981).

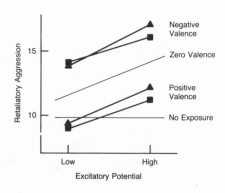

ineffective, even counterproductive, if the stimuli have negative valence and/or high excitatory potential. The combination of stimulus properties with parallel effects is additive. So is the combination of properties of opposite effects, except that the summative combination now operates toward neutralization.

Effect Patterns

The discussed research findings may be summarized as follows:

1. Bad moods associated with understimulation, boredom in particular, can be effectively diminished or terminated by consumption of arousing entertaining material.

2. Bad moods associated with overstimulation, stress in particular, can be effectively diminished or terminated by consumption of nonarousing, calming entertaining material.

3. Bad moods can be effectively diminished or terminated by consumption of highly involving entertaining material that has low behavioral affinity with the initially prevailing bad moods.

4. Bad moods can be effectively diminished or terminated by consumption of highly pleasant entertaining material.

5. Good moods can be effectively maintained or enhanced by consumption of minimally involving entertaining material.

6. Good moods can be effectively maintained or enhanced by consumption of entertaining material that has high behavioral affinity with the initially prevailing good moods.

7. Good moods can be effectively maintained or enhanced by consumption of highly pleasant entertaining material.

TESTS OF MOOD MANAGEMENT

The exploration of mood management through entertainment consumption has begun only recently (e.g., Zillmann, Hezel, & Medoff, 1980). As a first step, procedures for the behavioral assessment of consumption choices and consumption per se had to be developed and refined. The design of these procedures aimed at a high degree of ecological validity. So did the construction of classes of available entertainment choices. Such intentions worked against achieving maximum control over the properties of the messages among which respondents could choose. Various critical message properties (e.g., hedonic valence, excitatory potential, absorption capacity) tend to be confounded—making rigorous tests of hypotheses very difficult, if not impossible. Some of the confoundings in question seem unavoidable, and it is not necessarily fair to speak of them in an accusatory manner. For instance, highly absorbing messages tend to be arousing also; similarly, highly pleasant ones tend to be both arousing and absorbing. Confoundings may thus have to be accepted and hypotheses might have to be integrated so as to take these confoundings into consideration. On the other hand, some recent investigations have gone beyond the exploratory stage and have addressed specific hypotheses (e.g., Bryant & Zillmann, 1984).

In this overview of research on mood management via entertainment, tests of specific proposals are intertwined with exploratory endeavors. The overview cannot give complete coverage to the available research and should be seen as an effort to illustrate significant aspects of the phenomenon under investigation.

Managing Excitedness

Sympathetic excitation is greatly variable. In some experiential states it reaches extreme levels. The so-called active emotions (e.g., fear and anger) are associated with greatly elevated levels of excitation. Extended overstimulation produces the same effect. The resulting experiential state is usually referred to as *stress*. Conceptually, *boredom* is the opposite experiential state. It results from extended understimulation and is associated with extremely low levels of sympathetic activity. Both boredom and stress are states that experiencers tend to construe as aversive. They are, in other words, bad moods to be gotten rid of. The question is whether individuals experiencing such moods manage their "entertainment environment" in a way that helps them to diminish and to terminate these moods. Specifically, do bored individuals display a preference for varied, exciting stimulation that would effectively normalize their excitatory state? And do stressed individuals display the opposite preference for unvaried, unexciting stimulation that would effectively normalize their state?

Bryant and Zillmann (1984) conducted an investigation to test these possibilities. Subjects were placed into a state of boredom or stress and then allowed to watch television, ostensibly while they were waiting for the experiment to continue. Boredom was accomplished by having the subjects perform monotonous tasks for an extended period of time, such as threading washers onto a lace without any performance pressures being applied. Stress was induced by the administration of GRE/SAT type exams, and performance pressures were continually applied. As the individually tested subjects waited for a second study to begin, they could, but did not have to, watch television. However, the experimenter enticed them to watch. He pointed out that various programs could be received from a new cable service, and he sampled from six available programs before leaving the subjects alone for a quarter hour. Actually, the programs that were available on the monitor were received from playbacks in the adjacent room. The subjects' entertainment consumption was ascertained in this room, too. Choice of channel and time of exposure to each channel were recorded for the entire test period.

Six programs were simultaneously available. In a pretest with subjects who were neither bored nor under stress, these programs had been evaluated on a battery of scales. The analysis of the ratings yielded three programs that were considered exciting and three that were considered relaxing. The exciting ones presented an action-packed adventure drama, a professional football game, and a play-off quiz show; the relaxing ones presented underwater nature scenes, classical lullabies from a concert, and a travelogue on restful vacationing.

It was expected, of course, that bored subjects would choose exposure to exciting materials over exposure to relaxing ones, and that stressed subjects would exhibit the opposite preference. These are the choices that serve excitatory homeostasis and therefore constitute effective mood management.

As there was no theoretical interest in exposure to the individual programs, exposure times were accumulated across programs within the categories of the exciting/relaxing dichotomy. These aggregate data were subjected to analysis. The findings, which apply to both genders equally, are shown in Fig. 8.3. As can be seen, bored subjects very much avoided exposure to relaxing programs and showed a strong inclination to watch exciting materials. This is exactly as expected. Stressed subjects conformed less well with expectations. They elected to expose themselves as much to exciting as to relaxing fare. An explanation for this might be a strong disdain for nonexciting, "dull" programs by young people. The distaste might be strong enough to prevent the selection of such materials in situations where the selection has benefits. However, although an ideal transverse interaction pattern was not obtained, the divergent interaction displayed in Fig. 8.3 gives ample evidence of effective mood management. After all, bored subjects elected to consume significantly more exciting programs than did stressed subjects; and stressed subjects elected to consume significantly more relaxing programs than did bored subjects.

Excitatory homeostasis is, of course, not the only excitatory condition to be served by entertainment choices. Such choices often serve the evocation of

FIGURE 8.3. Selective exposure to exciting and relaxing television programs as a function of prior boredom and stress. Respondents chose from among six available offerings. Three were exciting, three relaxing. Selective exposure was measured in accumulated time of channel selection (adapted from Bryant & Zillmann, 1984).

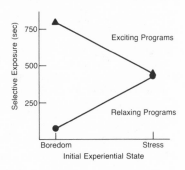

positive affective states of the greatest intensity possible. But extreme intensity requires that excitation climbs to considerable heights, if only for short periods of time (Zillmann, 1980). Interestingly, individuals habituate to the stimuli that evoke strong excitatory reactions, and this well established circumstance (cf. Grings & Dawson, 1978) promotes the selection of similar yet different stimuli for the continued evocation of strong excitatory reactions that characterize positive moods of great intensity. The processes in question have been explored in considerable detail for erotica (e.g., Zillmann & Bryant, 1984). Erotic stimuli initially produce strong sympathetic reactions. With repeated exposure to the stimuli, these reactions tend to become modest, if not negligible. As the excitatory reactions become flat, positive moods become shallow and drab.

The consequences of such excitatory habituation for mood management by consumption of erotica are obvious. The evocation of intense, pleasant sexual excitedness requires exposure to novel stimuli to which individuals have not yet habituated; individuals are forced away from common erotica and enticed to consume less common fare, such as material showing uncommon sexual practices.

Selectivity of this kind has recently been demonstrated in an investigation by Zillmann and Bryant (1986). Both male and female subjects were massively exposed to common, nonviolent erotic films or had no such exposure. Ostensibly while waiting, they were given a private opportunity to watch videos. They could choose from among G- and R-rated materials as well as from among X-rated fare. Explicit erotica were standard (i.e., material to which massively exposed subjects had excitationally habituated) or not. The latter type showed bondage, sadomasochistic behaviors, or bestiality involving human females. Use of videos was unobtrusively recorded. The findings are summarized in Fig. 8.4. They show that both women and men, but especially men, who had excitationally habituated to common erotic fare selected and consumed (in terms of time of exposure) significantly more of the uncommon erotic materials than did non-habituated women and men. Diminished excitatory responding, then, fosters choices of alternative entertainment contents. Specifically, it invites the consumption of materials that hold the greatest promise of producing strong excitatory reactions as intensifiers of positive transitory mood states.

Managing the Hedonic Component

The initial research on mood management through entertainment choices focused on the behavior of persons in good versus bad moods, with persons in no particular mood as a control group (Zillmann, Hezel, & Medoff, 1980). Bad mood is, of course, the condition of particular interest, as individuals experiencing such a mood should be motivated to diminish the hedonic quality of this mood, to escape it altogether, and, if possible, to enter into the hedonically opposite state—all this through consumption of entertaining material. Indi-

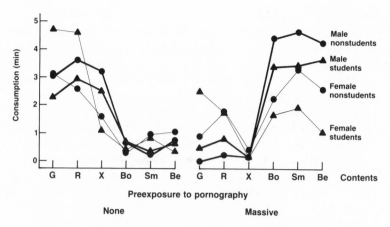

FIGURE 8.4. Selective exposure to different contents as a function of preexposure to common pornography, subject gender, and subject population. The contents are G-rated (G), R-rated (R), X-common (X), X-bondage (Bo), X-sadomasochism (Sm), and X-bestiality (Be). Heavy lines describe consumption by males, thin ones consumption by females. Triangles describe consumption by students, circles by non-students (from Zillmann & Bryant, 1986).

viduals in bad moods should therefore be partial to consuming highly absorbing, pleasant fare that features activities with little affinity to their experiential state. By the same token, they should be inclined to avoid exposure to uninvolving, serious material, especially the kind whose content has affinity to their experiential state. Individuals in good moods, in contrast, have no cause to avoid uninvolving material, and, if anything, they should be partial to content with affinity to their state. These projected preferences were explored under conditions designed to achieve a high degree of ecological validity, not only in the exposure situation, but also in the categorization of selectable stimulus materials. The latter was accomplished by recording a week's prime-time offerings, and by classifying the contents of all recorded programs. From the resulting pools, situation comedies, action dramas, and game shows were drawn at random. Subjects were eventually confronted with unique triplets of programs from which they could choose. The procedure thus involved prime-time programming in a representative fashion and allows generalizations about the appeal of the three content classes as a function of the viewers' mood.

The first part of the experiment served the induction of a bad, a good, or no particular mood state. Subjects performed an emotion–recognition test. After proper recognition of emotion was emphasized as an important social skill, they were exposed to a series of slides showing ambiguous facial expressions. They chose one of four emotions and stated their solution. The experimenter informed them whether it was right or wrong (irrespective of actual correctness) and

161

recorded their responses. In the bad-mood condition he failed the subjects, asserting that they got almost all expressions wrong. Additionally, he insinuated that they would be lacking a critical social skill. In the good-mood condition, in contrast, he led them to believe that they got almost everything right. Additionally, he praised them as being highly sensitive to facial expressions. The subjects' performance in the no-mood conditions was mixed and was said to be at the level of most other persons.

Following this induction of mood, subjects were informed of a delay and invited to pass the time by watching television in the experimenter's room. The experimenter explained that, thanks to a new cable service, prime-time programs could be received now. He flipped through the channels, stopped at an empty one, and left the subject. As described before (Bryant & Zillmann, 1984), playbacks in the adjacent room fed the monitor, and the subjects' choices were recorded there.

What exposure behavior can be expected under these circumstances? The programs' excitatory potentials hardly allow specific predictions. Comedy, drama, and game shows can all be highly arousing, and clearcut differences do not exist. The same seems to be the case for the programs' involvement potentials. The situation is somewhat different for behavioral affinity. Game shows pertain to performance. Contestants succeed or fail and are praised or consoled. This admixture of success and failure makes for a stimulus in which behavioral affinity exists about as often as its opposite: information that counters the conditions linked to the bad mood in question. Persons in a bad mood because of failure might find some relief in the exhibition of others' success (although envy might make this unlikely), but they are probably reminded of their own dilemma when seeing others fail. Mixtures of success and failure, then, seem not to offer a good way out of bad mood. Only the consideration of hedonic valence allows reasonably specific predictions. Both action drama and game shows offer suspense, tension, and many sad moments along with a few happy ones. Comedy, in contrast, is designed to induce laughter, merriment, and euphoria. In short, it is designed to place viewers into a positive, good mood.

Based on these considerations, it may be expected that persons in a bad mood exhibit a strong preference for situation comedies over action dramas and game shows. Persons in a good mood are less in need of being cheered up. They can be expected to consume more of the alternatives to comedy. The same applies to persons in no particular mood. Their consumption can be considered normative.

Moods were found to exert a considerable degree of influence on the consumption of comedy, drama, and games. However, the influence was not as expected. Whereas exposure to comedy was, as predicted, lower for subjects in a good mood than for those in no particular mood, subjects in a bad mood did not exhibit the strong preference for comedy that they were expected to display. Not only did they not prefer comedy, they clearly shunned it.

The data on drama and game shows are of interest in that they show significant changes over time. Subjects in a good mood who had initially elected to watch game shows apparently became disenchanted with this type of program and deserted it in favor of drama. Subjects in a bad mood who had initially chosen drama went the opposite route, deserting drama in favor of game shows. These unforeseen shifts may be explained as the result of program format. Under the assumption that upset persons are less patient than relaxed ones, it can be expected that the subjects in a bad mood who elected to watch drama were not patient enough to make sense of the slowly unfolding dramatic events. After all, the plot of serial action drama spans an hour. Game shows, in contrast, are short-formatted. They are composed of numerous rather autonomous segments, and viewers can quickly and without too much cognitive effort catch onto the events and become absorbed by them. Subjects in a good mood, on the other hand, apparently had the needed patience to stay with drama. But this reasoning leaves unexplained why, over time, they deserted game shows.

The unexpected finding that subjects in a bad mood avoided comedy, compared to those in other moods, becomes less puzzling when the nature of situation comedy in primetime is considered. It has been established (Stocking, Sapolsky, & Zillmann, 1977; Zillmann, 1977) that the predominant form of humor in prime-time comedy is hostile humor that thrives on teasing and put-downs, on belittlement and demeaning treatments. Given such salience of hostility in prime-time comedy, the behavior of the subjects in a bad mood can be understood in terms of the proposals concerning behavioral affinity. These subjects had just suffered failure and belittlement themselves, and exposure to others' belittlement, although humorous, was likely to perpetuate their annoyance. The avoidance of such material, then, might constitute effective mood management after all.

This interpretation was put to the test in a follow-up study by Medoff (1979; see also Zillmann, Hezel, & Medoff, 1980). Behavioral affinity was manipulated in two ways. First, subjects were placed into a bad mood either by frustration only or by frustration and provocation. Subjects were neither frustrated nor provoked in a control condition. Second, subjects were confronted with a choice situation in which either hostile or nonhostile comedy competed against drama. Under these circumstances, behavioral affinity is pronounced only for the choice of hostile comedy by provoked subjects. Only in this case can humorous debasement reinstate experienced debasement. Only these subjects should shun hostile comedy. Subjects who were merely frustrated (i.e., unable to complete a task) should be free to seek out hostile comedy, as affinity between contents and experience is rather poor. Nonhostile comedy, finally, should appeal to both frustrated and provoked subjects.

The manipulation of mood states was analogous to that already described (Zillmann, Hezel, & Medoff, 1980). The original procedure confounded failure (i.e., frustration) and insult (i.e., attack, provocation). This confounding was now undone and frustration produced by failure and provocation by failure plus insult. Also, subjects could choose among drama and comedy only. The drama was kept constant. Comedy was either hostile or not hostile.

The findings, presented in Fig. 8.5, show strong, unexpected gender differences. The behavior of the female respondents is quite consistent with the stated theoretical expectations. First, these respondents consumed nonhostile comedy as predicted. Selective exposure to nonhostile comedy by provoked females is above the level of frustrated females, and that level, in turn, is above that of females in the no-mood control condition. Second, frustrated females did not avoid hostile comedy, but provoked females clearly did. All this is in line with affinity considerations. In contrast, the behavior of the male respondents accords with expectations on one point only: Frustrated men were drawn to hostile comedy. Provoked men tended to avoid comedy, but no more so than the men in the control condition. However, the troubling findings that run counter to expectations concern the consumption of nonhostile comedy. Both frustrated and provoked males, compared to no-mood males, should have sought out nonhostile comedy, but instead exhibited a strong disdain for it. Could it be that frustrated and angry men are so preoccupied with the circumstances of their experience, especially with what to do about it, that they do not feel like laughing? Research on gender differences in the response to provocation would support such an account (e.g., Sapolsky, Stocking, & Zillmann, 1977; Zillmann, 1979). But this research also suggests that gender differences vanish as provocation becomes severe. It is conceivable that both males and females, if sufficiently agitated, would find it difficult to escape into merriment by exposure to comedy or to entertainment generally. Counter to the contention that watching television enter-

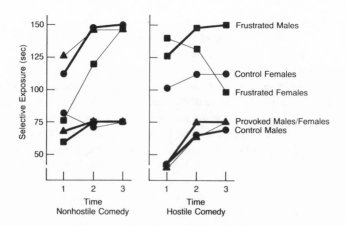

FIGURE 8.5. Selective exposure to hostile and nonhostile comedy as a function of mood. Comedy competed against drama. Exposure was unobtrusively recorded over time. Each time block is comprised of 150 seconds (adapted from Medoff, 1979).

tainment offers an escape from acute problems (e.g., van den Haag, 1960), severely annoyed persons would probably avoid distraction altogether and concentrate on what they can do about their predicament. The recent observation by Christ and Medoff (1984) that acutely annoyed women elected to watch less television fare overall than did their good-mood counterparts seems supportive of such a proposal.

It can be said that the consumption of entertaining stimuli is characterized by pronounced gender differences (cf. Zillmann & Bryant, 1984). On the whole, men exhibit a greater liking for violent entertainment (e.g., Fenigstein, 1979; Gunter, 1983); and they show greater fondness for sexual stimuli of any kind, especially for sexual images (e.g., Zillmann & Bryant, 1986; Zillmann & Mundorf, in press). In managing negative moods, these male preferences occasionally seem to get in the way of effective strategies. Upset men who would do well to stay away from exciting fare laden with sexual and violent events are likely to elect exposure nonetheless because of strong consumption habits that, presumably, have been formed in good moods. It appears that women, overall, are less caught up in such preferences and are free to make consumption choices that manage mood more effectively. It also appears that women are less inclined than men, for better or worse, to resolve bad moods through hostile confrontations with likely inducers (cf. Zillmann, 1979). Women seem to have developed a greater readiness for managing aversive moods by nonhostile means (e.g., Hokanson, 1970). Consuming entertainment is, of course, such a means. This is not to say that women avoid confrontations when they offer the most direct and efficient coping response. It is to say, however, that women who are experiencing bad moods that cannot be blamed on anybody's deliberate actions will not hesitate to combat these moods with entertainment at their disposal.

Managing Anticipated Moods

Research on the partiality for entertaining information likely to comfort rather than to irritate has been aggregated in the realm of crime drama. Gerbner and his associates (e.g., Gerbner & Gross, 1976; Gerbner, Gross, Jackson-Beeck, Jeffries-Fox, & Signorielli, 1978) reported a positive relationship between consumption of television and apprehensions about personal safety and gave these data a causal interpretation: Heavy viewing of television fare, because of the high degree of violence and victimization contained in it, was said to produce these apprehensions. The relationship, should it exist (cf. Hirsch, 1980; Hughes, 1980), can be interpreted quite differently, however. It has been suggested that any causal linkage might be opposite to that proposed by Gerbner et al. (Zillmann, 1980). Instead of exposure breeding fear, it could be that fear promotes exposure. Such a reverse projection makes little sense as long as the premise is accepted that crime drama on television is laden with atrocious violent transgressions and nothing else. If this were so, heavy viewers should indeed get the impression that the streets are dangerous. But such an impression would clash with a vested interest in safe streets, and this makes it difficult to see how programs of sheer destructive violence could hold great appeal to large audiences. The prime message of crime drama is somewhat different, however. Violent transgressions are admittedly plentiful. But they are almost invariably rectified. Unlike in the real world, the transgressors are promptly apprehended, brought to justice, and duly punished. The overall message in crime drama is that the criminals are put away and that the streets are made safer. Crime drama, by and large, is not a celebration of violent chaos, but one of justice in that transgressions are met with punishment. This triumph of good over evil should, of course, hold considerable appeal for those who are apprehensive about crime. It should be music to their ears.

The relationship between the strength of beliefs in a just world and consumption of action-adventure drama has been explored by Gunter and Wober (1983) and found to be positive. The fact that heavy viewers believed the world to be a just place challenges the contention that heavy viewing creates fears of becoming the victim of violent crime. But the findings leave open the possibility that exposure may have cultivated the perception of a just world. Irrespective of this, the findings can also be interpreted as showing that persons who believe in a just world seek to confirm their beliefs by exposing themselves to crime drama more frequently than do others.

Wakshlag, Vial, and Tamborini (1983) provided a direct test of the suggested management of fear by crime-drama consumption. In a laboratory experiment, these investigators placed male and female subjects in a state of apprehension and later gave them entertainment choices. Apprehensions were made manifest and created by exposure to a police documentary on crime. In a control condition, subjects watched a documentary on the Himalayas. Entertainment choices were made from a list of film synopses. These synopses had been pretested and received scores for the degree to which a film was perceived to feature violent victimization and/or punitive restoration of justice. Measures of the appeal of violence and justice could thus be attained by summing the scores across selected films.

The findings are presented in Fig. 8.6. Clearcut gender differences emerged in the appeal of violent victimization. Females exhibited less desire for watching violent drama than did males. Additionally, a greater tendency for females to select drama that promises just resolutions is apparent. Notwithstanding these gender differences, however, both apprehensive males and apprehensive females are equally sensitive to the discussed aspects of drama. Persons who were apprehensive about crime selected drama that was comparatively low in violent victimization and comparatively high in justice restoration. This is, of course, exactly what is expected on the basis of the proposed management of anticipated moods. Persons apparently minimize exposure to entertainment that contains

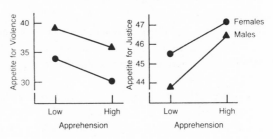

FIGURE 8.6. Selection of drama that emphasizes violent victimization or the punitive restoration of justice as a function of apprehensions about crime (adapted from Wakshlag, Vial, & Tamborini, 1983).

disquieting information, and they apparently maximize exposure to entertainment that carries a supportive, comforting message.

COMPLICATING FACTORS

Taken together, the findings that have been presented can be considered to have established that on numerous occasions individuals manage their moods by selecting appropriate forms of entertaining stimulation. The theoretical model of mood management that was developed to forecast such selection proved useful also. It projected many of the observed selections accurately. However, it would appear that several of the message properties on which the model bases its predictions are insufficiently specified and isolated, if not insufficiently understood. The prediction of some selections, as will be recalled, met with great difficulties. The disinterest in humorous material by male respondents in bad moods, in particular, was highly inconsistent with expectations.

What can be done to overcome these difficulties and to improve the model's predictive accuracy? It appears that several refinements are necessary.

First, as many of the message properties that have been conceptually isolated are confounded in all practical situations of interest, their interrelationships need to be understood in empirical terms. Once these interrelationships are ascertained, they can be used to integrate stimulus properties, and predictions can be based on sets of these properties rather than on individual properties.

Second, it would seem that the introduction of personality considerations should improve the model's predictive accuracy. For instance, it should be imperative to consider individual differences in sensation-seeking or sensation-tolerating (Zuckerman, 1979; see also the chapter in this volume) in the management of excitedness. Consideration of the appeal of violence (cf. Gunter & Wober, 1983) as a gender-transcending trait should prove similarly useful.

Third, it will have to be recognized that mood management often combines

167

the consumption of entertainment with alternative means, such as mood alteration by drugs. Drug usage of this kind has been shown to impact entertainment preferences considerably. For instance, alcoholic intoxication has been found to shift the enjoyment of humor away from refined, subtle forms toward raw and potentially brutal forms (Weaver, Masland, Kharazmi, & Zillmann, 1985).

Fourth, the social circumstances of consuming entertainment can not be ignored. Consumption choices are often not free, but constitute a compromise with co-consumers (e.g., Heeter & Greenberg, 1985). Less obviously, enjoyment often depends on consumption companions. Their presence and, more importantly, their behavior can systematically influence the appeal of entire genres of entertainment. For instance, the enjoyment of horror movies has recently been found to be greatly influenced by the companion's affective expressiveness (Zillmann, Weaver, Mundorf, & Aust, 1986). Social conditions, then, are capable of fostering enjoyment and preferences that seem otherwise unlikely, and predictions that are insensitive to these social influences are bound to be imprecise.

Finally, misassessments of the appeal of particular forms of entertainment are often invited by conditions inherent to that form. In making predictions, obtrusive secondary elements may be mistaken for the conditions of primary appeal. The appeal of thrillers, for instance, might be attributed to continually impending disaster and mayhem, where in fact it derives from the satisfying resolution of conflict and torment (cf. Zillmann, 1980). For the more accurate prediction of entertainment choices as mood management it will have to be determined exactly what consumption experience individuals expect from particular pieces of entertainment, because it is these individuals' perception of things to come that makes them seek out or avoid exposure to the pieces in question.

REFERENCES

Anderson, J. R., & Bower, G. H. (1973). *Human associative memory.* Washington, DC: Winston.

Baron, R. A. (1974). The aggression-inhibiting influence of heightened sexual arousal. *Journal of Personality and Social Psychology, 30,* 318–322.

Baron, R. A. (1977). *Human aggression.* New York: Plenum Press.

Baron, R. A., & Ball, R. L. (1974). The aggression-inhibiting influence of nonhostile humor. *Journal of Experimental Social Psychology, 10,* 23–33.

Berkowitz, L. (1970). Aggressive humor as a stimulus to aggressive responses. *Journal of Personality and Social Psychology, 16,* 710–717.

Bryant, J., & Zillmann, D. (1977). The mediating effect of the intervention potential of communications on displaced aggressiveness and retaliatory behavior. In B. D. Ruben (Ed.), *Communication yearbook 1* (pp. 291–306). New Brunswick, NJ: ICA-Transaction Press.

Bryant, J., & Zillmann, D. (1984). Using television to alleviate boredom and stress: Selective exposure as a function of induced excitational states. *Journal of Broadcasting, 28*(1), 1–20.

Carruthers, M., & Taggart, P. (1973). Vagotonicity of violence: Biochemical and cardiac responses to violent films and television programmes. *British Medical Journal, 3,* 384–389.

Christ, W. G., & Medoff, N. J. (1984). Affective state and selective exposure to and use of television. *Journal of Broadcasting, 28*(1), 51–63.

Collins, A., & Loftus, E. (1975). A spreading-activation theory of semantic memory. *Psychological Review, 82,* 407–428.

Day, K. D. (1980). *The effect of music differing in excitatory potential and hedonic valence on provoked aggression.* Unpublished doctoral dissertation, Indiana University.

Donnerstein, E., & Hallam, J. (1978). Facilitating effects of erotica on aggression against women. *Journal of Personality and Social Psychology, 36,* 1270–1277.

Fenigstein, A. (1979). Does aggression cause a preference for viewing media violence? *Journal of Personality and Social Psychology, 37,* 2307–2317.

Geen, R. G. (1975). The meaning of observed violence: Real vs. fictional violence and consequent effects on aggression and emotional arousal. *Journal of Research in Personality, 9,* 270–281.

Geen, R. G., & Rakosky, J. J. (1973). Interpretations of observed violence and their effects on GSR. *Journal of Experimental Research in Personality, 6,* 289–292.

Gerbner, G., & Gross, L. (1976). Living with television: The violence profile. *Journal of Communication, 26*(2), 173–199.

Gerbner, G., Gross, L., Jackson-Beeck, M., Jeffries-Fox, S., & Signorielli, N. (1978). Cultural indicators: Violence profile no. 9. *Journal of Communication, 28*(3), 176–207.

Grings, W. W., & Dawson, M. E. (1978). *Emotions and bodily responses: A psychophysiological approach.* New York: Academic Press.

Gunter, B. (1983). Do aggressive people prefer violent television? *Bulletin of the British Psychological Society, 36,* 166–168.

Gunter, B., & Wober, M. (1983). Television viewing and public trust. *British Journal of Social Psychology, 22,* 174–176.

Heeter, C., & Greenberg, B. (1985). Cable and program choice. In D. Zillmann & J. Bryant (Eds.), *Selective exposure to communication* (pp. 203–224). Hillsdale, NJ: Lawrence Erlbaum Associates.

Hirsch, P. M. (1980). The "scary world" of the non-viewer and other anomalies: A reanalysis of Gerbner et al.'s findings on cultivation analyses. *Communication Research, 7,* 403–456.

Hokanson, J. E. (1970). Psychophysiological evaluation of the catharsis hypothesis. In E. I. Megargee & J. E. Hokanson (Eds.), *The dynamics of aggression: Individual, group and international analyses* (pp. 74–86). New York: Harper & Row.

Hughes, M. (1980). The faults of cultivation analysis: A re-examination of some effects of television watching. *Public Opinion Quarterly, 44,* 287–302.

Kendall, P. C., & Hollon, S. D. (Eds.). (1979). *Cognitive-behavioral interventions: Theory, research, and procedures.* New York: Academic Press.

Landman, J., & Manis, M. (1983). Social cognition: Some historical and theoretical perspectives. In L. Berkowitz (Ed.), *Advances in experimental social psychology* (Vol. 16, pp. 49–123). San Francisco: Academic Press.

Lang, P. J. (1979). A bio-informational theory of emotional imagery. *Psychophysiology, 16,* 495–512.

Levi, L. (1965). The urinary output of adrenalin and noradrenalin during pleasant and unpleasant emotional states: A preliminary report. *Psychosomatic Medicine, 27,* 80–85.

Levi, L. (1969). Sympatho-adrenomedullary activity, diuresis, and emotional reactions during visual sexual stimulation in human females and males. *Psychosomatic Medicine, 31,* 251–268.

Medoff, N. J. (1979). *The avoidance of comedy by persons in a negative affective state: A further study in selective exposure.* Unpublished doctoral dissertation, Indiana University.

Nevin, J. A. (Ed.). (1973). *The study of human behavior: Learning, motivation, emotion, and instinct.* Glenview, IL: Scott, Foresman.

Ramirez, J., Bryant, J., & Zillmann, D. (1982). Effects of erotica on retaliatory behavior as a function of level of prior provocation. *Journal of Personality and Social Psychology, 43,* 971–978.

Sapolsky, B. S., Stocking, S. H., & Zillmann, D. (1977). Immediate vs delayed retaliation in male and female adults. *Psychological Reports, 40,* 197–198.

Skinner, B. F. (1969). *Contingencies of reinforcement: A theoretical analysis.* New York: Appleton-Century-Crofts.

Stocking, S. H., Sapolsky, B. S., & Zillmann, D. (1977). Sex discrimination in prime time humor. *Journal of Broadcasting, 21,* 447–457.

Thorndike, E. L. (1911). *Animal intelligence.* New York: Macmillan.

Thorndike, E. L. (1932). *The fundamentals of learning.* New York: Columbia University, Teachers College, Bureau of Publications.

van den Haag, E. (1960, Spring). A dissent from the consensual society. *Daedalus,* pp. 315–324.

Wadeson, R. W., Mason, J. W., Hamburg, D. A., & Handlon, J. H. (1963). Plasma and urinary 17-OHCS responses to motion pictures. *Archives of General Psychiatry, 9,* 146–156.

Wakshlag, J., Vial, V., & Tamborini, R. (1983). Selecting crime drama and apprehension about crime. *Human Communication Research, 10,* 227–242.

Weaver, J. B., Masland, J. L., Kharazmi, S., & Zillmann, D. (1985). Effect of alcoholic intoxication on the appreciation of different types of humor. *Journal of Personality and Social Psychology, 49,* 781–787.

Zillmann, D. (1971). Excitation transfer in communication-mediated aggressive behavior. *Journal of Experimental Social Psychology, 7,* 419–434.

Zillmann, D. (1977). Humour and communication. In A. J. Chapman & H. C. Foot (Eds.), *It's a funny thing, humour* (pp. 291–301). Oxford: Pergamon Press.

Zillmann, D. (1979). *Hostility and aggression.* Hillsdale, NJ: Lawrence Erlbaum Associates.

Zillmann, D. (1980). Anatomy of suspense. In P. H. Tannenbaum (Ed.), *The entertainment functions of television* (pp. 133–163). Hillsdale, NJ: Lawrence Erlbaum Associates

Zillmann, D. (1982). Television viewing and arousal. In D. Pearl, L. Bouthilet, & J. Lazar (Eds.), *Television and behavior: Ten years of scientific progress and implications for the eighties: Vol. 2. Technical reviews* (pp. 53–67). U.S. Public Health Service Publication No. ADM 82-1196. Washington, DC: U.S. Government Printing Office.

Zillmann, D. (1983). Transfer of excitation in emotional behavior. In J. T. Cacioppo & R. E. Petty (Eds.), *Social psychophysiology: A sourcebook* (pp. 215–240). New York: Guilford Press.

Zillmann, D., & Bryant, J. (1984). Effects of massive exposure to pornography. In N. M. Malamuth & E. Donnerstein (Eds.), *Pornography and sexual aggression* (pp. 115–138). Orlando, FL: Academic Press.

Zillmann, D., & Bryant, J. (1985). Affect, mood, and emotion as determinants of selective exposure. In D. Zillmann & J. Bryant (Eds.), *Selective exposure to communication* (pp. 157–190). Hillsdale, NJ: Lawrence Erlbaum Associates.

Zillmann, D., & Bryant, J. (1986). Shifting preferences in pornography consumption. *Communication Research, 13,* 560–578.

Zillmann, D., Bryant, J., Comisky, P. W., & Medoff, N. J. (1981). Excitation and hedonic valence in the effect of erotica on motivated intermale aggression. *European Journal of Social Psychology, 11,* 233–252.

Zillmann, D., Hezel, R. T., & Medoff, N. J. (1980). The effect of affective states on selective exposure to televised entertainment fare. *Journal of Applied Social Psychology, 10,* 323–339.

Zillmann, D., Hoyt, J. L., & Day, K. D. (1974). Strength and duration of the effect of aggressive, violent, and erotic communications on subsequent aggressive behavior. *Communication Research, 1,* 286–306.

Zillmann, D., & Johnson, R. C. (1973). Motivated aggressiveness perpetuated by exposure to aggressive films and reduced by exposure to nonaggressive films. *Journal of Research in Personality, 7,* 261–276.

Zillmann, D., & Mundorf, N. (in press). Image effects in the appreciation of video rock. *Communication Research.*

Zillmann, D., Weaver, J. B., Mundorf, N., & Aust, C. F. (1986). Effects of an opposite-gender companion's affect to horror on distress, delight, and attraction. *Journal of Personality and Social Psychology, 51,* 586–594.

Zuckerman, M. (1979). *Sensation seeking: Beyond the optimal level of arousal.* Hillsdale, NJ: Lawrence Erlbaum Associates.

9

Behavior and Biology: Research on Sensation Seeking and Reactions to the Media

Marvin Zuckerman
University of Delaware

The most vital aspect of consciousness is attention, for without an adequate mechanism for focusing mental effort and an adequate program of priorities we cannot learn, communicate, or adapt to the changing contingencies of the environment. Consider the dilemma of the schizophrenic who cannot selectively filter out irrelevant stimuli, and when in a high state of arousal cannot differentiate internal from external, or meaningful from nonmeaningful, stimuli. In our modern urban environment there are many competing demands for attention from one instant to the next. But a reactive attention mechanism is part of our biological makeup. One of our hominid ancestors in a relatively relaxed state on a plain in Africa might have little engagement of attention by the environment, but the sound of something moving in the brush, the sight of something moving in distance, or a new smell wafting about, must have had the instant capacity to engage attention and arouse the brain. Novel stimuli do have this intrinsic capacity to stop ongoing activity and to engage the attention mechanism.

Novelty is not always a signal of danger and is not associated solely with negative affect. Any predators, like dogs or cats, are attracted to novel movement as a potential source of food or, if not particularly hungry, play. Young members of many predator species, including the human, engage in stalk and pounce or rough and tumble play. Chimpanzees may use improvised toys in their play like noise making cans or tree branches used for mock threat effects (Goodall 1971). What is uniquely human in play stems from our time-expanded imagination and vast potential for vicarious play or experience.

A human who finds hunting of interest may seek out the kind of stimulating experience involved in that activity. However, direct experience is limited by restricted hunting seasons, limited availability of game, and other demands on attention and time. In prehistoric times, early humans painted hunting scenes on the walls of their caves. In modern times, the hunter's attention may be engaged by books, magazines, newspaper accounts, films (fictional or nonfictional), television programs, or directly related accounts of hunting. Those whose appetites for experience involve adventure, sports, or sex have a similar choice of vicarious experience addressed at their particular tastes and interests. Although such play may no longer be biologically adaptive, it may be based on fundamental biological mechanisms that once were directly adaptive in practice for the activities involved in reproduction and foraging. I suggest that the appetite for arousing stimulation and experience, whether direct or vicarious, is based in significant part on biological mechanisms, and individual differences in this appetite are based on variations in the underlying biological mechanisms as well as the outcomes of experience associated with such stimuli.

Arousal Potential of Stimuli

What qualities of stimuli are arousing? Berlyne (1971) used the term *arousal potential* to describe "the 'psychological strength' of a stimulus pattern, the degree to which it can take over control of behavior and overcome the claims of competing stimuli" (p. 70). Later, Berlyne and Madsen (1973) defined *arousal potential* partly in terms of the physiological arousal produced by stimuli: "It [arousal potential] represents something like overall power to excite the nervous system, to command attention, and to influence behavior" (p. 14). The properties of stimuli that cause arousal and demand attention include: intensity, novelty, complexity, change and suddeness of change, surprisingness, incongruity, uncertainty, size, color, sensory modality, affective connotations, and relevance to basic rewards or punishments (Berlyne, 1960, 1971).

Berlyne suggested that the hedonic value of stimuli was related to their arousal potential in a curvilinear manner: low-arousing stimuli elicit little but indifference; moderately arousing stimuli produce pleasurable affect up to some maximal level of arousal, but beyond this level added arousal produces decreasing pleasantness and eventually negative affect. Although Berlyne was not particularly interested in individual differences, a number of theorists (Eysenck, 1963, 1967; Fiske & Maddi, 1961; Gray, 1964; Zuckerman, 1969) proposed that differences in optimal levels of stimulation and arousal might be the basis of a fundamental personality trait.

Sensation Seeking Scales

In 1964 we (Zuckerman, Kolin, Price, & Zoob, 1964) published the first form of a questionnaire called the Sensation Seeking Scale (SSS). The scale was based on the idea that persons differ reliably in their preferences for or aversions to stimuli or experiences with high-arousal potential. The immediate use of the scale was to predict responses to experimental sensory deprivation conditions.

High sensation seekers were shown to be more restless in monotonous confinement situations (Zuckerman et al., 1966). The low sensation seekers became more anxious and aroused in a social confinement situation with another person and access to auditory and visual stimuli (Zuckerman, Persky, Link, & Basu, 1968). After a couple of hours of sensory deprivation, the highs responded more than the lows for varied visual stimuli (Lambert & Levy, 1972).

On the basis of these and other results, the first theory of a sensation-seeking motive was formulated (Zuckerman, 1969). The first postulate incorporated Berlyne's arousal potential qualities of stimulation plus the factors that reduce arousal potential such as stimulus repetition, constancy, and overfamiliarity. The third postulate suggested that "every individual has characteristic optimal levels of stimulation (OLS) and arousal (OLA)" (p. 429) that vary with constitutional characteristics of the central nervous system, age, learning experiences, recent levels of stimulation, task demands, and phase of the diurnal arousal cycle.

The SSS form II used a General scale consisting of diverse kinds of items related to the construct of sensation seeking and loading on the first unrotated factor derived from a factor analysis. Subsequent factor analytic studies revealed four sensation-seeking factors and scales were constructed to measure them (form IV, Zuckerman, 1971; form V, Zuckerman, Eysenck, & Eysenck, 1978). These same factors have been generally found in studies done in England (Zuckerman et al., 1978), Australia (Ball, Farnill, & Wangeman, 1984), Canada (Rowland & Franken, 1986), and Israel (Birenbaum, 1986). The four subscales are described here:

Thrill and Adventure Seeking (TAS):: a desire to seek sensation through physically risky activities that provide unusual sensations and novel experiences, e.g. parachuting and scuba diving

Experience Seeking (ES): a desire to seek sensation through a non-conforming lifestyle, travel, music, art, drugs, and unconventional friends.

Disinhibition (Dis): a desire to seek sensation through social stimulation, parties, social drinking, and variety of sex partners.

Boredom Susceptibility (BS): an aversion to boredom produced by unchanging conditions or persons and a great restlessness when things are the same for any period of time.

Form IV of SSS also contains the General scale from Form II. Form V contains a Total Sore, which is the sum of the four subscales.

PERCEPTUAL AND MEDIA PREFERENCES

If our theory of sensation seeking is correct then sensation seekers' preferences should be related to the arousal potential of sensations or experiences. In the realm of sports (Zuckerman, 1983a), sensation seekers tend to engage in activities that involve sensations of speed, flying, and out of the ordinary experi-ence such as parachuting, hang-gliding, scuba diving, skiing, mountain climb-ing, and auto racing. Even those who do not race cars as a sport report driving their cars at high speeds (Zuckerman & Neeb, 1980). In contrast, gymnasts, physical education majors, and runners are not high sensation seekers, and the runners appear to be lower on some of the SS scales than non-runners. Apart from the risk involved in the sports favored by sensation seekers, the activities provide novel kinds of sensation. Parachutists, for instance, like the sensations of free fall that lower sensation seekers must compare to the unpleasant feelings they experience in a rapidly descending elevator.

Preference for Visual Complexity

A very simple test of the preference for complexity is based on preferences among polygons that vary in the number of turns. Looft and Baranowski (1971) found that General SS correlated positively with preferences for the more com-plex polygons. Zuckerman, Bone, Neary, Mangelsdorff, and Brustman (1972) investigated preferences for designs from the Welsh (1959) Figure Preference Test. Figure 9.1 shows the designs preferred more by high sensation seekers and Fig. 9.2 shows the designs preferred more by low sensation seekers. There is an

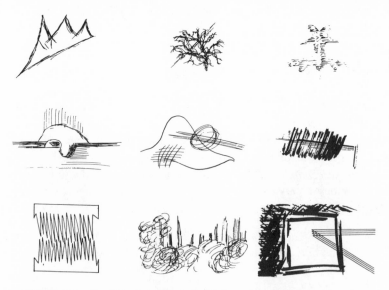

FIGURE 9.1.   Designs liked more by high sensation seekers than by lows. From "What is the sensation seeker? Personality and experience correlates of the Sensation Seeking Scales" by M. Zuckerman, R. N. Bone, R. Neary, D. Mangelsdorff, & B. Brustman, 1972, *Journal of Consulting and Clinical Psychology, 39,* p. 317, Copyright 1972 by the American Psychological Association.

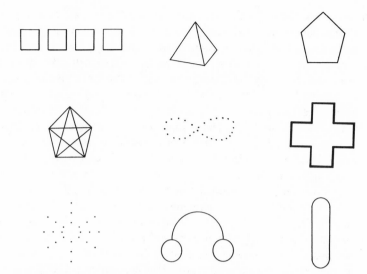

FIGURE 9.2. Designs liked more by low sensation seekers than by highs. From "What is the sensation seeker? Personality and experience correlates of the Sensation Seeking Scales" by M. Zuckerman, R. N. Bone, R. Neary, D. Mangelsdorff, & B. Brustman, 1972, *Journal of Consulting and Clinical Psychology 39,* p. 318, Copyright 1972 by the American Psychological Association.

obvious difference in the complexity of the two sets of designs, but there are also other factors like symmetry, shading, sketchiness, suggestive associations, and emotional symbolism that distinguish the two sets of designs. Osborne and Farley (1970) studied preferences for modern paintings that had been rated for complexity. The preferences for high complexity paintings was not related to sensation seeking. However, complexity is not the only factor influencing the arousal potential of paintings. Modern artists often use very simple forms but achieve dramatic effects though colors and size of forms. Zuckerman and Ulrich (1983) studied preferences for 19th century landscape and seascape paintings ranging in style from realistic to impressionistic and surrealistic. The high sensation seekers had an overall greater liking for paintings of all types but highs and lows differed in particular classifications. The highs liked surrealistic or impressionistic paintings that are ambiguous in content or form. Lows liked peaceful and realistic landscape scenes.

Music Preferences

Zuckerman and Hopkins (1965) gave subjects in a sensory deprivation experiment the option of listening to music, pressing a button for slides, or no stimulation at all. Before the experiment began they were given their choice of three kinds of music: classical, jazz, or a bland Muzak type of popular music. The high sensation seekers chose either classical or jazz and the lows chose the bland Muzak type of music. Watson, Anderson, and Schulte (1977) used five musical selections rated for how grating, exciting, or bland they were. High sensation seekers among their subjects (psychiatric patients) tended to like all kinds of music more than lows but the differences were particularly marked for music rated as "grating." Glascow, Cartier, and Wilson (1985) compared high and low sensation seekers' responses to short selections of classical music ordered along dimensions of familiarity and complexity. The preferences of sensation seekers were not related to these dimensions. The study was limited because it only used classical music selections and only considered two possible dimensions related to arousal. Intensity of the music was not controlled. Considering the fact that high sensation seekers are more tolerant of high levels of loudness (Buchsbaum & Molino, Personal communication, 1974; Farley & Kline, 1972; Kish, Frankel, Masters, & Berry, 1976) this dimension of music may be more salient for the difference in preferences of highs and lows. Litle and Zuckerman (1986) developed a Music Preference Scale based on reported likings for a variety of categories of popular and classical music. Sensation seeking correlated positively with a liking for all types of rock music and negatively with a liking for bland soundtrack or Muzak type music. One feature distinguishing rock music from other types of music is loudness. Soundtrack music, in contrast to rock, is usually less intense because it is intended as background for other media such as film, or activities in the work place.

Media Preferences

Brown, Ruder, Ruder, and Young (1974) correlated the Change Seeker Index (CSI), a sensation-seeking type scale that correlates highly with the SSS, with the incidence of reported activities related to the media. Change seeking correlated positively with time spent listening to music, frequency of movie attendance in general and attendance of X-rated (pornographic) movies in particular, reading in general and reading of fiction books in particular. The SSS has also been related to consumption of X-rated magazines and movies, in a study by Schierman and Rowland (1985), and attendance of X-rated movies in the study by Zuckerman and Litle (1986). An interest in erotic portrayals in the media is not a substitute for experience but is in fact related to extent of sexual experience (Zuckerman, 1976a). Sensation seekers report a greater degree of sexual experience than low sensation seekers in terms of both activities and partners (Zuckerman, Tushup, & Finner, 1976) and a greater willingness to look at erotic stimuli.

Zuckerman and Litle (1986) also found that sensation seekers, particularly those high on the disinhibition subscale, reported more attendance of horror movies. High sensation seekers of both sexes scored higher on scales of general curiosity about morbid events and sexual events. In these scales, they reported a greater interest in reading about or witnessing violence or sex at first hand or in media presentations. Low sensation seekers tend to avoid depictions of either violent or sexual themes in the media. Correlations between entertainment preferences and sensation seeking in the Schierman and Rowland (1985) study indicate that high male sensation seekers tend to read news magazines, non-fiction books, and watch TV news reports more than low sensation seekers. This may reflect the focus on violent events in the news media, but the relations between these activities and sensation seeking was not found in females. Low SS males tend to like musical movies and romantic fiction more than highs; low SS females like theater comedies and dramas more than highs. High SS females report going to pubs, lounges, and nightclubs for entertainment and attending rock music concerts.

Schierman and Rowland (1985) studied the actual viewing behavior of subjects given the choice of watching 30 minute segments of five movies: an action movie, rated as the most highly arousing one, a horror movie. a comedy, a drama, and a romantic film. Subjects were allowed to switch channels whenever they liked and the extent of channel switching, among those who switched channels at all, correlated highly with sensation seeking in both males and females. High sensation-seeking subjects tended to spend more time watching the action film; lows spent more time watching the comedy. These results are consistent with the high sensation seeker's liking for violence in the media found in the Zuckerman and Litle (1986) study. Comedy is a relatively innocuous form of arousal apparently preferred by low sensation seekers.

Zaleski (1984) examined the choices of most liked among 21 pictures, 7 were rated as arousing positive feelings, 7 as arousing negative emotions, and 7 were neutral in arousal. Most of the pictures rated as high in arousal of negative emotions had morbid themes like scenes of torture, executions, and corpses. High positive arousal pictures were pleasant portrayals of celebration and affection, but none were explicitly sexual. The high sensation seekers showed a relatively greater preference for the negative arousal pictures and the lows showed a greater liking for the positive arousal ones. There were no differences in preferences for the neutral or low arousal pictures. Apart from confirming the greater liking for morbid themes by high sensation seekers, the results of the study are relevant to arousal theory. High sensation seekers tended to like the more emotionally arousing stimuli regardless of whether they were positive or negative in content. For lows the content was crucial; they liked the positively arousing stimuli but disliked the negatively arousing stimuli even more than the neutral stimuli. If the arousal potential of the stimuli were measured we would probably find that the morbid stimuli were most arousing, the positive stimuli next most arousing, and the neutral stimuli least arousing. The low sensation seekers preferred the stimuli that were probably intermediate in arousal, while the highs, preferred the most arousing stimuli regardless of their negative content. It is an unfortunate fact of life, well recognized in those who select stories for the media, that "bad news" is intrinsically more interesting (because it is more arousing) than "good news."

Sex and Age Differences

Sensation seeking as a trait (General or Total scores) is higher in males than females in all countries and at all ages (Zuckerman, 1979a). After peaking in the late teens or early 20s, sensation seeking declines with age. The sex and age differences are most pronounced on the TAS and Dis subscales, but the sex difference is never found on the ES scale. Sex differences in media preferences are consistent with sex differences on sensation seeking. In the study by Zuckerman and Litle (1986), males scored higher than females on the Curiosity about Morbid Events and Curiosity about Sexual Events Scales and reported greater attendance at both horror and sex films. In the Schierman and Rowland (1985) study, males watched the action film more than females and high sensation seekers of both sexes watched it more than highs. In the study by Zaleski (1984), males tended to prefer the stimuli that aroused negative emotions, whereas females preferred the positively arousing stimuli, the same direction of differences between high and low sensation seekers within gender groups. Whatever it is that accounts for these differences in media preferences of high and low sensation seekers may be the same thing that accounts for the gender differences in media tastes.

AROUSAL AND AROUSABILITY

Sensation seekers clearly prefer stimuli that are novel, complex, ambiguous, and that elicit strong emotional reactions. The question of why they prefer such stimuli brings us to the biological basis of the sensation-seeking motive. In the introduction to this chapter it was suggested that sensation seekers might be characterized by strong attention reactions and the capacity to readily shift attention to a novel stimulus. Sensation seekers seem to sample widely from their environment. Some unpublished work by Exline (personal communication, 1986) shows that sensation seekers shift their gaze about frequently in a novel environment. The response to a novel stimulus has been called the *orienting reflex* (OR). In animals, it is characterized by an inhibition of ongoing activity and an orientation of the receptors toward the source of stimulation. The behavioral inhibition is usually accompanied by internal changes in physiological arousal. In humans, the OR has been measured by psychophysiological responses such as an increase in skin conductance or a deceleration of heart rate in the seconds immediately following the stimulus. A number of studies have been done measuring the strength of the OR in high and low sensation seekers.

Neary and Zuckerman (1976) found that male high sensation seekers tended to show stronger skin conductance responses (SCRs) than lows to visual and auditory stimuli (tones) on first presentations of the stimulus. However, when the stimulus was repeated the high sensation seekers' responses dropped to the SCR level of the lows. Whenever, a new stimulus was presented the highs again gave a stronger OR than the lows. This finding was replicated for auditory stimuli by Feij, Orlebeke, Gazendam, and van Zuilen (1985), Robinson and Zahn (1983), Smith, Perlstein, Davidson, and Michaels (1986), and for visual stimuli by Smith et al. (1986). Stelmack, Plouffe, and Falkenberg (1983) found that sensation seeking correlated positively with SCRs to printed words, but negatively with SCRs to pictures. Failures to replicate the differences in the SCR OR have been reported by Cox (1977), Ridgeway and Hare (1981), and Zuckerman, Simons, and Como (1986). In contrast to most of the other studies, Smith et al. (1986) used complex, meaningful stimuli designed to be salient to high sensation seekers. These "loaded" words, pictures, and videotaped scenes elicited stronger SCRs than neutral stimuli in all subjects, but the differences in response to loaded and neutral stimuli was greater for high sensation seekers than for lows.

More consistent findings have emerged using heart rate (HR) deceleration as a measure of the OR. The advantage of using HR is that the OR (deceleration of HR) can be distinguished from the defensive reflex (acceleration of HR). The defensive reflex (DR) is a characteristic response to stimuli that are painful or intense. Orlebeke and Feij (1979) found that subjects scoring high and low on the Disinhibition subscale of the SSS differed in their responses to an 80 db tone on the first two stimulus presentations. High sensation seekers showed a decelerating HR, characteristic of an OR, whereas lows showed an accelerating HR interpreted as a DR. Ridgeway and Hare (1981) found similar differences in HR response to a 60 db tone. Robinson and Zahn (1983) found stronger HR ORs in high sensation seekers responding to novel tones. Zuckerman et al. (1986) found that high disinhibitors had a stronger HR OR to a 50 db tone, whereas the low disinhibitors had a stronger DR to a 95 db tone.

Lacey, Kagan, Lacey, and Moss (1963) have described the HR deceleration as indicating an attitude of "environment acceptance" (attention), whereas the pattern of acceleration is more indicative of an attitude of "environment rejection" (attention to thoughts or preparation for flight or avoidance of stimulation). If these patterns of psychophysiological response are reliable, they may represent one source of difference in the attitudes of high and low sensation seekers. The high sensation seeker is receptive to novel stimuli; the low tends to reject them, prefering the more familiar and less complex. The high sensation seeker's optimal level of stimulation may depend on the levels set by the characteristic level of arousal produced by novel stimuli. Anything producing lower arousal levels may be considered "boring."

STIMULUS INTENSITY TOLERANCE AND CORTICAL EVOKED POTENTIALS

Apart from the voluntary avoidance of high intensities of stimulation, the low sensation seeker may have a type of nervous system that rejects such stimulation or inhibits cortical reactivity to high intensity stimuli. Pavlov (1927/1960) defined a property of the nervous system as *strength* versus *weakness*. By strength he meant the ability of cortical cells to continue to work under conditions of intense or prolonged stimulation. Pavlov's successors, Teplov and Nebylitsyn, and a current Pavlovian theorist, Jan Strelau (1983), suggested that there is an inverse relationship between the capacity of cortical cells to work at high stimulus intensities and the sensitivity of the cells to low intensity stimulation. Strong nervous system types tolerate high intensities of stimulation but are relatively insensitive to low intensities of stimulation; the reverse is true for weak nervous system types. At the phenomenal level this seems to hold for high and low sensation seekers, assuming the former are strong nervous system types and the latter are weak nervous system types. Low sensation seekers have low auditory thresholds (Goldman, Kohn, & Hunt, 1983; Kish, Frankel, Master, & Berry, 1976) and low tolerance for high intensity sounds (Buchsbaum & Molino, Personal Communication, 1974; Farley & Kline, 1972); the reverse is true for high sensation seekers.

Psychophysical methods, involving human judgments of sensory events, and classical conditioning constituted the main approach to assessing individual differences in nervous system reactivity until the development of the cortical evoked potential (EP) method by Buchsbaum and Silverman (1968). The method consists of presenting stimuli a number of times at each intensity in a range of stimulus intensities from low to high, and recording the EEG during each stimulus presentation. The EEG reactions for each stimulus intensity are fed into a computer and averaged at successive points for a 500 msec post stimulus period. The averaging yields a clear signal called the *evoked potential*. The method uses an early component of this signal (P1–N1) representing the first impact of the stimulus on the higher cortical centers. The method developed by Buchsbaum and Silverman, described in more detail in Buchsbaum and Pfefferbaum (1971), defines a dimension of "augmenting–reducing" in terms of the relationship (slope) between stimulus intensity and amplitude of the P1N1 EP. Those who show a strong positive slope (increasing EP with increasing stimulus intensity) are called *augmenters* and those who show little positive slope or negative slopes define the reducing end of the continuum. Generally, the difference between augmenters and reducers is most evident at the highest stimulus intensities where the augmenters continue to show increase in EP amplitude while the lows show a marked reduction in EP amplitude relative to the next highest stimulus intensity.

Buchsbaum (1971) hypothesized that high sensation seekers would be augmenters and lows would be reducers, defining these terms by the EP method he developed. Zuckerman, Murtaugh and Siegel (1974) confirmed this hypothesis for the visual (flashing lights) evoked potential. One of the subscales of the SSS, Disinhibition, was most strongly related to EP augmenting. von Knorring (1981) confirmed this relationship between sensation seeking and visual EP augmenting with Swedish subjects. A second replication was reported by Lukas (1982) in America, and a third by Zuckerman, Simons, and Como (1986).

Augmenting–reducing of the auditory EP has also been related to Disinhibition sensation seeking in studies by Coursey, Buchsbaum, and Frankel (1975), Lukas and Mullins (1985), Mullins and Lukas (1984), Orlebeke, Kok, and Zeillemaker (1984), and Zuckerman et al. (1986). In one study (Lukas & Mullins, 1983) the investigators were unable to find a relationship between sensation seeking and auditory EP augmenting, but the relationship was found in a subsequent study in which subjects were required to attend to the stimulus.

What are the implications of this well-replicated finding for responses to the media? The obvious distaste of low sensation seekers for live or recorded rock music and their preference for subdued background music may relate in large part to the characteristic intensity differences between these two types of music. The differential responses to stimulus intensity, the reactions of high and low sensation seekers to morbid spectacles, and the lows' avoidance of such themes in live, film, television, or text form may have something to do with the way their nervous systems are constructed. There seems to be a congruence between the tendency of the nervous system to "tune out" stimuli that are too arousing, and the behavioral tendencies to do the same thing. The high sensation seeker appears to be open to all kinds of stimulation, no matter how novel, intense, or emotion provoking, and her nervous system is in full compliance. The low sensation seeker tries to avoid such stimuli and the brain itself furnishes a second line of defense, achieving a kind of biological denial through dearousal and consequent inattention and attenuation of intensity.

According to a comparative model for sensation seeking (Zuckerman, 1984a), if a personality trait in humans is related to a biological trait, then a similar kind of relationship might be predicted between individual differences in other species and that same biological trait. Cats show the same kind of individual differences in augmenting and reducing of the EP as humans and therefore have been used as subjects for comparative studies. Hall, Rappaport, Hopkins, Griffin, and Silverman (1970), Lukas and Siegel (1977), and Saxton, Siegel, and Lukas (in press) have found that augmenter cats are more active, exploratory, and emotionally reactive to novel stimuli than reducer cats. Saxton et al. also found that reducer cats were better able to learn to inhibit behavior for periods of time in order to obtain reward.

BIOCHEMICAL BASES OF SENSATION SEEKING

Gonadal Hormones

In a previous section, I noted how the same stimuli that are preferred by high sensation seekers compared to lows, are also preferred by men as compared to women. The parallel findings with sensation seeking and gender, as well as the differences on sensation seeking itself, led us to examine the relation of gonadal hormones to sensation seeking. Studies by Daitzman and Zuckerman (1980) and Daitzman, Zuckerman, Sammelwitz, and Ganjam (1978) have shown that males who score high on the Disinhibition subscale of the SSS are higher on testosterone, and estrogens (estradiol and estrone) than low disinhibitors. Mattson, Schalling, Olweus, Löw, and Svensson (1980) found that male delinquents who were high on testosterone scored higher than low testosterone males on Monotony Avoidance, a Swedish sensation-seeking scale. Testosterone also was related to verbal and attitudinal aggressiveness, vigorousness, interest in physical sports, extraversion, and a lack of defensiveness.

Monoamine Oxidase

Monoamine oxidase (MAO) is an enzyme that, in brain neurons, regulates the levels of three monoamine neurotransmitters by metabolizing the transmitter after the cell has fired and reuptake has occurred in the presynaptic neuron. In living humans, MAO is usually measured from blood platelets and such measures are considered by some to be a reasonable estimate of MAO type B in the brain. MAO shows evidence of strong genetic determination (Murphy, 1973; Nies, Robinson, Lamborn, & Lampert, 1973) and is a stable and reliable biological trait in humans. Newborn infants show a range of MAO values comparable to adults, and infants with low MAO levels are more active and behaviorally integrated that high MAO infants in the first 72 hours of life (Sostek, Sostek, Murphy, Martin, & Born, 1981).

Significant negative correlations between platelet MAO and the General SSS were first reported in studies by Murphy et al., 1977, and Schooler, Zahn, Murphy, and Buchsbaum (1978). These studies involved two groups of male and two groups of female students. The significant correlations were found in both male samples and one of the two female samples. Subsequent studies found significant negative correlations in a large sample of Swedish army conscripts (von Knorring, Oreland, & Winblad, 1984), and Spanish normal adults and patients (Arqué, Segurn, & Torrubia, 1985). The correlations in studies by Ballenger et al. (1983) and Schalling, Edman, and Asberg (1983) were not significant but were negative and in the case of Schalling et al. were quite close to significant. Furthermore, studies in Sweden using the Swedish Monotony

Avoidance scale (Perris, Eisemann, von Knorring, Oreland & Perris, 1984; Perris et al., 1980) and Schalling et al. (1983) found negative correlations between this sensation seeking scale and MAO.

The fact that high sensation seekers tend to have low MAO levels is consistent with other data contrasting low MAO with high MAO types in normal human populations. Low MAO males report more time spent in social activities, more of them smoke and use drugs and alcohol (Coursey, Buchsbaum, & Murphy, 1979; von Knorring & Oreland, 1985; von Knorring et al., 1984), and more of them are likely to have a history of serious trouble with the law (Coursey et al., 1979). Fowler, von Knorring, & Oreland, (1980) report that mountain climbers are higher on the SSS and have lower MAO levels than controls. Also consistent with the sensation seeking findings are the facts that females have higher levels of MAO than males at nearly all ages between 18 and 75 (Murphy et al., 1976) and MAO levels increase with age in human brain, platelets, and plasma (Robinson, Davis, Nies, Ravaris, & Sylvester, 1971).

Comparative studies of monkeys observed in a colony show that low MAO monkeys spend more time in social, play, aggressive and sexual activities than high MAO monkeys (Redmond, Murphy, & Baulu, 1979). All of these findings are consistent with results from studies of human sensation seekers.

The significance of the consistent findings linking MAO to sensation seeking points to the involvement of the monoamine systems regulated by MAO in the brain. There is a considerable literature linking these monoamine systems to activity, explorativeness, aggressiveness, lack of inhibition, consummatory behavior, sexual behavior, fear or lack of it, and sensitivity to reward and punishment in other species, primarily rodents (Zuckerman, 1984a). Most of what we know about these systems in humans come from psychopharmacological studies of abnormal populations. From these studies of patients and the few studies of biochemical correlates of personality traits in normals, we are beginning to grasp the biochemical basis of personality.

Monoamines, Related Enzymes, and Sensation Seeking

In the noradrenergic neurons, the enzyme dopamine-beta-hydroxylase (DBH) converts dopamine to noradrenaline (NA) and therefore is crucial in production of new NA and prevention of depletion in an active system. Three studies (Ballenger et al., 1983; Kulcsar, Kutor, & Arató, 1984; Umberkoman-Wiita, Vogel, & Wiita, 1981) have reported negative correlations between serum or plasma DBH and sensation seeking. These findings are consistent with the fact that low levels of serum DBH have been associated with augmenting of the EP (von Knorring & Perris, 1981), and augmenting of the EP is characteristic of high sensation seekers. On the assumption that DBH in blood is a reasonably reliable index of DBH in NA neurons in the brain, we would expect NA levels themselves to be low in high sensation seekers in an unstimulated state. Ballenger et al. (1983) found that NA in the cerebrospinal fluid (CSF) was negatively correlated with the SSS General scale in a group of normal males and females. Although we cannot assess NA activity in the brains of living humans, the NA in the cerebrospinal fluid, known to be increased by stimulation of the NA system in the brain, may be the closest we can come to an estimate of brain NA. As yet, no relationship has been found between sensation seeking and metabolites of dopamine or serotonin in human CSF.

The Biochemical Motive for Seeking Arousal

Little is known about the effect of vicariously aroused emotions on activity of monoamine systems in the brain. In animals, stress of any kind produces increased turnover of NA in the brain. However, the catecholamines NA and adrenaline in the peripheral nervous system have been increased by erotic, violent, and fear-provoking films, of the type favored by high sensation seekers (Levi, 1967, 1969). If such stimuli have similar effects on brain catecholamines, then we might explain the attraction of these films in terms of stimulating moderate arousal in systems that activate reward centers in the brain. There are, of course, more direct ways of activating these centers. Physical or social risk-taking activities are probably more effective than vicarious enjoyment of these activities in activating brain reward centers, although sensation seekers seem to enjoy both types of experience. Stimulant drugs like cocaine and amphetamine directly activate the catecholamine neurons in the brain and provide euphoric arousal. Sensation seeking is the primary personality trait involved in initial drug use and many high sensation seekers are also polydrug users (Zuckerman, 1983b).

Social-Learning Factors in Sensation Seeking

Most of what I have discussed so far concerns the biological basis for the sensation seeking trait. Evidence of high heritability for the trait (58% to 67% of the variance) comes from a study comparing identical and fraternal twins (Fulker, Eysenck, & Zuckerman, 1980). The heritability of the trait depends on the heritability of the underlying physiological mechanisms. However, at least one third of the variance in the trait comes from the environment. Surprisingly, (but as found for most other personality traits) it is not the distinctive family environment which is influential in sensation seeking trait, but the specific environment of peers, siblings, and the general society. The environment does not act on a passive individual; the person seeks out what he needs from the environment. Just as the availability of drugs is a major factor in their use, the availability of role models and sources of excitement are major factors in the forms sensation seeking will take. Children will seek it in play, some in more dangerous and some in safer games. Older children, adolescents, and adults may seek it in sports or media stimulation and social and sexual activities. In some neighborhoods, criminal activities and drugs are the primary sources of sensation rewards, whereas in the suburbs, parties and fast cars may provide the needed "jolts." Persons, who might not be predisposed to be high or even moderate sensation seekers may be drawn into social or antisocial activities because of their need to be accepted by more sensation seeking peers. Eventually, most persons will find their own optimal level of stimulation and arousal.

I have discussed how sensation seeking declines with age and how this may be based on biological changes such as reduced gonadal hormones and increased levels of MAO. However, extreme types of experience may also affect sensation seeking. Exposure to war or personal catastrophes may reduce the desire for stimulation and arousal and increase the need for stability, constancy, and predictability. A new form of the SSS (VI, Zuckerman, 1984b), which differentiates between past sensation seeking experience and future desires or intentions, enables us to investigate this hypothesis.

COMMENTS ON OTHER SYMPOSIUM PAPERS

After reading the contents of this volume, I wondered why I was asked to contribute because I am not well known for my communication, or cognition, at least as areas of personal research. After reading the chapters, I realized that there were two reasons for my presence. One is the persisting interest in the optimal level of stimulation and optimal level of arousal constructs as an explanation of reactions to the media, particularly the chapters by Crockett, Donohew, Finn, and Christ, and Zillmann. The second reason would seem to be that I was the token representative of an individual difference approach. Although several of the contributors to the volume have suggested that individual differences are a source of differential reactions to the media, none of them seem to have examined this problem in any depth.

As described in this chapter, the first sensation seeking scale was based on the idea that there are reliable, consistent individual differences in the optimal level of stimulation (Zuckerman et al., 1964) and these differences in OLS were based on differences in optimal levels of arousal (Zuckerman, 1969). However, comparisons of the SSS with other scales, like Pearson's (1970) Novelty Experiencing Scales, have indicated some definite boundaries for the construct of sensation seeking (see Table 6.3, p. 141 in Zuckerman, 1979a). Pearson divides her four scales along two dimensions: sensation and cognition, and internal and external. Sensation seeking correlates primarily with the External Sensation scale (exciting and risky activities), and secondarily with the Internal Sensation scale (inner experiences such as fantasies, feelings, and dreams). The correlations of the SSS with internal and external cognitive (problem-solving) experience seeking are mainly low and insignificant, and in some studies the correlations were negative with the External Cognitive scale. Sensation seekers, as defined by our scale, seek external or internal stimuli that provide unusual or novel sensations, but they do not necessarily seek stimulation through cognitive activities. For this reason, we would not expect to find differences between high and low sensation seekers produced by purely cognitive factors in textual materials like the discrepancy factor in the study by Donohew, Palmgreen, and Duncan (1980). However, textual material may appeal to high sensation seekers if it stimulates strong feelings in them. The study by Donohew et al. used the Pearson (1970) scale total score but they should have probably looked more closely at the cognitive scales.

On the other hand, the studies by Zillmann described in this volume, which primarily use external visual and auditory stimulation as means of manipulating arousal, could benefit more from the use of sensation seeking as the most pertinent dimension of personality. Reactions to the media are not determined just by current stressors, which are the main focus of Zillmann's work. As we have shown in this chapter, there seem to be reliable differences between high and low sensation seekers in the content of their media preferences. Zillmann recognizes the role of stable sex differences in media tastes in determining choices of entertainment. Males show little change in preference as a result of stress, continuing to view their usual favorites, violence and sex. Women, however, are more likely to attempt to reduce stress by selecting more innocuous comedies. The study by Zuckerman and Litle (1986) showed both sex and sensation-seeking differences on curiosity about morbid and sexual events, and attendance of violent horror movies and X-rated erotic films.

One curious absence in the studies described by Zillmann is the lack of any measures of mood reactions to the experimental manipulations. Mood would seem to be an important intervening variable in selection of media in these studies, but Zillmann just describes the changes in operant behavior as a function of his experimental manipulations. Individual differences in affective reactions to stress are a notorious source of variance. If one is going to assess this type of reaction, it would be best to use state measures that are standardized and psychometrically sound rather than one-item, ad hoc self-rating scales of dubious reliability. The new revised Multiple Affect Adjective Check List (Zuckerman & Lubin, 1985) has the advantage of being quick and simple to administer, uses factor analytically derived scales, most of which show excellent reliability, and measures positive affect as well as negative affects.

Obviously, if one is to make sense of the data on the influence of the media on mood or attitude, one must consider personality as well as gender differences. I have certainly concentrated too much on the individual difference side and neglected the experimental manipulation of mood and behavior. As can be seen in some of the studies described in this chapter, we are beginning to move in that direction. Zillmann's chapter has provided some useful ideas as to how we might procede to examine the interactions between stress induced moods, reactions to media presentations and sensation seeking.

Cognition is of great interest to me and we have investigated some of the cognitive differences between high and low sensation seekers (Zuckerman, 1976b, 1979b). Sensation seekers see less objective risk in the activities they tend to favor even before they have tried such activities. They also expect to experience less anxiety and more positive affect while engaged in these activities than low sensation seekers, even when the risk estimate is the same for highs and lows. Expected emotional reactions are probably a major source of approach or avoidance to most activities. Noone expects to be physically damaged by watching a violent or erotic film, but low sensation seekers may avoid these types of films because they would expect to experience unpleasant affects.

When affect or cognition and behavioral responses are measured after some treatment we cannot assume a causal role for affect or cognition. In these cases, cognitions and affects are correlates of behavioral responses not their causes. Furthermore, one cannot assume a causal priority to either cognition or affect. As Crockett (this volume) points out, affect may influence schemas just as schemas may influence affective responses. A state of fear, whatever its source, may change one's appraisal of risk in a sensation-seeking situation, and one's appraisal of risk may make one fearful in the same situation. Affect states may arise from conditioned and generalized reactions that have little, if any, cognitive content, or the cognitive content may not be related to the affect (as when a phobic admits that he knows there is no threat in the situation and that his fear is unrealistic).

In the broader sense, I am opposed to the type of cognitive theory that insists that cognitions determine all behaviors even if the person is incapable of verbalizing the particular cognition. Although not a radical behaviorist, I must agree with Skinner (1953) that cognitions are inferred (internal) behaviors that, like overt behavior, must be explained by antecedent events and their outcomes. Unlike Skinner, I would add that many cognitions must have a biological component in their origin, as well as an environmental one. If we ask why a high sensation seeker tends to underestimate risk or a low sensation seeker tends to overestimate risk in a novel situation, the answer rarely lies in their different patterns of experience outcomes. Rather, the unique points of view of sensation seekers are partly explained by the way they are made, or inherited differences in nervous system structure and function. In addition to this biological component, which seems to account for at least half of the variance in most broad personality traits (Eysenck & Eysenck, 1985), we may speculate on environmental influences like modeled behavior. However, a true heredity-environment interactional position must recognize that what we learn from personal experience, or the models we choose to emulate from the range of models available, depends on our genetic constitution as well as our unique experiences.

REFERENCES

Arqué, J., Segurn, R., & Torrubia, R. (1985, June). *Biochemical correlates of sensation seeking and susceptibility to punishment scales: A study in individuals with somatoform disorders and normals.* Paper presented at the second meeting of the International Society for the Study of Individual Differences, San Felieux, Spain.

Ball, I. L., Farnill, D., & Wangeman, J. F. (1984). Sex and age differences in sensation seeking: Some national comparisons. *British Journal of Psychology, 75,* 257–265.

Ballenger, J. C., Post, R. M., Jimerson, D. C., Lake, C. R., Murphy, D. L., Zuckerman, M., & Cronin, C. (1983). Biochemical correlates of personality traits in normals: An exploratory study. *Personality and Individual Differences, 4,* 615–625.

Berlyne, D. E. (1960). *Conflict, arousal and curiosity.* New York: McGraw Hill.

Berlyne, D. E. (1971). *Aesthetics and psychobiology.* Engelwood Clifts, NJ: Prentice-Hall.

Berlyne, D. E., & Madsen, K. B. (1973). *Pleasure, reward, preference: Their nature, determinants and role in behavior.* New York: Academic Press.

Birenbaum, M. (1986). On the construct validity of the sensation seeking scale in a non-English-speaking culture. *Personality and Individual Differences, 7,* 431–434.

Brown, L. T., Ruder, V. G., Ruder, J. H., Young, S. D. (1974) Stimulation seeking and the Change Seeker Index. *Journal of Consulting and Clinical Psychology, 42,* 311.

Buchsbaum, M. S. (1971). Neural events and the psychophysical law. *Science, 172,* 502.

Buchsbaum, M. S., & Pfefferbaum, A. (1971). Individual differences in stimulus-intensity response. *Psychophysiology, 8,* 600–611.

Buchsbaum, M. S., & Silverman, J. (1968). Stimulus intensity control and the cortical evoked response. *Psychosomatic Medicine, 30,* 12–22.

Coursey, R. D., Buchsbaum, M. S., & Frankel, B. I. (1975). Personality measures and evoked responses in chronic insomniacs. *Journal of Abnormal Psychology, 84,* 239–249.

Coursey, R. D., Buchsbaum, M. S., & Murphy, D. L. (1979). Platelet MAO activity and evoked potentials in the identification of subjects biologically at risk for psychiatric disorders. *British Journal of Psychiatry, 134,* 372–381.

Cox, D. N. (1977). *Psychophysiological correlates of sensation seeking and socialization during reduced stimulation.* Unpublished doctoral dissertation, University of British Columbia, Vancouver, Canada.

Daitzman, R. J., & Zuckerman, M. (1980). Disinhibitory sensation seeking, personality and gonadal hormones. *Personality and Individual Differences, 1,* 103–110.

Daitzman, R. J., Zuckerman, M., Sammelwitz, P. H., & Ganjam, V. (1978). Sensation seeking and gonadal hormones. *Journal of Biosocial Science, 10,* 401–408.

Donohew, L., Palmgreen, P., & Duncan, J. (1980). An activation model of information exposure. *Communication Monographs, 47,* 295–303.

Eysenck, H. J. (1963). *Experiments with drugs.* New York: Pergamon.

Eysenck, H. J. (1967). *The biological basis of personality.* Springfield, IL: Charles C. Thomas.

Eysenck, H. J., & Eysenck, M. W. (1985). *Personality and individual differences: A natural science approach.* New York: Plenum Press.

Farley, F. H., & Kline, K. (1972). *Noise and light tolerance thresholds and the stimulation seeking motive.* Unpublished manuscript.

Feij, J. A., Orlebeke, J. F., Gazendam, A., & van Zuilen, R. (1985). Sensation seeking: Measurement and psychophysiological correlates. In J. Strelau, F. Farley, & A. Gale (Eds.), *Biological bases of personality and behavior* (Vol. 1, pp. 195–210). Washington, DC: Hemisphere Press.

Fiske, D. W., & Maddi, S. R. (1961). *Functions of varied experience.* Homewood, IL: Dorsey Press.

Fowler, C. J., von Knorring, L., & Oreland, L. (1980). *Psychiatry Research, 3,* 273–279.

Fulker, D. W., Eysenck, S. B. G., & Zuckerman, M. (1980). The genetics of sensation seeking. *Journal of Personality Research, 14,* 261–281.

Glascow, M. R., Cartier, A. M., & Wilson, G. D. (1985). Conservatism, sensation seeking and music preferences. *Personality and Individual Differences, 6,* 395–396.

Goldman, D., Kohn, P. M., & Hunt, R. W. (1983). Sensation seeking, augmenting-reducing and absolute auditory threshold: A strength-of-the-nervous-system perspective. *Journal of Personality and Social Psychology, 45,* 405–411.

Goodall, J. (1971). *In the shadow of man.* New York: Dell.

Gray, J. A. (1964). Strength of the nervous system and levels of arousal: A reinterpretation. In J. A. Gray (Ed.), *Pavlov's typology* (pp. 289–364). New York: MacMillan.

Hall, R. A., Rappaport, M., Hopkins, H. K., Griffin, R. B., & Silverman, J. (1970). Evoked response and behavior in cats. *Science, 170,* 998–1000.

Kish, G. B., Frankel, A., Masters, J. J., & Berry, R. A. (1976). Augmenting-reducing and sensation seeking: A test of Sales' hypothesis. *Journal of Clinical Psychology, 32,* 302–305.

von Knorring, L. (1981). Visual evoked responses and platelet monoamine oxidase in patients suffering from alcoholism. In H. Begleiter (Ed.), *The biological effects of alcohol* (pp. 270–291). New York: Plenum Press.

von Knorring, L., & Oreland, L. (1985). Personality traits and platelet monoamine oxidase in tobacco smokers. *Psychological Medicine, 15,* 327–334.

von Knorring, L., Oreland, L., & Winblad, B. (1984). Personality traits related to monoamine oxidase activity in platelets. *Psychiatry Research, 12,* 11–26.

von Knorring, L., & Perris, C. (1981). Biochemistry of the augmenting-reducing response in visual evoked potentials. *Neuropsychobiology 7,* 1–8.

Kulcśar, Z., Kutor, L., & Arató, M. (1984). Sensation seeking, its biochemical correlates, and its relation to vestibulo-ocular functions. In H. Bonarius, G. van Heck, & N. Smid (Eds.), *Personality psychology in Europe: Theoretical and empirical developments* (pp. 327–346). Lisse, The Netherlands: Swets & Zeitlinger.

Lacey, J. I., Kagan, J., Lacey, B. C., & Moss, H. A. (1963). The visceral level: Situational determinants and behavioral correlates of autonomic response patterns. In P. H. Knapp (Ed.), *Expressions of emotions in man.* New York: International Universities Press.

Levi, L. (1967). Stressors, stress tolerance, emotions and performance in relation to catecholamine excretion. In L. Levi (Ed.), *Emotional stress: Physiological and psychological reactions: medical industrial and military implications* (pp. 192–201). New York: American Elsevier.

Levi, L. (1969). Sympatho-adrenomedullary activity, diuresis and emotional reactions during visual sexual stimulation in human females and males. *Psychosomatic Medicine, 31,* 251–268.

Lambert, W., & Levy, L. H. (1972). Sensation seeking and short term sensory isolation. *Journal of Personality and Social Psychology, 24,* 46–52.

Litle, P., & Zuckerman, M. (1986). Sensation seeking and music preferences. *Personality and Individual Differences, 4,* 575–578.

Looft, W. R., & Baranowski, M. D. (1971). An analysis of five measures of sensation seeking and preferences for complexity. *Journal of General Psychology, 85,* 307–313.

Lukas, J. H. (1982). Human augmenting-reducing and sensation seeking. *Psychophysiology, 19,* 333–334.

Lukas, J. H., & Mullins, L. F. (1983). Auditory augmenting-reducing and sensation seeking. *Psychophysiology, 20,* 457 (Abstract).

Lukas, J. H., & Mullins, L. F. (1985). Auditory augmenters are sensation seekers and perform better under high work-loads. *Psychophysiology, 22,* 580–581 (Abstract).

Lukas, J. H., & Siegel, J. (1977). Cortical mechanisms that augment or reduce evoked potentials in cats. *Science, 196,* 73–75.

Mattson, A., Schalling, D., Olweus, D., Löw, H., & Svensson, J. (1980). Plasma testosterone, aggressive behavior, and personality dimensions in young male delinquents. *Journal of the American Academy of Child Psychiatry, 19,* 476–490.

Mullins, L. F., & Lukas, J. H. (1984). Auditory augmenters are sensation seekers if they attend the stimuli. *Psychophysiology, 21,* 589 (Abstract).

Murphy, D. L. (1973). Technical strategies for the study of catecholamines in man. In E. Usdin & S. Snyder (Eds.), *Frontiers in catecholamine research* (pp. 1077–1082). Oxford: Pergamon Press.

Murphy, D. L., Belmaker, R. H., Buchsbaum, M. S., Martin, N. F., Ciaranello, R., & Wyatt, R. J. (1977). Biogenic amine related enzymes and personality variations in normals. *Psychological Medicine, 7,* 149–157.

Murphy, D. L., Wright, C., Buchsbaum, M. S., Nichols, A., Costa, J. L., & Wyatt, R. J. (1976). Platelet and plasma amine oxidase activity in 680 normals: Sex and age differences and stability over time. *Biochemical Medicine, 16,* 254–265.

Neary, R. S., & Zuckerman, M. (1976). Sensation seeking, trait and state anxiety, and the electrodermal orienting reflex. *Psychophysiology, 13,* 205–211.

Nies, A., Robinson, D. C., Lamborn, K. R., & Lampert, R. P. (1973). Genetic control of platelet and plasma monoamine oxidase activity. *Archives of General Psychiatry, 28,* 834–838.

Orlebeke, J. F., & Feij, J. A. (1979). The orienting reflex as a personality correlate. In H. D. Kimmel, E. H. van Olst, & J. F. Orlebeke (Eds.), *The orienting reflex in humans* (pp. 567–585). Hillsdale, NJ: Lawrence Erlbaum Associates.

Orlebeke, J. F., Kok, A., & Zeillemaker, C. W. (1984). Augmenting-reducing (disinhibition) and the processing of auditory stimulus intensity. *Psychophysiology, 21,* 591 (Abstract).

Osborne, J. W., & Farley, F. H. (1970). The relationship between aesthetic preference and visual complexity in abstract art. *Psychonomic Science, 19,* 69–70.

Pavlov, I. P. (1960). *Conditioned reflexes: An investigation of the physiological activity of the cerebral cortex.* (Trans. G. V. Anrep). New York: Dover. (originally published 1927).

Pearson, P. H. (1970). Relationships between global and specified measures of novelty seeking. *Journal of Consulting and Clinical Psychology, 34,* 199–204.

Perris, C., Eisemann, M., von Knorring, L., Oreland, L., & Perris, H. (1984). Personality traits and monoamine oxidase activity in platelets in depressed patients. *Neuropsychobiology, 12,* 201–205.

Perris, C., Jacobsson, L., von Knorring, L., Oreland, L., Perris, H., & Ross, S. B. (1980). Enzymes related to biogenic amine metabolism and personality characteristics in depressed patients. *Acta psychiatrica Scandinavica, 61,* 477–484.

Redmond, D. E. Jr., Murphy, D. L., & Baulu, J. (1979). Platelet monoamine oxidase activity correlates with social affiliative and agonistic behaviors in normal rhesus monkeys. *Psychosomatic Medicine, 41,* 87–100.

Ridgeway, D., & Hare, R. D. (1981). Sensation seeking and psychophysiological responses to auditory stimulation. *Psychophysiology, 18,* 613–618.

Robinson, D. S., Davis, J. M., Nies, A., Ravaris, C. L., & Sylvester, D. (1971). Relation of sex and aging to monoamine oxidase activity of human brain, plasma, and platelets. *Archives of General Psychiatry, 24,* 536–539.

Robinson, T. N. Jr., & Zahn, T. P. (1983). Sensation seeking, state anxiety and cardiac and EDR orienting reactions. *Psychophysiology, 20,* 465 (Abstract).

Rowland, G. L., & Franken, R. E., (1986). The four dimensions of sensation seeking: A confirmatory factor analysis. *Personality and Individual Differences, 7,* 237–240.

Saxton, P. M., Siegel, J., & Lukas, J. H. (in press). Visual evoked potential augmenting/reducing slopes in cats. 2. Correlations with behavior. *Personality and Individual Differences.*

Schalling, D., Edman, G., & Asberg, M. (1983). Impulsive cognitive style and inability to tolerate boredom. In M. Zuckerman (Ed.), *Biological bases of sensation seeking, impulsivity and anxiety* (pp. 125–147). Hillsdale, NJ: Lawrence Erlbaum Associates.

Schierman, M. J., & Rowland, G. L. (1985). Sensation seeking and selection of entertainment. *Personality and Individual Differences, 5,* 599–603.

Schooler, C., Zahn, T. P., Murphy, D. L., & Buchsbaum, M. S. (1978). Psychological correlates of monoamine oxidase in normals. *Journal of Nervous and Mental Disease, 166,* 177–186.

Skinner, B. F. (1953). *Science and human behavior.* New York: MacMillan Company.

Smith, B. D., Perlstein, W. M., Davidson, R. A., & Michaels, K. (1986). Differential effects of relevant novel stimulation on electrodermal activity. *Personality and Individual Differences, 4,* 445–452.

Sostek, A. J., Sostek, A. M., Murphy, D. L., Martin, E. B., & Born, W. S. (1981). Cord amine oxidase activities relate to arousal and motor functioning in human newborns. *Life Sciences. 28,* 2561–2568.

Stelmack, R. M., Plouffe, L., & Falkenberg, W. (1983). Extraversion, sensation seeking and electrodermal response: Probing a paradox. *Personality and Individual Differences, 4,* 607–614.

Strelau, J. (1983). *Temperament, personality, activity.* London: Academic Press.

Umberkoman-Wiita, B., Vogel, W. H., & Wiita, P. J. (1981). Some biochemical and behavioral (sensation seeking) correlates in healthy adults. *Research Communications in Psychology, Psychiatry and Behavior, 6,* 303–316.

Watson, C. G., Anderson, R., & Schulte, D. (1977). Responses of high- and low-emotional deficit patients to exciting, grating, and neutral stimuli. *Journal of Clinical Psychology, 33,* 552–554.

Welsh, G. S. (1959). *Preliminary manual for the Welsh Figure Preference Test.* Palo Alto, CA: Consulting Psychologists Press.

Zaleski, Z. (1984). Sensation seeking and preference for emotional and visual stimuli. *Personality and Individual Differences, 5,* 609–611.

Zuckerman, M. (1969). Theoretical formulations: I. In J. P. Zubek (Ed.), *Sensory deprivation: Fifteen years of research* (pp. 407–432). New York: Appleton-Century-Crofts.

Zuckerman, M. (1971). Dimensions of sensation seeking. *Journal of Consulting and Clinical Psychology, 36,* 45–52.

Zuckerman, M. (19976a). Research on pornography. In W. W. Oaks, G A. Melchiode, & I. Ficher (Eds.), *Sex and the life cycle* (pp. 147–161). New York: Grune & Stratton.

Zuckerman, M. (1976b). Sensation seeking and anxiety, traits and states, as determinants of behavior in novel situations. In I. Sarason & C. D. Speilberger (Eds.), *Stress and Anxiety* (Vol. 3). Washington, DC: Hemisphere.

Zuckerman, M. (1979a). *Sensation seeking: Beyond the optimal level of arousal.* Hillsdale, NJ: Lawrence Erlbaum Asociates.

Zuckerman, M. (1979b). Sensation seeking and risk taking. In C. E. Izard (Ed.), *Emotions in personality and psychopathology* (pp. 163–197). New York Plenum Press.

Zuckerman, M. (1983a). Sensation seeking and sports. *Personality and Individual Differences, 4,* 285–292.

Zuckerman, M. (1983b). Sensation seeking: The initial motive for drug abuse. In E. Gottheil, K. A. Druley, T. E. Skolada, & H. M. Waxman (Eds.), *Etiological aspects of alcohol and drug abuse.* Springfield, IL: Charles C. Thomas.

Zuckerman, M. (1984a). Sensation seeking: A comparative approach to a human trait. *The Behavioral and Brain Sciences, 7,* 413–471.

Zuckerman, M. (1984b). Experience and desire: A new format for sensation seeking scales. *Journal of Behavioral Assessment, 6,* 101–114.

Zuckerman, M., Bone, R. N., Neary, R., Mangelsdorff, D., & Brustman, B. (1972). What is the sensation seeker? Personality trait and experience correlates of the Sensation Seeking Scales *Journal of Consulting and Clinical Psychology, 39,* 308–321.

Zuckerman, M., Eysenck, S. B. G., & Eysenck, H. J. (1978). Sensation seeking in England and America: Cross-cultural, age, and sex comparisons. *Journal of Consulting and Clinical Psychology, 46,* 139–149.

Zuckerman, M., & Hopkins, T. R. (1965) Unpublished study.

Zuckerman, M., Kolin, E. A. Price, L., & Zoob, I. (1964). Development of a Sensation-Seeking Scale. *Journal of Consulting Psychology, 28,* 477–482.

Zuckerman, M., & Litle, P. (1986). Personality and curiosity about morbid and sexual events. *Personality and Individual Differences, 7,* 49–56.

Zuckerman, M., & Lubin, B. (1985). *Manual for the MAACL-R, The Multiple Affect Adjective Check List-Revised.* San Diego, CA: Educational and Industrial Testing Service.

Zuckerman, M., Murtaugh, T. T., & Siegel, J. (1974). Sensation seeking and cortical augmenting–reducing. *Psychophysiology, 11,* 535–542.

Zuckerman, M., & Neeb, M. (1980). Demographic influences in sensation seeking and expressions of sensation seeking in religion, smoking, and driving habits. *Personality and Individual Differences, 1,* 197–206.

Zuckerman, M., Persky, H., Hopkins, T. R., Murtaugh, T., Basu, G. K., & Schilling, M. (1966). Comparison of stress effects of perceptual and social isolation. *Archives of General Psychiatry, 14,* 356–365.

Zuckerman, M., Persky, H., Link, K. E., & Basu, G. K. (1968). Experimental and subject factors determining responses to sensory deprivation, social isolation, and confinement. *Journal of Abnormal Psychology, 73,* 183–194.

Zuckerman, M., Simons, R. F., & Como, P. G. (1986). *Sensation seeking and stimulus intensity as modulators of cortical, cardiovascular, and electrodermal response: A cross-modality study.* Manuscript submitted for publication.

Zuckerman, M., Tushup, R., & Finner, S. (1976). Sexual attitudes and experience: Attitude and personality correlates and changes produced by a course in sexuality. *Journal of Consulting and Clinical Psychology, 44,* 7–19.

Zuckerman, M., & Ulrich, R. (1983). *Sensation seeking and preferences among 19th century nature paintings.* Paper presented at Conference on Psychology and the Arts. Cardiff, Wales.

10 "The Nature of News" Revisited: The Roles of Affect, Schemas, and Cognition

Lewis Donohew
University of Kentucky

Seth Finn
University of North Carolina at Chapel Hill

William G. Christ
Trinity University

In exposure to the news, as in other areas of life, individuals appear to seek an optimal or medium level of stimulation (Berlyne, 1971; Martindale, 1981; Wundt, 1894). When the level of stimulation exceeds or drops below this optimal level, pleasure may turn to displeasure.

This does not imply, however, that individuals will read, watch, or listen to only those news items that maintain arousal levels within desired boundaries. Although arousal needs do appear to guide them in their selections, they may choose to override these affective tugs for any of a number of reasons, such as desire to learn more about a topic of importance to them in which they perceive themselves to be deficient (McCombs & Weaver, 1985). A number of these processing goals are described by Bargh (this volume). As Martindale (1981) notes in explaining other similar behaviors, "There are any number of tasks that we must perform either poorly or at the cost of considerable displeasure" (p. 26).

From a physiological perspective, humans are continuously involved in a search for stimulation, driven by pleasure centers of the midbrain (Campbell, 1973; Martindale, 1981; Olds & Forbes, 1981; Young, 1978). According to Young, often the brain

> follows a routine program under the control of the activating system, so that we hardly notice our daily surroundings. But we are quickly alerted by new and interesting objects or occurrences. There is a continuous interaction between sig-

195

nals flowing up and down these immensely intricate nervous pathways, (and) the activating system keeps the sensory system alert, looking all the time for interesting data in what goes on around (it). (p. 233)

Although need for arousal varies across individuals (Zuckerman, 1978, 1983 this volume), it is nonetheless fundamental to human behavior and serves an important function in the mechanisms guiding exposure to the mass media, including the separate processes of attracting and holding attention (Zillmann, 1982).

To understand more completely the processes that underlie the selection of "competing stimuli," one must be sensitive to the relationship between novel sensory inputs and physiological arousal (Berlyne, Craw, Salepeteck, & Lewis, 1963; Bryant & Zillmann, 1984; Christ, 1985; Christ & Medoff, 1984; Pribram & McGuinness, 1975; Skinner & Lindsley, 1973; Zillmann, 1982; Zillmann, Hezel, & Medoff, 1980) as well as the impact of schemas and other mental constructs that may guide information processing at a low level of awareness. (Fiske & Taylor, 1984; Schank & Abelson, 1977; Sypher & Applegate, 1984). For example, while engaging in pursuit of arousal, the newspaper reader or television viewer may be responding to subtle influences on the attention process of which he or she is not aware (Bryant & Zillmann, 1984; Christ & Biggers, 1984; Christ & Medoff, 1984; Zillmann et al., 1980). These sources of influence may have little or nothing to do with the subject matter, but rather may include such elements as the design of the message itself.

THE NATURE OF NEWS

Wilbur Schramm (1949) offered an explanation of the "nature of news" in which he stated that news is not an event but an entity that exists in the minds of readers, listeners, and viewers. He wrote that news

is not identical with the event, it is an attempt to reconstruct the essential frame-work of the event. . . . Then the news is trusted to ink or sound waves or light waves, and ultimately comes to an audience where it competes with the rest of the environment for favor. . . (I)tems of news are perceived by the individual as part of another gestalt—(the) environment and its competing stimuli, the state of (the) organism at the moment and . . . stored information and attitudes. (p. 259)

All of this led to a crucial question: Why do news consumers perceive one cue rather than another and select what they do?

Schramm drew upon Freud's pleasure and reality principles to provide a theoretic rationale for exposure to news as the seeking of immediate or delayed rewards. In a more controversial portion of the paper, he attempted to link individual needs for rewards with objective categories of "hard" and "soft" news content. Although noting that for any individual the boundaries between the two classes were not stable, he stated that in general news furnishing immediate rewards might be expected to include crime and corruption, accidents and disasters, sports and recreation, social events, and human interest. On the other hand, news of public affairs, economics, social problems, science, education, and health were expected to provide delayed rewards.

In the intervening years, Schramm's perspective on the nature of news has remained plausible (e.g., Pietila, 1969; Singletary, 1985; Stempel, 1963), but there has been a paucity of research attempting to integrate the three factors Schramm identified—"the environment," "the state of the organism," and "stored information"—as central to the consumer's selection and perception of the news. Since then, the news consumer's environment has changed radically as television has become the dominant news medium. But even more crucial to mass media research, advances in neurophysiology and cognitive psychology have greatly expanded our theoretical base for understanding how the state of the organism and its stored information may affect news-consuming behavior. Lacking these insights 40 years ago, the mainstream of mass communication research moved from studies of direct effects of mass media on individuals to studies of more diffuse networks of influence. These shifts involved changes in the perceived roles of individuals in the communication process, from passive receivers to proactive seekers of information.

However, recent research on automaticity in human information processing (Bargh, chapter 2; Berger, 1980; LaBerge & Samuels, 1974; Langer, 1980; Roloff, 1980; Shiffrin & Schneider, 1977)—in which individuals carry out over-learned tasks that have become routine for them while only dimly aware that they are doing so—directly challenges the somewhat idealistic conception of individuals as totally proactive (and "rational") seekers of information and indicates the need for a paradigm that involves direct effects as well (Donohew, Nair, & Finn, 1984).

This state has been found to occur in communication situations such as reading and even talking with others as well as in other familiar circumstances, like driving home from work. While in this state, individuals tend to follow previously learned routines and much of the guidance of their systems appears to be turned over to more or less automatic mechanisms—although intentionally so, as Bargh (chapter 2) cautions—which continue to operate until brought back to full attention by something novel or threatening in the environment. Such instances might include a siren and flashing lights on an emergency vehicle or simply the end of the learned sequence, such as arrival at home. Findings from this research have considerable implications for exposure to information.

COGNITIVELY TRIGGERED AROUSAL

The exact nature of the relationship between cognitive processing and cortical and autonomic arousal is still an open question. But at least two widely disseminated models (Mandler, 1982; Sokolov, 1960) are appropriate for exploring how novel sensory inputs may interact with stored information to generate arousal. The first of these is the theoretical model Sokolov (1960) provides in his explanation of the orienting reflex.

> [Sokolov] postulates a chain of cells in the cortex of the brain that preserve information about the intensity, the quality, the duration and the order of the presentation of stimuli. According to this hypothesis, the orienting reflex is evoked when a "new stimulus," entering via the specific sensory pathways does not coincide with the parameters of the neuronal model set up in the cortex. This discordance in the cortex then generates excitatory activity so that its well-known arousing influence evokes the orienting reflex. (Brazier, 1967, p. 63)

Of equal importance, however, is the obverse situation in which a sensory input in fact matches the neuronal model in the cortex. In this case, the cortex sends inhibitory discharges to the reticular activation system, thereby suppressing generalized arousal. Over the long term, of course, the repeated processing of a "new stimulus" will change the parameters of the neuronal model such that it too will generate a "match." In that case, what might have previously been an "old stimulus" is once again capable of activating the organism.

Although the casual reader may accept Sokolov's theory as an entirely plausible basis for explaining a common, but short-lived psychophysical phenomenon, it is vital to recognize that the model is appropriate for explaining the involuntary focusing of attention to any combination of sensory inputs that generates conflicts with information stored in memory (Martindale, 1981). Thus, it is no surprise that the fundamental match–mismatch mechanism of Sokolov's neurophysiological theory should appear in a more cognitively based model of human emotion proposed by Mandler (1982).

Mandler hypothesizes that activation of the autonomic nervous system occurs in response to incongruities between incoming sensory information and the expectations that are associated with schemas held in long-term memory. Although we may expect individuals to prefer cognitively consistent information, Mandler argues—much like Sokolov—that congruent information is so easily assimilated that it generates no physiological response, providing only "cold" positive value. To generate the sort of emotional intensity we identify with the autonomic nervous system, the mind must experience some degree of incongruity between sensory inputs and stored information. Only when "affective intensity" is generated do we experience emotion tinged with a positive or a negative value depending on "an evaluation of the meaning of the conditions and contexts in which individuals find themselves" (Mandler, 1982, pp. 21–22).

The most notable difference between Sokolov's explanation of the orienting reflex and Mandler's schematic incongruity model is their focus, of course, on different forms of arousal. Sokolov's focus on cortical arousal simplifies discussion, because the positive and negative consequences of information processing can be predicted on the basis of purely quantitative measures. The relationship between amounts of arousal and optimal behavior is assumed to take the shape of the classic inverted U-curve (Yerkes & Dodson, 1908). Accordingly, individuals seek to maintain a moderate level of arousal, because of its adaptive value.

By contrast, Mandler's model incorporates both a level of arousal and an evaluative sign reflecting the positive and negative valences normally attributed to emotions and feeling states. What we find interesting, however, is that Mandler's model implicitly suggests an inverted-U curve as well. Although Mandler hypothesizes that slight incongruities between sensory inputs and schemas— resulting in low levels of affective intensity—are uniformly positive in their impact on mood, the probability of successfully accessing or improvising new schemas to accommodate discrepant information steadily declines as schematic incongruity, and therefore the strength of affective intensity, increases. To paraphrase Hebb (1955, p. 250), it appears that, up to a certain point, schematic incongruity has positive motivating value, beyond that point negative value. Indeed, high levels of affective intensity could only occur when high levels of cortical arousal are also present, which would add a negative bias to cognitive assessments.

RECENT STUDIES OF AROUSAL AND NEWS EXPOSURE

Measures of arousal have been used for a number of years by commercial research organizations as a yardstick in previewing television shows, evaluating broadcast commercials, predicting hits in the record industry, and even in gauging the appeal of television newscasters (Chagall, 1977; Fletcher, 1985; Mariani, 1979). However, until recently this approach has attracted little attention as a possible way of assessing effects of the news stories themselves, even though Zillmann (1982) has speculated that television news coverage of "wars, natural disasters, tragic events such as plane crashes, or 'bad news' about political happenings or the state of the economy may be assumed to foster reactions associated with substantial increases in arousal" (p. 57).

Donohew and his associates have provided preliminary empirical support for the use of arousal measures to evaluate the effectiveness of various types of newswriting in the print and broadcast media. They have found in a number of studies that the way news stories were written affected the level of physiological arousal (Donohew, 1979, 1981, 1982), and affective states as well as preferences for continued exposure (Donohew, Palmgreen, & Duncan; 1980) and television preferences (unpublished data).

Theoretically, although readers or viewers may turn away from a source of stimulation when their arousal level becomes too high, the primary problem with printed messages would appear to be at the lower end of the continuum. In the absence of physical elements such as color and movement, the readers must be stimulated almost entirely by the style and the import of the message. In the first of these studies (Donohew 1979, 1981, 1982), news stories written in a narrative style generated significantly more arousal than did those presented in a more traditional inverted-pyramid newspaper style, even though both contained the same set of facts. The narrative style was edited from an actual account of an event (the mass suicides in Guyana) appearing in *Newsweek* magazine. The traditional style involved presentation of the most important facts first, followed by other information approximately in the order of its importance. This form of presentation, sometimes known as the inverted pyramid style, involved the same news event, edited from a version appearing in the *New York Times*.

Although the narrative story presented information about a tragic event, and thus might have been expected to evoke more unpleasant responses than the more blandly presented story, the opposite was true (see Fig. 10.1). Not only did arousal level (solid bar) drop below the starting baseline among subjects reading the traditional version, but in verbal reports on their feelings described in before–after administrations of a mood scale (hash marks), they described their responses as more negative. One interpretation of this finding is that stories gener-

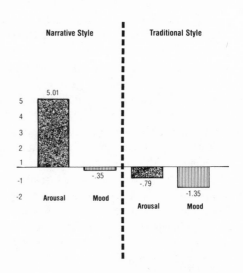

FIGURE 10.1.   Arousal and mood responses to news stories written in narrative and traditional styles.

ating more arousal are likely to be considered more pleasurable, regardless of content, provided they do not directly threaten the receiver (Donohew, 1984). Such an interpretation has important implications as well for previous studies of newswriting style in which a narrative "story-telling" style generated better readership (Rarick, 1967) and greater comprehension (Graesser, Higginbotham, Robertson, & Smith, 1978; Green, 1979; Thorndyke, 1979) than traditional journalistic approaches.

Another study conducted by Donohew and his associates (1980) raises questions about how exciting this presentation should be. What attracted some individuals repelled others, as indicated in interaction effects. The study examined effects of exposure to messages in which levels of importance and discrepancy-support were manipulated. Subjects were divided into those indicating a high need for stimulation (Pearson, 1970) and those with low needs. The first stage of the study examined affective responses—changes in mood in a positive and negative direction as indicated on a self-report instrument—to the message manipulations by the two types of subjects, and the second stage examined effects of these affective responses on decisions to stop or continue reading the messages.

For readers with low needs for arousal, stories on unimportant topics and those supporting the views of the respondents generated significantly more positive mood change and greater preferences for continued exposure than those on important topics (as judged by the readers) and those containing discrepant information. For individuals with high needs for arousal, more important topics generated more positive mood change and greater preferences for continued exposure. Even for high need subjects, however, the need for arousal was exceeded when subjects were exposed to discrepant information, resulting in preferences for discontinuing exposure. An affective state main effect was found at the second stage. For subjects with either high or low needs, as negative affect increased, preferences for continued exposure to the source of stimulation (news stories) dropped (see Fig. 10.2).

These findings indicate another practical problem of news reporting which needs to be addressed in further research: Is it possible to write stories that are exciting enough to hold easily bored readers without turning away readers who are easily stressed?

One of our experiments just described showed a narrative style to be more arousing and therefore more likely to hold the reader on one of the most tragic stories of the decade. One might ask, however, if the same would hold true on more difficult and less emotional subject matter, such as economics or science, as referred to earlier. We also might ask which technique leads to greater comprehension of the material and if the level of presumed interest indicated by arousal is, in fact, related to the "holding power" of the stories when boredom or threat susceptibility of readers is taken into account.

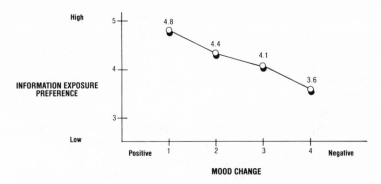

FIGURE 10.2. Main effect of mood change on information-exposure preference.

Multiple-Level Processing

To delve into these matters further requires a more rigorous framework. As we have seen, one way is to divide news consumers on the basis of high and low needs for stimulation. In recent years, the need for arousal has been identified as a fairly stable trait in distinguishing personality types (see Zuckerman, 1978, this volume). Zillmann (this volume) and Zillmann and Bryant (1985) also have provided convincing evidence that television exposure often is directed by the viewer's immediate need to establish a more satisfactory stimulus environment. Clearly television news is not to be excluded from the mix of mass media programming available for mood management. But what about the stimulative effects of news reports themselves? Must news consumers have certain information stores available in order to be affected by particular messages? Can diverse sources of arousal be isolated within individual news reports? Are all sources of arousal summed before positive or negative affect is attributed, or does the news consumer discriminate between sources of arousal, labeling each individually and guiding behavior on the basis of a multifaceted evaluation?

One way to help disentangle some of these problems is to adopt an information-theoretic approach, which is implicit in the probabilistic models of cognitively triggered cortical (Sokolov) and autonomic (Mandler) arousal previously discussed. An information-theoretic perspective need not lead to a technical dead end as long as one remains mindful of the opportunities afforded living systems to add to or reconfigure their memory store, thereby altering "the competence with which they process information" (Pribram & McGuiness, 1975, p. 135; Finn & Roberts, 1984). In fact, Pribram and McGuinness (1975) have underscored the appropriateness of conceptualizing "organisms subject to arousal as 'information processing systems,' where input is matched against some residual in the organism of his past experience, or some competence" (p. 117).

One immediate consequence of this capability is the capacity of the human reader to grasp messages on any one or all of several superimposed levels (Moles, 1966). Unexpected sensory inputs may arise from novel type faces, curious spelling errors, complex syntactic structures, peculiar arrangements of paragraphs and white space as well as unpredictable semantic content. As a result, attention may be disproportionately focused on different aspects of the text depending on whether the human information processor is a pre-schooler learning the alphabet, a proofreader, a grammarian, a layout editor, or the so-called "average" reader. Thus, the primary advantage of an information-theoretic perspective is that it sensitizes communication researchers to the existence of multiple sources of information within the same message, each capable of generating arousal depending on the competence, the intentions, and the expectations of the specific "information-processing system."

It should be readily acknowledged, however, that many non-semantic codes embedded in a text normally will be processed automatically, thereby assuring a higher degree of regularity in reader responses than the potentially chaotic situation just suggested. Nevertheless, high or low levels of arousal may reflect an individual's commitment to the task (high or low involvement), whereas positive and negative evaluations may be made in response to specific goals (reducing uncertainty or regulating mood). In this regard, self-reports of perceived arousal or mood change may be more informative than measures of strictly physiological phenomena (Leventhal, 1980; Mehrabian, 1980).[1]

MODELS FOR RESEARCH ON THE NATURE OF NEWS

At this point, a body of theory exists to support research into questions such as those just raised. This work has grown largely out of the research described here as well as research in related areas. Illustrative of this work are two models that assume a search for pleasurable stimulation as a major motivation for exposure to news.

The first model to be described here is Finn's information-theoretic model of

---

[1] The complications that arise in using physiological measures alone are well illustrated by the results previously presented in Figure 1. A slightly elaborated interpretation from the one offered previously is that the use of "narrative style" in presenting the news story facilitated information processing at the decoding stage, thereby permitting the reader to focus more intently on the novel semantic content of the story. As a result, the narrative story generated higher levels of arousal and did not engender the substantial negative shift in mood that reading the traditional news story did. Looking at the physiological data in isolation, however, one might argue that the narrative story was, in fact, the more difficult to process, because one might expect physiological arousal to be correlated with mental effort as well as attention (Kahneman, 1974). More refined notions of mental effort (Pribram & McGuiness, 1975) would lead one to question the fundamental assumptions of the second interpretation, but the example points out the need for coherent models and remaining sensitive to the many levels at which attention may be focused.

reader enjoyment (Finn, 1983, 1985b). The model (see Fig. 10.3) portrays news consumption as a multi-level form of information processing that may be activated by either informational or entertainment needs. The model is distinguished by its emphasis on the entertainment needs of the reader and its attempt to correlate textual unpredictability with assessments of reader enjoyment. Keeping in mind Moles' (1966) dictum that a text is really a series of superimposed messages, the model identifies three essential modes of information processing: decoding, entertainment-seeking, and information-seeking—paying particular attention to the diverse ways in which unpredictable elements in the message can affect the reader.

The model is configured to portray decoding as the basic action that ultimately enables the reader to process a text in terms of its semantic content. However, decoding itself is comprised of a set of subroutines—such as the recognition of letter features, words, and syntactic relationships—that the fluent reader more often than not employs without conscious attention (LaBerge & Samuels, 1974). At the decoding stage, then, unpredictable elements in the message tend to complicate and even interrupt automatic processing while familiar vocabulary and predictable syntax contribute to greater reading ease and increased reader enjoyment.[2]

Given a satisfactory level of decoding, the reader can evaluate the semantic content of the text in regard to either its entertainment or its information value or both. If the reader is primarily engaged in entertainment-seeking, the model predicts that reader enjoyment should be correlated with semantic unpredictability inasmuch as mismatches between sensory inputs and stored information should generate pleasurable levels of mental stimulation. However, the situation is considerably more complex if the reader is operating in an information-seeking mode. Although new information can resolve uncertainty, there is no guarantee that it will. Whether reader enjoyment is enhanced by unpredictable content at the information-seeking level in large part depends on the reader's ability to accommodate incongruous information in a positive fashion. Mandler's (1982) model would seem to be especially instructive on this point. It suggests that the probability of achieving some form of positive accommodation diminishes as the degree of cognitive incongruity increases. Thus, increased uncertainty and anxiety are likely outcomes if the reader is in an information-seeking mode.

Finn (1985a, 1985b) has partially validated this model in two studies by partitioning cloze procedure scores (Taylor, 1953, 1954) into syntactic and semantic components. Specifically, he has used the cloze scores of deleted func-

---

[2]There is, of course, the possibility that stylistic innovation can generate pleasurable affect for readers or viewers who are especially attuned to form as well as content. However, in the case of journalistic presentations, forms are highly standardized to assure the foregrounding of specific types of content. Otherwise, reporters would develop writing styles as diverse as those of columnists, critics and essayists.

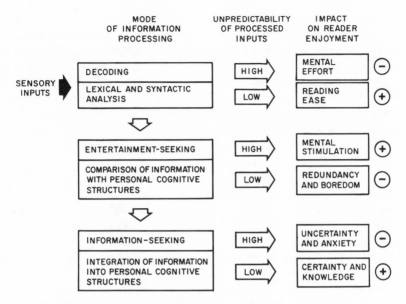

FIGURE 10.3. An information-theoretic model of reader enjoyment.

tion words to demonstrate the contribution that syntactic predictability makes to reading ease at the decoding stage and the cloze scores of deleted content words to illustrate the contribution that semantic unpredictability makes to reading enjoyment when readers are processing a text in an entertainment-seeking mode. So far, however, no attempt has been made to validate the model's fundamental distinction between the stimulative impact of novelty that stems from comparing new sensory inputs with cognitive structures and the negative consequences that might occur if these novel perceptions cannot be easily accommodated within a reader's higher order cognitive structures.[3] Instead, the two studies just cited relied on passages about quasi-scientific events that were unlikely to threaten a reader's cognitive equilibrium or generate aversive responses.

The second model presented here is a two-stage activation theory of information exposure (Donohew et al., 1980). The basic assumption of this theory is that

---

[3]An unexplored, but interesting parallel exists between Finn's distinction about "comparing" and "integrating" sensory inputs and Higgins and King's (1981) distinction between "identifying with some (mental) construct" and "identifying as" an instance of the construct. To use their example of meeting "a person who possesses many of the characteristic attributes of one's father" (p. 73), one can readily appreciate the pleasurable stimulative effects that may be derived from making comparisons. On the other hand, if the man were introduced as the new husband of one's mother, this individual must be "identified as" an instance of the construct of father. In such a case, every newly observed characteristic of the individual must be successfully integrated into what was once a highly stable construct. Novelty can no longer be enjoyed for its own sake.

205

individuals have an optimum level of activation (arousal) at which they feel most comfortable. As illustrated in Fig. 10.4, some individuals (a) have low needs and are not likely to expose themselves to a significant amount of novel, varied, or threatening sources of stimulation but turn toward that which is more routine for them, whereas others (b) tend to do the opposite. Others (c) may shrink from substantial exposure to either, whereas still others (d) may handle both quite comfortably. One can imagine that the former person would need to live in a protected media environment. It is types (a) and (b) however, that appear to be most common and that make the theory predictive.

All of this leads us to an activation theory of information exposure growing out of two fundamental assumptions: (a) the previously mentioned assumption that individuals have an optimum level of arousal at which they feel most comfortable, and (b) the assumption that they enter information-exposure situations with the expectation of achieving or maintaining this optimal state.

From these assumptions we may deduce two principal propositions: (1) that individuals will experience a positive affect when the optimal state is achieved, and (2) that they will experience a negative affect when (a) arousal drops below the optimum level, or when (b) arousal exceeds the optimal level. Ultimately this leads to predictions that individuals experiencing a positive affect will continue to expose themselves to an information source, whereas individuals experiencing a negative affect will discontinue their exposure to an information source.

In other words, as illustrated in Fig. 10.5, when an individual's arousal level is exceeded—for example, when a news story contains a message that is too threatening or otherwise too exciting—he or she will become uncomfortable and face internal pressures. Similarly, when the desired level is not reached—the message is too boring—the person also will be likely to turn away. It is only

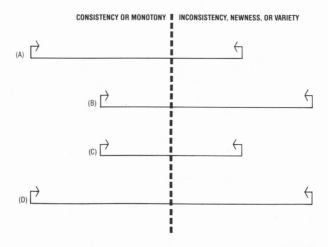

FIGURE 10.4.   Hypothetical consistency-variety "baselines."

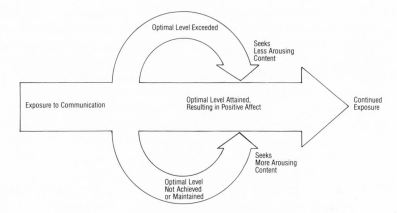

FIGURE 10.5. An activation theory of information exposure.

when the message satisfies a desired level of arousal that individuals are likely to stay with it.

Competition Between Models

Although the two models of news-reading behavior described here share an underlying correspondence to the traditional inverted-U curves that are used to represent the curvilinear relationships between arousal and hedonic tone (Berlyne, 1971; Wundt, 1894) as well as arousal and optimal mental performance (Hebb, 1955; Yerkes & Dodson, 1908), each model was derived independently and incorporates a distinctive orientation. Donohew's activation model is oriented toward a reader who is exploiting qualities of the environment to achieve an optimal level of arousal. Although effects of message styles have been studied, its emphasis is on the cognitive and affective needs of the individual as he or she approaches the information. Thus, his program of research often has been focused on the differences in affective responses that occur because individual readers each possess their own arousal curve, each distinguished by a single point at which optimal arousal occurs.[4] Finn's model, however, is oriented toward the qualities of the text itself that generate positive or negative feeling

---

[4]While this conceptualization makes it appear as if arousal can be, by nature, pleasurable, neurophysiological concepts of arousal do not permit such positive or negative labelling of the phenomenon itself. We would argue, however, that individuals are clearly capable of making a conscious decision that all novel sensory inputs—up to a point—are to be labelled positively regardless of more discriminating criteria that might be invoked in other circumstances. The same consciousness would be equally capable of recognizing, we think, that especially in the case of sensory inputs that signalled a mediated reality, the organism is scarcely putting itself at risk to pursue such exercises of the mind.

states and makes no allowance for individual differences. Theoretically, conflicts between elements in the text and the reader's information store generate arousal on many different planes. But its impact on reading enjoyment is tied to the mode of processing in which it arises.

Regardless of these differences in orientation, however, to the extent that Finn's and Donohew's models overlap, they also compete to explain the same phenomena. Rather than avoiding this inherent conflict, we would like to pursue it in the belief that multiple interpretations of data will help us further understand the processing and selection phenomena at issue in our research. The data reported in a monograph by Donohew et al. (1980) provide a unique opportunity to analyze results in terms of both models.

This experiment employed a 2 × 2 × 2 factorial design in an attempt to demonstrate the impact of individual needs for low or high activation under four conditions. The participating students were divided into two groups based on their responses to Pearson's (1970) Novelty Experiencing Scale and then asked to read one of four essays chosen to effect different levels of activation:

1. Important/Discrepant Condition: a high-importance topic with an argument contrary to the student's views;

2. Important/Supportive Condition: a high-importance topic with an argument supportive of the student's views;

3. Unimportant/Discrepant Condition: a low-importance topic with an argument contrary to the student's views; and

4. Unimportant/Supportive Condition: a low-importance topic with an argument supportive of the student's views.

Changes in affect were measured using a paper-and-pencil verbal test of the students' changes in mood (Greenberg & Tannenbaum, 1962).

Although Donohew and his associates used these data originally to demonstrate individual differences in needs for arousal, it seems to us now that the textual variables outlined above operationalize key components in Finn's model as well.

Figure 10.6, in particular, charts the interaction between changes in reader affect and the two textual variables—discrepancy and importance—without regard to the activation needs of the participants. For the purposes of comparison, the criteria for evaluation that might be invoked at the high- and the low-importance conditions would seem to parallel those used in information-seeking and entertainment-seeking as designated by Finn's model. Similarly, discrepant information would seem to be analogous with ''uncertainty'' or ''unpredictability'' depending on whether information-seeking or entertainment-seeking criteria

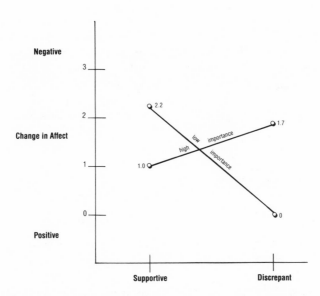

FIGURE 10.6. Discrepancy by importance interaction reported by Donohew et al. (1980).

were invoked, whereas supportive information would relate to "certainty" and "predictability" as outlined in Finns' model.

The results are intriguing. What we find is that the condition with the greatest change in positive affect—in fact the only non-negative change in pre- and posttest mood scores—is the combination of conditions analogous to unpredictability in an entertainment-seeking mode. By contrast, the conditions that roughly reflect predictability in an entertainment-seeking mode result in the greatest negative shift in affect.

The use of Finn's model to analyze this data set provides an alternative explanation as well for the anomalous results exhibited in Fig. 10.7. Donohew's model, which is premised on a distinction between low- and high-activation needs, failed to predict the negative affect that occurred when members of the high-activation group read an article of high importance that conveyed discrepant information. Donohew et al. analyzed the unforeseen result in a way that is consistent with the unidimensional conception of arousal that is implicit in Hebb's inverted-U curve.

Apparently the arousal value of the discrepant information employed was farther from the preferred arousal of high need for activation subjects than was the arousal value of supportive information. The opposite had been assumed. If, however, we continue to reconceptualize this experiment in terms of Finn's

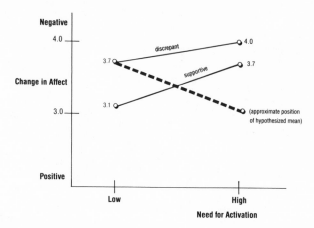

FIGURE 10.7. Means for hypothesized discrepancy by need for activation interaction reported by Donohew et al. (1980).

model, we have students engaging in an information-seeking level (high-importance) task, processing a message that increases uncertainty (discrepant condition). Stated as such, the negative change in their moods is highly likely. On the other hand, Finn's model would not have predicted differential responses from individuals with high and low needs for activation.

THE IMPACT OF MENTAL EFFORT

One continuing anomaly in the data we have presented is the generally negative deflection of mood observed whenever pre- and posttest measures of participants' mood states were compared. Thus, even under the conditions in which Finn's model would predict maximum reader enjoyment—readers processing discrepant information about a topic of low importance—the predicted positive shift in mood turned out to be positive only to the extent that the reading of a news story did not diminish the participants' initially "positive" feelings. Under all other conditions, the reading experience had, in fact, effected negative shifts in mood.

If we hypothesize that the reader's motivation for processing information is to forestall a negative shift in mood, it appears that for this sample of student participants, reading the newspapers is not an especially effective coping mechanism. Although such a conclusion has practical implications about newswriting style and content, it also raises the likelihood that the decoding effort plays a contributory role in determining the affective impact of printed messages. Zipf (1949) may have been closer to the mark than most researchers acknowledged when he proposed that human behavior was often guided by what he called the "principle of least effort." That human information processors are often cognitive misers also has been aptly noted in the social cognition literature (Fiske & Taylor, 1984; Taylor & Fiske, 1978).

A NOTE ON TELEVISION AS A SOURCE OF NEWS

This discussion of mental effort provides an especially appropriate occasion to address the question of television as a source of news. It is clear that television enjoys an obvious advantage in reducing mental effort (Salomon, 1984), first because a significant step in decoding the message is eliminated when verbal information is presented aurally (Horowitz & Samuels, 1985), and second because the visual channel is not only rich in information, but provides additional context to aid in interpreting the verbal message. By contrast, the printed page constitutes a minimal source of information. The sense of closure we attain when reading occurs only because of an immense store of information in the reader's memory from which messages are constructed with reference to signs found on the printed page. Comprehension can be achieved only if appropriate mental structures can be accessed or improvised as sensory inputs are processed. Ironically, the richness of television's visual channel permits the viewer to derive pleasurable stimulation from novel elements of the video picture, even if they are in fact extraneous to the news story itself.

IMPLICATIONS FOR FUTURE RESEARCH

If there has been a major change in perspective on the nature of news since Schramm's original article, it has been toward teasing out the subtle interaction between cognition and affect that occurs during information processing. Underlying that relationship is a tacit assumption that the affective response is a product of arousal and cognitive labeling that is further complicated by misattributions that arise from excitation transfer (Zillmann, 1971, 1983). There is however, an ironic twist of events that is often overlooked if we are correct that arousal stems from mismatches between sensory inputs—the news—and stored information. News consumers are not only engaged in cognitive processes to label their physiological activation, but the arousal itself is the end product of a cognitive matching process that occurs in many cases automatically. Such an intricate phenomenon has interesting implications for the study of news at both a theoretical and practical level.

With regard to journalistic practice, it seems highly likely that one of a journalist's most important skills is the ability to linguistically code information in a fashion that facilitates the recognition and heightens the impact of these cognitive mismatches. For instance, it is a standard practice in journalism that information essential to establishing a cognitive incongruity be moved ahead to the lead of a news story rather than revealing it in its natural chronological order, which would be the traditional method for organizing a narrative. Rivers (1975) has characterized this ''straight news story'' strategy as one of presenting ''conclusions first, emphasizing results'' (p. 69), which he asserts would be wholly artificial for a fiction writer. We have noted elsewhere in this chapter that this traditional journalistic presentation may be counterproductive; that is, stories presented in narrative style may be easier to process because their chronological, story-like structures are more familiar to the reader. But in any event, news consumers would seem to benefit from greater awareness of the psychological underpinnings of these attention-getting and arousal-generating strategies.

That the affective responses to news are highly dependent on cognitive processes suggests that the rate at which information is presented may be an important variable in predicting audience response. Evidence indicating that a recipient has expended higher than average mental effort to process sensory inputs suggests that the recipient of the message lacked appropriate schema to handle the new information. He or she was forced to process it in a piecemeal fashion that precluded the opportunity to experience the sort of instantaneous macro-comparisons from which relatively high degrees of arousal might be generated. For the inept decoder, one would envision a general slow down in the processing of sensory inputs. Print media would lead the news consumer to move more slowly through the text. For members of the broadcast audience who cannot control the rate of information flow, the only recourse may be to intermittently withhold attention. But in either case, the intensity of affective responses would be substantially diminished.

Several researchers, interested in the impact of news, have initiated ambitious research programs focusing on the underlying role of *schemas* and *scripts* in determining the comprehension, recall, or even the accessibility of particular types of news (van Dijk, 1983; van Dijk & Kintsch, 1983; Findahl & Hoijer, 1985; Graber, 1984). Evidence that they play an essential role in generating arousal adds a critical new dimension to such research. Finn (1986) has suggested that the traditional notion of *sensationalism* as applied to journalistic practice should be redefined to encompass the act of reporting novel events within the frameworks of familiar, but empirically or historically inappropriate schemas purely to heighten their affective impact. In the aftermath of Watergate, for example, rather small-scale cases of political misconduct were dubbed with titles such as ''Koreagate'' and ''Debategate.''

EPILOGUE: THE NATURE OF SOCIAL COGNITION

Although, as Simon (1982) has put it, ''every novelist depends on cognitive processes applied to the printed page. . . to evoke mood and emotion'' (p. 382), it seems that the dominant trend in social cognition ''has been to push cognitive explanations as far as possible to see where they illuminate new ground not clarified by previous approaches" (Fiske, 1982, p. 56). Even when social situations clearly include affective dimensions, the focus usually is on the impact of affect on cognitions, but not the reverse. That is not to say, however, that the social-cognition literature is unrelated to our research interests. As we have indicated earlier, many of the unconscious biases that shape exposure to news and the editorial judgments made by professional journalists may be but specific instances of what Taylor and Fiske (1978) have characterized as "top of the head" phenomena. We would urge that future research not only attempt to explain cognitive mechanisms, but also the affective consequences of such effortless processing that seem to enhance its appeal.

The social-cognition literature has been especially instructive as well in helping us refine notions of automaticity. Although we have been quick to adopt Langer's notion of "mindless" behavior (Langer, 1980; Langer, Blank, & Chanowitz, 1978), we do not wish to overlook the high probability that persons engaging in this behavior may be "mindful" of their decision to do so. Thus, we are essentially in agreement with Bargh (1984, this volume), who has clarified this point by observing that "when people exert little conscious effort in examining their environment they are at the mercy of automatically-produced interpretations" (1984, p. 35).

What we find especially intriguing is the notion that human information processors adjust their level of attention to new sensory inputs on the basis of stored information in long-term memory—often preferring to rely upon an available schema and its associated detail rather than raw sensory data. This preference for previously encoded data over new inputs from the environment would seem to be crucial in directing news consumption. It has directed our attention to the need to differentiate between two types of "automaticity." The first form is the classic type as suggested by LaBerge and Samuels (1974): It occurs when subroutines of higher order information-processing tasks are performed without conscious attention to free up cognitive capacity for more integrative activities. The second form is a more conscious manifestation of cognitive miserliness that occurs when individuals substitute stored information for raw sensory data, because they want to avoid what they consider to be the needless commitment of mental effort and capacity to endeavors of little consequence.

Finally we would like to acknowledge the research program initiated by Isen and her associates (Clark & Isen, 1982; Isen, 1984; Isen, Clark, Shalker, & Karp, 1978). Although Isen's work parallels that of other social-cognition researchers in that its thrust is on the impact of initial affect on subsequent cognitions—a focus that is just the reverse of ours—her research program coincides with ours on a number of major points. First, she approaches behavioral situations with an underlying assumption that individuals are intrinsically motivated toward achieving positive feeling states. Second, her notion of what she calls "feeling states" as distinct from emotions seems to capture accurately the intensity of the mood most commonly generated by attending to mass media messages. And third, she evokes these positive feeling states through the distribution of "surprise gifts" to random subjects in naturalistic settings, which seems analogous in impact to the sort of semantic visual "surprises" that may be embedded in mass media messages.

As communication researchers, we are most interested, of course, in information-seeking and entertainment-seeking behaviors, which we believe to be motivated by the individual's search for optimal states of well-being. Generally, in news consumption, we see information seekers as individuals attempting to reduce uncomfortably high levels of arousal, and entertainment seekers as individuals attempting to overcome uncomfortably low levels of arousal (or boredom). Until now, we have tended to conceptualize these two types of motivation as nearly symmetrical. That is, that high arousal motivates some sort of attenuation, and low arousal motivates some form of enhancement. We remain intrigued, however, with the notion that these are not solely levels of low and high arousal, but that the body may respond with greater urgency to uncertainty and anxiety than boredom or low activation. Thus, the behavioral impact of positive and negative affect may be asymmetric.

Isen and her associates have explored these asymmetric patterns, focusing on experimental results that demonstrate similar behavioral outcomes generated by dissimilar affective feeling states. Our intuition suggests that this asymmetry may stem from not so subtle conflicts between limbic and neocortical systems of the brain (Koestler, 1964; MacLean, 1979; Martindale, 1981). It appears to us that teasing out the interplay between these two systems is central to any attempt to draw a more fine-grained picture of why news consumers select and process only some of the "competing stimuli" available to them.

REFERENCES

Bargh, J. A. (1984). Automatic and conscious processing of social information. In R. S. Wyer & T. K. Srull (Eds.), *Handbook of social cognition* (Vol. 3, pp. 1–44). Hillsdale, NJ: Lawrence Erlbaum Associates.

Berger, C. R. (1980). Self-consciousness and the adequacy of theory in relationship development. *Western Journal of Speech Communication, 44*, 93–96.

Berlyne, D. (1971). *Aesthetics and psychobiology.* New York: Appleton-Century-Crofts.

Berlyne, D., Craw, W. H., Salepeteck, P., & Lewis, J. (1963). Novelty, complexity, incongruity, extrensic motivation, and the GSR. *Journal of Experimental Psychology, 66*, 560–567.

Brazier, M. A. B. (1967). Neurophysiological contributions to the subject of human communication. In F. E. X. Dance (Ed.), *Human communication theory* (pp. 61–69). New York: Holt, Rinehart & Winston.

Bryant, J., & Zillmann, D. (1984). Using television to alleviate boredom and stress: Selective exposure as a function of induced excitational states. *Journal of Broadcasting, 28*, 1–20.

Campbell, H. J. (1973). *The pleasure areas: a new theory of behavior.* New York: Delacorte Press.

Chagall, D. (1977). Only as good as his skin tests. *TV Guide*, March 26, pp. 5–10.

Christ, W. G. (1985). The construct of arousal in communication research. *Human Communication Research, 11*, 575–592.

Christ, W. G., & Biggers, T. (1984). An exploratory investigation into the relationship between television program preference and emotion-eliciting qualities—a new theoretical perspective. *Western Journal of Speech Communication, 48*(3), 293–307.

Christ, W. G., & Medoff, N. J. (1984). Affective state and the selective exposure to and use of television. *Journal of Broadcasting, 28,* 51–63.

Clark, M. S., & Isen, A. M. (1982). Toward understanding the relationship between feeling states and social behavior. In A. H. Hastorf & A. M. Isen (Eds.), *Cognitive social psychology* (pp. 73–108). New York: Elsevier North Holland.

van Dijk, T. A. (1983). Discourse analysis: Its development and application to the structure of news. *Journal of Communication, 33*(2), 20–43.

van Dijk, T. A., & Kintsch, W. (1983). *Strategies in discourse analysis.* New York: Academic Press.

Donohew, L. (1979). *Newswriting styles: What arouses the reader?* A report of a study conducted under a grant from the News Research Council, American Newspaper Publishers Association.

Donohew, L. (1981). Arousal and affective responses to writing styles. *Journal of Applied Communication Research, 9,* 109–119.

Donohew, L. (1982). Newswriting styles: What arouses the reader? *Newspaper Research Journal, 3,* 3–6.

Donohew, L. (1984). *Why we expose ourselves to morbid news.* Paper presented at the symposium on "Morbid curiosity and mass media." Gannett Foundation and College of Communications, University of Tennessee, Knoxville.

Donohew, L., Nair, M., & Finn, S. (1984). Automaticity, arousal, and information exposure. In R. Bostrom (Ed.), *Communication yearbook 8* (pp. 267–284). Beverly Hills, CA: Sage.

Donohew, L., Palmgreen, P., & Duncan, J. (1980). An activation model of information exposure. *Communication Monographs, 47,* 295–303.

Findahl, O., & Hoijer, B. (1985). Some characteristics of news memory and comprehension. *Journal of Broadcasting and Electronic Media, 29,* 379–396.

Finn, H. S. (1983). An information theory approach to reader enjoyment of print journalism (Doctoral dissertation, Stanford University, 1982). *Dissertation Abstracts International, 43,* 2481A–2482A.

Finns, S. (1985a). Unpredictability as a correlate of reader enjoyment of news articles. *Journalism Quarterly, 62,* 334–339, 345.

Finn, S. (1985b). Information-theoretic measures of reader enjoyment. *Written Communication, 2,* 358–376.

Finn, S. (1986). *Sensational and informational processing: Evidence for a cognitive link.* Paper presented at the conference on "Sensationalism and the Mass Media," University of Michigan, Ann Arbor.

Finn, S., & Roberts, D. F. (1984). Source, destination, and entropy: Reassessing the role of information theory in communication research. *Communication Research, 11,* 453–476.

Fiske, S. T. (1982). Schema-triggered affect: Applications to special perception. In M. S. Clark & S. T. Fiske (Eds.), *Affect and cognition: The 17th Annual Carnegie Symposium on Cognition* (pp. 55–78). Hillsdale, NJ: Lawrence Erlbaum Associates.

Fiske, S. T., & Taylor, S. E. (1984). *Social cognition.* Reading, MA: Addison-Wesley.

Fletcher, J. (1985). Physiological responses to the media. In J. Dominick & J. Fletcher (Eds.), *Broadcasting research methods* (pp. 89–104): Boston: Allyn & Bacon.

Graber, D. (1984). *Processing the news: How people tame the information tide.* New York: Longman.

Graesser, A., Higginbotham, M., Robertson, S. E. & Smith, W. (1978). A natural inquiry into the National Enquirer: Self-induced versus task-induced reading comprehension. *Discourse Processes, 1,* 355–372.

Green, G. (1979). *Organization, goals, and comprehensibility in narratives: Newswriting: A case study* (Technical Report No. 132). Urbana-Champaign, IL: Center for the Study of Reading, University of Illinois at Urbana-Champaign.

Greenberg, B. S., & Tannenbaum, P. B. (1962). Communicator performance under cognitive stress. *Journalism Quarterly, 39,* 169–178.

Hebb, D. O. (1955). Drives and the CNS (conceptual nervous system). *Psychological Review, 62,* 243–254.

Higgins, E. T., & King, G. (1981). Accessibility of social constructs: Information-processing consequences of individual and contextual variability. In N. Cantor & J. F. Kihlstrom (Eds.), *Personality, cognition, and social interaction* (pp. 69–121). Hillsdale, NJ: Lawrence Erlbaum Associates.

Horowitz, R., & Samuels, S. J. (1985). Reading and listening to expository text. *Journal of Reading Behavior, 3,* 185–198.

Isen, A. M. (1984). Toward understanding the role of affect in cognition. In R. S. Wyer & T. K. Srull (Eds.), *Handbook of social cognition* (Vol. 3, pp. 179–236). Hillsdale, NJ: Lawrence Erlbaum Associates.

Isen, A. M., Clark, M., Shalker, T. E., & Karp, L. (1978). Affect, accessibility of material in memory, and behavior: A cognitive loop? *Journal of Personality and Social Psychology, 36,* 1–12.

Koestler, A. (1964). *The act of creation.* New York: Macmillan.

LaBerge, D., & Samuels, S. (1974). Toward a theory of automatic information processing in reading. *Cognitive Psychology, 6,* 293–323.

Langer, E. J. (1980). Rethinking the role of thought in social interaction. In H. Harvey, W. Ickes, & R. Kidd (Eds.), *New directions in attribution research* (Vol. 2, pp. 35–58). Hillsdale, NJ: Lawrence Erlbaum Associates.

Langer, E. J., Blank, A., & Chanowitz, B. (1978). The mindlessness of ostensibly thoughtful action: The role of "placebic" information in interpersonal interaction. *Journal of Personality and Social Psychology, 36,* 635–642.

Leventhal, H. (1980). Toward a comprehensive theory of emotion. In L. Berkowitz (Ed.), *Advances in experimental social psychology* (Vol. 13, pp. 139–207). New York: Academic Press.

MacLean, P. (1979). Paul Maclean and the triune brain. *Science, 204,* 1066–1068.

Mandler, G. (1982). The structure of value: Accounting for taste. In M. S. Clark & S. T. Fiske (Eds.), *Affect and cognition: The 17th annual Carnegie symposium on cognition* (pp. 3–36). Hillsdale, NJ: Lawrence Erlbaum Associates.

Mariani, J. (1979). Can advertisers read—and control—our emotions? *TV Guide, March 31.*

Martindale, C. (1981). *Cognition and consciousness.* Homewood, IL: Dorsey.

Mehrabian, A. (1980). *Basic dimensions for a general psychological theory (Implications for personality, social, environmental, and developmental studies).* Cambridge. MA: Oelgeschlager, Gunn and Hain.

McCombs, M., & Weaver, D. (1985). Toward a merger of gratifications and agenda-setting research. In K. E. Rosengren, L. A. Wenner, & P. Palmgreen (Eds.), *Media gratifications research: current perspectives.* Beverly Hills, CA: Sage.

Moles, A. (1966). *Information theory and esthetic perception.* Urbana: University of Illinois Press.

Olds, M. E., & Fobes, J. (1981). The central basis of motivation: intracranial self-stimulation studies. *Annual Review of Psychology, 32,* 523–574.

Pearson, P. H. (1970). Relationships between global and specified measures of novelty-seeking. *Journal of Consulting and Clinical Psychology, 37,* 23–30.

Pietila, V. (1969). immediate versus delayed reward in newspaper reading. *Acta Sociologica, 12,* 199–208.

Pribram, K., & McGuinness, D. (1975). Arousal, activation, and effort in the control of attention. *Psychological Review, 82,* 116–149.

Rarick, G. (1967). *Field experiments in newspaper item readership.* Eugene, OR: Division of Communication Research, School of Journalism, University of Oregon.

Rivers, W. L. (1975). *The mass media: Reporting, writing, editing* (2nd ed.). NY: Harper & Row.

Roloff, M. (1980). Self-awareness and the persuasion process: Do we really know what we are doing? In M. Roloff & G. Miller (Eds.), *Persuasion: New directions in theory and research* (pp. 29–66). Beverly Hills, CA: Sage.

Salomon, G. (1984). Television is "easy" and print is "tough": the differential investment of mental effort in learning as a function of perceptions and attributions. *Journal of Educational Psychology, 76,* 647–658.

Schank, R. C., & Abelson, R. P. (1977). *Scripts, plans, goals, and understanding: An inquiry into human knowledge structures.* Hillsdale, NJ: Lawrence Erlbaum Associates.

Schramm, W. (1949). The nature of news. *Journalism Quarterly, 26,* 259–269.

Shiffrin, R. M., & Schneider, W. (1977). Controlled and automatic information processing, II: Perceptual learning, automatic attending, and a general theory. *Psychological Review, 84,* 127–190.

Simon, H. (1982). Affect and cognition: Comments. In M. S. Clark & S. T. Fiske (Eds.), *Affect and cognition: The 17th annual Carnegie symposium on cognition* (pp. 332–342). Hillsdale, NJ: Lawrence Erlbaum Associates.

Singletary, M. W. (1985). Reliability of immediate reward and delayed reward categories. *Journalism Quarterly, 62,* 116–120.

Sokolov, E. N. (1960). Neuronal models and the orienting reflex. In M. A. B. Brazier (Ed.), *The central nervous system and behavior: Transactions of the third conference* (pp. 186–276). New York: Josiah Macy Jr. Foundation.

Stempel, G. (1963). *An experimental study of the nature of news.* Paper presented at Association for Education in Journalism convention, Lincoln.

Sypher, H. E., & Applegate, J. L. (1984). Organizing communication behavior: The role of schemas and constructs. In R. N. Bostrom (Ed.), *Communication yearbook 8* (pp. 310–329). Beverly Hills, CA: Sage.

Taylor, S. E., & Fiske, S. T. (1978). Salience, attention, and attribution: Top of the head phenomena. In L. Berkowitz (Ed.), *Advances in experimental social psychology* (Vol. 11, pp. 249–288). New York: Academic Press.

Taylor, W. L. (1953). "Cloze procedure": A new tool for measuring readability. *Journalism Quarterly, 30.* 415–433.

Taylor, W. L. (1954). *Application of "cloze" and entropy measures to the study of contextual constraint in samples of continuous prose.* Unpublished doctoral dissertation, University of Illinois.

Thorndyke, P. W. (1979). Knowledge acquisition from newspaper stories. *Discourse Processes, 2,* 95–112.

Wundt, W. (1894). *Grundzuge der physiologischen Psychologie.* Leipzig: Engelmann.

Yerkes, R. M., & Dodson, J. D. (1908). The relation of strength of stimulus to rapidity of habit formation. *Journal of Comparative and Neurological Psychology, 18,* 459–482.

Young, J. Z. (1978). *Programs of the brain.* London: Oxford University Press.

Zillmann, D. (1971). Excitation transfer in communication-mediated aggressive behavior. *Journal of Experimental Social Psychology, 7,* 419–434.

Zillmann, D. (1982). Television viewing and arousal. In D. Pearl, L. Bouthilet, & J. Lazar (Eds.), *Television and behavior: Ten years of scientific progress and implications for the eighties* (Vol. 2, pp. 53–67). Rockville, MD: National Institute of Mental Health.

Zillmann, D. (1983). Transfer of excitation in emotional behavior. In J. T. Cacioppo & R. E. Petty (Eds.), *Social psychophysiology* (pp. 215–240). New York: Guilford.

Zillmann, D., & Bryant, J. (1985). Affect, mood and emotion as determinants of selective exposure. In D. Zillmann & J. Bryant (Eds.), *Selective exposure to communication* (pp. 157–180). Hillsdale, NJ: Lawrence Erlbaum Associates.

Zillmann, D., Hezel, R. T., & Medoff, N. J. (1980). The effect of affective states on selective exposure to televised entertainment fare. *Journal of Applied Social Psychology, 10,* 323–339.

Zipf, G. (1949). *Human behavior and the principle of least effort.* Reading, MA: Addison-Wesley.

Zuckerman, M. (1978). *Sensation seeking: beyond the optimal level of arousal.* Hillsdale, NJ: Lawrence Erlbaum Associates.

Zuckerman, M. (1983). A biological theory of sensation seeking. In M. Zuckerman (Ed.), *Biological bases of sensation seeking, impulsivity, and anxiety* (pp. 37–76). Hillsdale, NJ: Lawrence Erlbaum Associates.

11 Communication, Social Cognition, and Affect: A Psychophysiological Approach

John T. Cacioppo
University of Iowa

Richard E. Petty
Ohio State University

Louis G. Tassinary
University of Iowa

Despite early obstacles and misunderstandings regarding the psychophysiological enterprise, psychophysiological procedures have the potential of extending the traditional verbal and behavioral measures of communication, affect, and social cognition and thereby provide a continuous and noninvasive means of tracking the means by which the social world impinges on individual action and experience. The history of psychophysiological research on social processes is traced briefly, and research illustrating how one can make strong inferences about a person's cognition and affect from physiological response profiles within structured situations is reviewed.

BACKGROUND

Traditionally, social psychologists have been interested in the reportable and behavioral effects of human association, communication, and interaction. Social psychology, like the field of communication, is partitioned into conceptual areas of research such as persuasion, mass media effects, interpersonal attraction, group processes, and so forth. The standard dependent measure has been verbal report, and the emphasis in research has been on observations in naturalistic settings or on highly controlled experimental settings and manipulations (e.g.,

219

see Mayo & LaFrance, 1977). These traditions, which have had a major impact on the field of communications as well, were bequeathed by the very founders of the field of social psychology. For example, Allport (1947), in his Divisional Presidential address before the first annual meeting of the Division of Personality and Social Psychology, equated psychophysiology with simplistic mechanistic thinking and criticized it (along with animal and infant research) as being reductionistic, inadequate, and a waste of time and energy for those interested in relevant social behavior. Allport's influential Presidential address and subsequent writings provided an important defense of the cognitive orientation of early social psychologists against the juggernaut of American behaviorism, but it also cast verbal reports in the starring role of social processes and cast psychophysiological concepts and measures as irrelevant to the study of social processes and behavior generally and communication in particular (e.g., Allport, 1947, 1969; Bem, 1972; Valins, 1966).

Psychophysiology, in contrast, evolved out of the efforts of electrical engineers, physiologists, experimental psychologists and clinical psychologists and psychiatrists (e.g., Porges & Coles 1976; Kaplan & Bloom, 1960). The diverse goals and interests of these individuals, coupled with the formidable technical obstacles confronting these early investigators, led predictably to a partitioning of the discipline not into conceptual areas of research, but rather into anatomical areas (e.g., electrodermal, cardiovascular, electrocortical). The one common thread among early psychophysiologists was their equipment and recording technique, and accordingly the early definitions of psychophysiology were in operational terms such as research in which the polygraph was used (e.g., Ax, 1964).

Our research has focused primarily on attitudes and persuasion (see Petty, Cacioppo, Kasmer, this volume), but psychophysiology was of interest not only because the physiological knowledge base and noninvasive quantitative measurements held the potential of providing a means of testing and extending existing theories, but also because it held the potential for a mutually stimulating interdisciplinary enterprise wherein one considers the inherent biological and social nature of behavior and for tracking cognitive, emotional, and behavioral processes as they unfolded (Cacioppo & Petty, 1981a, 1986; Cacioppo & Sandman, 1981; Petty & Cacioppo, 1983). This multifaceted perspective representing social, psychological, and physiological levels of events is far from new, however, dating at least as far back as the third century B.C., when the Greek physician Erastratos used psychophysiological observations such as the disruption of a regular heart beat in a young man when his stepmother visited to isolate the social cause of the individual's malady—"lovesickness" (Mesulam & Perry, 1972).

Moreover, psychophysiological studies of communicative behavior began appearing in the psychological literature over half a century ago when, for instance: (a) Riddle (1925) studied deception and small group behavior by monitoring the respiratory rhythms of people bluffing during a poker game to study deception and stress; (b) Smith (1936) studied social influence by monitoring the skin resistance responses (SRRs) of individuals as they were confronted by the information that their peers held attitudes that were discrepant from their own; and (3) Rankin and Campbell (1955) studied racial prejudice by monitoring the SRRs of individuals as they were exposed to white and black experimenters. Despite the interesting findings of each of these investigations, the emphasis in early research was either on the construct of general physiological arousal (see Cacioppo & Petty, in press) or on the application of psychophysiological procedures to validate theoretical constructs and measures. Regarding the former, Fowles (1980) noted in his review of the literature that:

> The effect of attempting to assimilate all of these traditions to a single arousal theory was to create a model in which the reticular activating system was assumed to serve as a generalized arousal mechanism which responded to sensory input of all kinds, energized behavior, and produced both EEG and sympathetic nervous system activation. . . . As is well-known, this model failed the empirical test rather badly. (p. 88)

The promise of psychophysiological procedures for purposes of construct validation, however, appeared more considerable:

> At the very simplest level, the attraction of social psychologists to physiological techniques is not hard to understand. The techniques provide nonverbal, objective, relatively bias-free indices of human reaction that have some of the same appeal as gestural, postural, and other indicators of covert response. (Shapiro & Schwartz, 1970, pp. 89–90)

The key phrase here is *relatively* bias-free indices, however. Although physiological measures may be less susceptible to direct cognitive control than verbal or overt behaviors, physiological responses are vulnerable to instructional sets, intentional distortion, and social biases (e.g., see Fridlund & Izard, 1983; Sternbach, 1966; Tognacci & Cook, 1975).

PSYCHOPHYSIOLOGICAL PERSPECTIVES

Moreover, the fact that physiological indices are not linked invariantly to psychological processes or states proved a disappointment to some and resulted in suggestions that psychophysiology had failed to fulfill its promise (e.g., Allport, 1947; Stewart, 1984). This is because the establishment of a dissociation between a physiological marker and a psychological process or state invalidates the psychophysiological enterprise when the original investigation is designed to demonstrate invariant correlates. However, this also represents an outdated,

overly simplistic, and reductionistic conceptualization of the psychophysiological enterprise (Cacioppo & Petty, 1986). As Donchin (1982) has noted:

> it is more sensible to view the psychophysiological measures as manifestations of
> processes evoked, or invoked, in the organism. Such processes may, or may not,
> be part of some information processing activity. When they are, their attributes
> may, or may not, be monotonic functions of some, arbitrarily selected, perfor-
> mance measure. When such functions are found they are of use to the extent that it
> is possible to address issues of theoretical import by employing psychophysio-
> logical measures as a source of data about the organism. (pp. 457–458)

This alternative, albeit less spectacular, view of the psychophysiological enterprise makes no pretense of promising someday to describe human behavior as
a list of invariant physiological correlates of psychological events. Nevertheless,
it is quite feasible to make strong inferences about a person's cognition and affect
from physiological response profiles, but these inferences can only be made
within the framework of a very structured situation. Expertise in forming the
psychophysiological questions as well as an understanding of the physiological
and bioelectrical basis of the phenomena are, therefore, critical to the success of
any application of psychophysiology to the study of social or communication
processes.

Facial Response System.   The research we have been conducting on the
messages carried in covert facial signals is a case in point. The somatic nervous
system is the final pathway through which people interact with and modify their
physical and social environments. That the pattern of efference is not always as
intended (e.g., as when one performs clumsily), not always a veridical reflection
of goals (e.g., as when one deceives), and not always obvious (e.g., as when one
hides feelings) is important to recognize when specifying under what conditions
a given pattern of efference will mark a particular psychological process. But
without efference, individuals do not communicate, do not affiliate, do not
proliferate, do not interact—in short, are not social. Even efferent discharges
that are too subtle or fleeting to be observeable under normal conditions of social
interaction may be of interest, therefore, because these are less likely to undergo
the same distortions as overt expressions and actions and therefore may reflect
incipient but socially relevant events.

Theoretical analyses of efferent activity during problem solving, imagery, and
emotion have shared assumptions regarding the specificity and adaptive utility of
somatic responses. In reviewing this research several years ago, Cacioppo and
Petty (1981a) found evidence for the following five principles:

1. There are foci of somatic activity in which changes mark particular psychological processes (e.g., linguistic vs. nonlinguistic processing; positive
   vs negative affect);

2. inhibitory as well as excitatory changes in somatic activity can mark a psychological process;
3. changes in somatic activity are patterned temporally as well as spatially;
4. changes in somatic activity become less evident as the distance of measurement from the focal point increases; and
5. foci can be identified a priori by (a) analyzing the overt reactions that initially characterized the particular psychological process of interest but which appeared to drop out with practice, and (b) observing the somatic sites that are involved during the "acting out" of the particular psychological process of interest.

Moreover, from a communications perspective the muscles of facial expression may be especially noteworthy in that these somatic effectors are linked to connective tissue and fasciae rather than to skeletal structures; their influence on the social environment, therefore, is often mediated by the construction of facial configurations rather than by direct action through the movement of the skeletal structure (Rinn, 1984). Tomkins (1962), Izard (1971), and Ekman and Friesen (1975) have pioneered work on the face as a multisignal/multimessage response system.

Ekman and Friesen (1975), for instance, have conceptualized the face as the source of: (a) static, (b) slow, (c) artificial, and (d) rapid signals.

Carried by the rapid signals alone are a variety of messages, most over which individuals have a good deal of control. The perioral musculature, for instance, is heavily and contralaterally innervated by the facial (seventh cranial) nerve and is capable of extraordinary specificity and flexibility (e.g., as in the case of verbal articulation). Nonverbal facial messages include emblems (symbolic communication—e.g., wink), manipulators (self-manipulative associated movements—e.g. lip bite), illustrators (actions accompanying/highlighting speech—brows), regulators (nonverbal modulators—e.g., nods), and distinctive emotions (Ekman & Friesen, 1975).

Regarding the latter, the states of happiness, sadness, fear, anger, disgust, and surprise have been linked to distinctive facial displays across cultures and infants, whereas variability in facial efference and emotion has been linked to several sources, including differences in the emotion(s) evoked by a stimulus, differences in the timing of the emotional reaction, and to display rules (e.g., Ekman, 1972, 1982; Izard, 1977; Scherer & Ekman, 1982; Steiner, 1979).

Facial Efference. Of course, not all intra- or interpersonal processes are accompanied by visually or socially perceptible expressive facial actions, and this fact has limited the utility of research linking facial actions to underlying psychological processes (e.g., Graham, 1980; Love, 1972; Rajecki, 1983). It is therefore noteworthy that:

facial expressions are principally the result of stereotyped movements of facial skin and fascia (connective tissue) due to contraction of the facial muscles in certain combinations. Such contractions create folds, lines, and wrinkles in the skin and cause movement of facial landmarks such as mouth corners and eyebrows. (Rinn, 1984, p. 52)

Electromyography (EMG) is a psychophysiological technique that allows the measurement of both covert and overt facial efference. Briefly, each muscle consists of millions of fibers housed in connective tissue and is activated by a specific motor nerve. The motor nerve, in turn, consists of many tiny motoneurons, which terminate on muscle fibers at a region called the *motor end-plate.* These motoneurons have differential critical firing thresholds, such that progressively larger units are added to, or progressively smaller units are subtracted from, the total output of a motoneuron pool (size principle; Henneman, 1980). When a particular motoneuron is depolarized, a neural impulse travels to the end-plate region, and the chemical transmitter acetylcholine initiates a self-propogating muscle action potential (MAP), which activates the physiochemical mechanism causing the fiber to contract. Whenever a MAP passes along a muscle fiber, an electrical potential is created that can be measured at the skin. The acetylcholine is quickly eradicated by the enzyme cholinesterase, and MAP activity and muscle fiber contraction ceases without additional neural activity. Contraction of muscle fibers also activates skin receptors, which provide afferent feedback about facial muscle activity. Although the details of the individual MAPs are lost in surface EMG recordings, the discrete microvolt discharges from individual MAPs summate spatially and temporally during motor unit recruitment to yield an aggregate that, with proper placement and amplification, can indicate the action (or inaction) or motoneuron pools. (For further information about EMG recording, see Fridlund & Cacioppo, 1986.)

Consistent with the model of skeletomuscular patterning just outlined, research using facial EMG recordings has revealed several interesting somatic consequences of communication, social cognition, and affect:

1. *Cognitive dimension*—somatic activity over the perioral region is greater during cognitive deliberations (e.g., symbolic processing involving semantic material) than during automatic or visual processing;

2. *Affective dimension*—somatic activity is heightened over the zygomatic region and lessened over the corrugator region during positive emotions, whereas the opposite is the case during negative emotions; and

3. *Intensity dimension*—the amount of somatic activity over the perioral region varies as a function of the extent of cognitive deliberation; and the amount of activity over the corrugator (and possibly the zygomatic) muscle region varies as a function of the intensity of an emotional reaction.

Skeletomuscular Patterning During Action and Imagery. In an illustrative study (Cacioppo, Petty, & Marshall-Goodell, 1984), subjects were led to believe they were participating in a study on involuntary neural responses during "action and imagery." Subjects on any given trial either: (a) lifted a "light" (16 gram) or "heavy" (35 gram) weight (action); (b) imagined lifting a "light" (16 gram) or "heavy" (35 gram) weight (imagery); (c) silently read a neutral communication as if they agreed or disagreed with its thesis (action); or (d) imagined reading an editorial with which they agreed or disagreed (imagery). Based on the model of skeletomuscular patterning, we expected the following: (a) orbicularis oris (perioral) EMG activity would be greater during the communicative attitudinal tasks than during the physical tasks, and (b) the affective processes invoked by the positive and negative attitudinal tasks would lead to distinguishable patterns of EMG activity over the corrugator supercilii, zygomatic major, and possibly the levator labii superioris (which is involved in expressions of disgust) regions (see Fig. 11.1), whereas the simple physical tasks would lead to distinguishable EMG activity over the superficial forearm flexors (whose actions control flexion about the wrist).

Imagining performing rather than actually performing the tasks was, of course, associated with lower mean levels of EMG activity. More importantly, and consistent with the model of skeletomuscular patterning, multivariate analyses revealed that the site and overall form of the task-evoked EMG responses were generally similar across the levels of this factor. Analyses further revealed support for both predictions. First, perioral EMG activity was higher during the attitudinal than physical tasks even though the tasks required no overt verbalization (see Fig. 11.2).

Second, EMG activity over the corrugator supercilii, zygomatic major, and levator labii superioris muscle regions in the face varied as a function of whether subjects thought about the topic in an agreeable or disagreeable manner (see Fig. 11.3), EMG activity over the superficial forearm flexors was higher during the physical than attitudinal tasks, and EMG activity over the forearm (but not over the facial muscles) varied across the simple physical tasks (see Fig. 11.4).

To probe whether subjects had suspicions regarding facial efference being the focus of the study, subjects were interviewed at the end of each session and were asked specifically what they believed to be the experimental hypothesis. Because subjects might reason that they should not disclose how much they "knew," we emphasized that it was important that they respond honestly and accurately. The post-experimental interviews failed to reveal any evidence for the operation of experimental demands. All subjects appeared convinced of the cover story (e.g., that the sensors were used to detect involuntary physiological reactions), and no subject articulated anything resembling the experimental hypothesis. Instead, the post-experimental interviews of subjects indicated that they tended to organize the experimental trials in terms of whether they imagined or performed some task

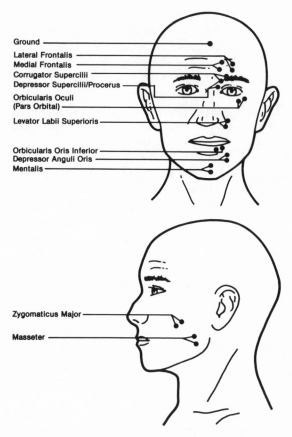

Ground
Lateral Frontalis
Medial Frontalis
Corrugator Supercilii
Depressor Supercilii/Procerus
Orbicularis Oculi
(Pars Orbital)
Levator Labii Superioris
Orbicularis Oris Inferior
Depressor Anguli Oris
Mentalis

Zygomaticus Major
Masseter

FIGURE 11.1. Recording sites for bipolar electromyographic recording over various facial muscle regions (adapted from Fridlund &
Cacioppo, 1986).

(e.g., lifting a weight or silently reading a text) rather than in terms of whether
the task was physical or attitudinal.

Finally, following the study two judges viewed videotapes of subjects during
trials on which the subjects performed positive and negative attitudinal tasks.
The judges' task was to guess the valence of the task performed each trial based
on their observations of the subjects' facial displays during the trial. Judges
performed at chance level. It is unlikely that subjects chose to support the
experimental hypothesis by making socially imperceptible facial responses to the
attitudinal tasks. Indeed, Hefferline, Keenan, and Harford (1959) found they
could operantly condition an invisibly small thumb-twitch even though subjects
remained ignorant of their behavior and its effect; and they reported that subjects
could not produce this covert behavior in the absence of EMG feedback when

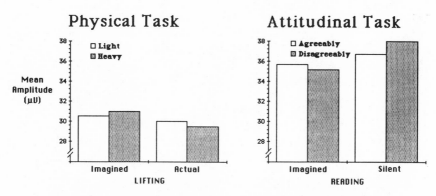

FIGURE 11.2. EMG activity over the perioral (orbicularis oris) muscle region during physical and attitudinal tasks (adapted from Cacioppo, Petty, & Marshall-Goodell, 1984).

deliberately trying to do so. Together these data suggest both that experimental demands are not necessary for the selective facial EMG activation observed during affective processing and imagery and, more interestingly, that social cognition and affect can have discriminable effects on facial EMG patterning.

Perioral EMG Activity as a Function of Self-Referent Processing. The data displayed in Fig. 11.2 are also consistent with the notion that problem solving and silent language processing influence perioral EMG activity (see reviews by Garrity, 1977; McGuigan, 1970). However, these data, like previous research, are not particularly informative regarding the specificity of the relationship between perioral EMG activity and information processing because the type of stimulus presented and/or the type of subject employed has been varied along with the extent of linguistic processing presumably manipulated. For instance, although poor readers show greater perioral EMG activity while reading than good readers (e.g., Edfeldt, 1960; Faaborg-Anderson & Edfeldt, 1958), it is unclear whether this effect is caused by differences in the cognitive work involved in comprehending or in encoding the material, the manner in which the material is being processed, attentional differences in the readers, differences in self-monitoring between the readers, and/or differences in apprehension. Because the literature on communication and persuasion is characterized both by theories based on the premise that people commonly engage in cognitive deliberations regarding the content of persuasive appeals (Fishbein & Ajzen, 1975; Greenwald, 1968) and by theories based on the contrasting premise that social influence can be achieved much of the time mindlessly (Langer, Blank, & Chanowitz, 1978), automatically (Chaiken, in press; Cialdini, 1984) and possibly without awareness (Kunst-Wilson & Zajonc, 1980), we have proposed the elaboration likelihood model (ELM) as a general framework to organize the

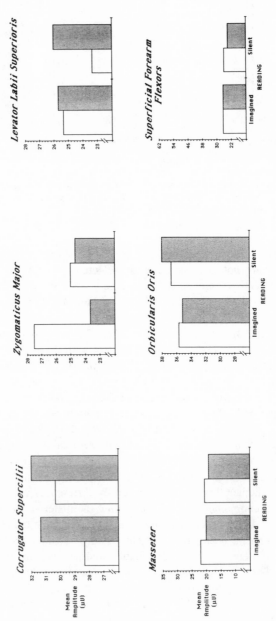

FIGURE 11.3. EMG activity over mimicry muscle regions (top row), and over masseter, perioral, and forearm (bottom row) muscle regions as a function of attitudinal tasks (adapted from Cacioppo, Petty, & Marshall-Goodell, 1984).

Physical Task

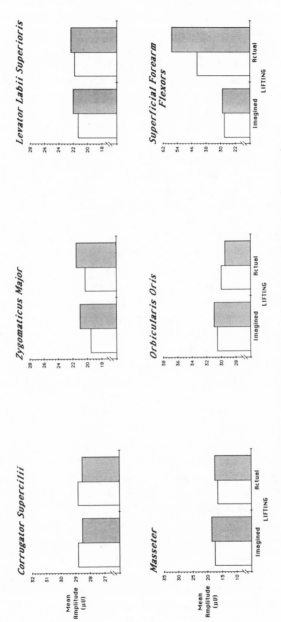

FIGURE 11.4. EMG activity over mimicry muscle regions (top row), and over masseter, perioral, and forearm (bottom row) muscle regions as a function of physical tasks (adapted from Cacioppo, Petty, & Marshall-Goodell, 1984).

processes postulated by these various theories, and we have attempted in our psychophysiological research to extend the model of skeletomuscular patterning to determine precisely how facial efference generally and perioral EMG activity in particular serves as a marker for cognitive and affective processing.

In most of our initial investigations of perioral EMG activity, we employed the instructional manipulations used commonly to study encoding operations. The paradigm involves presenting target words (e.g., trait adjectives) to subjects while randomly varying the question pertaining to each trait word (Craik & Tulving, 1975). In this paradigm, somatic responses attributable to features of subjects and stimuli are assigned to the error term, and what generally remains is variance due to the instructional factor (the "cue-question"), which serves as the operationalization of the predominant type of informational analysis operating during the presentation of the target word (cf. Baddeley, 1978; Cermak & Craik, 1979). Results of research in this paradigm have generally shown that the more semantic (i.e., meaning-oriented) the cued analysis, the more likely subjects are to remember the stimulus word (see review by Craik, 1979), although these effects are especially evident when semantic processes are cued both at the time of encoding and at the time of retrieval (Morris, Bransford, & Franks, 1977; Tulving, 1978). These data have been interpreted as indicating the existence of qualitatively different processes by which incoming information is related to one or more existing domains of knowledge (Cermak & Craik, 1979; Craik, 1979).

The purpose of our initial study was to determine whether perioral (orbicularis oris) EMG activity was higher when subjects performed tasks that required that they think about the meaning and self-descriptiveness of a word rather than about the orthographic appearance of the word (Cacioppo & Petty, 1979b). EMG activity over a nonoral muscle region (superficial forearm flexors of the non-preferred arm) was also recorded to determine whether task-evoked changes in EMG activity were specific or general (e.g., part of an arousal response). Subjects were shown cue-questions asking them whether or not the succeeding trait-adjective was printed in upper-case letters, or whether or not the word was self-descriptive. Half of the trait adjectives were printed in upper-case letters and half were printed in lower case; and half of the trait adjectives were highly self-descriptive, whereas half were were not at all self-descriptive. Subjects responded yes or no by pressing one of two microswitches. Results revealed several interesting results (see Fig. 11.5). First, the self-referent task led to better recall than the orthographic task, replicating previous studies in social psychology (e.g., Rogers, Kuiper, & Kirker, 1977). Second, the self-referent task led to greater increases in perioral EMG activity than the orthographic task. Third, EMG activity over a nonoral muscle group did not vary as a function of the orienting task, making it unlikely that the association between self-referent processing and perioral EMG activity was due to subjects being generally more aroused or tense when performing the self-referent than orthographic task.

This orienting-task paradigm has also been used to investigate possible dif-

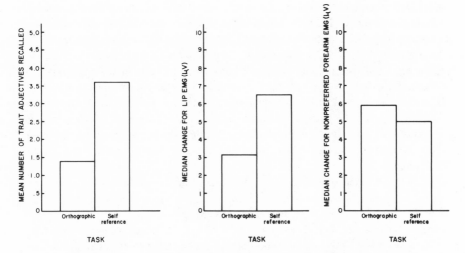

FIGURE 11.5. EMG activity over the perioral region as a function of orthographic and self-referent processing (from Cacioppo & Petty, 1981a).

ferences in the existence of different processes by which incoming information is related to one or more existing domains of social knowledge. Studies have shown that trait words are better recalled when rated for their descriptiveness of oneself or one's best friend than of people about whom one has little or no direct knowledge (e.g., Bower & Gilligan, 1979; Keenan & Baillet, 1980). These data have been interpreted as indicating structural differences in domains of social knowledge in memory. As Ferguson, Rule, and Carlson (1983) note, the do-mains of knowledge (e.g., one's self) accessed by tasks (e.g., self-referent task) that produce relatively better recall of the incoming stimuli are thought to be characterized by greater elaboration (i.e., more associates), integration (i.e., stronger interassociative bonding), and/or differentiation (i.e., more chunking of associates into distinct, but related subsets). Ferguson et al. further reported data from this paradigm using a between-subjects design showing that self-referent and evaluative orienting tasks yielded similar response latencies and levels of recall. They argued that: (a) evaluation constitutes a central dimension along which incoming information such as trait words is categorized and stored, and (b) both evaluative and self-referent tasks facilitated the use of the evaluative dimension and minimized the use of other irrelevant dimensions in rating traits. This led them to conclude that, given the centrality of the evaluative dimension in the organization of memory, "no unique memorial status need be attributed to the self or familiar others" (Ferguson et al., 1983, p. 260).

In an experiment bearing upon both the effects of information processing on perioral EMG activity and on Ferguson et al.'s analysis, subjects were exposed to 60 trait adjectives spanning a range of likeability (Cacioppo & Petty, 1981b; see, also, Cacioppo, Petty, & Morris, 1985). Each trait adjective was preceded by one of five cue-questions, which defined the processing task. The cue questions were: (a) Does the following word rhyme with ---'' (Rhyme), (b) "Is the following word spoken louder than this question?" (Volume discrimination), (c) "Is the following word similar in meaning to ---?" (Association), (d) "Is the following word good (bad)? (Evaluation), and (e) "Is the following word self-descriptive?" (Self-reference). Finally, as in all of our facial EMG research, Subjects in this study knew bioelectrical activity was being recorded, but they did not realize that activity over which they had voluntary control was being monitored.

Results revealed that mean recognition confidence ratings were ordered as follows: self-reference, evaluation, association, rhyme, and volume discrimination (see Fig. 11.6). Importantly, all means except the last two differed significantly from one another. These data, which were obtained using a within-subjects rather than a between-subjects design, have been conceptually replicated by McCaul and Maki (1984) and argue against Ferguson et al.'s contention that evaluative and self-referent processing are fundamentally the same. In addition we found that: (a) the mean amplitude of perioral (orbicularis oris) EMG activity was lowest for the nonsemantic tasks of rhyme and volume discrimination, intermediate for the task of association, and equally high for the tasks of evaluation and self-reference (in a subsequent section of this chapter, we show that

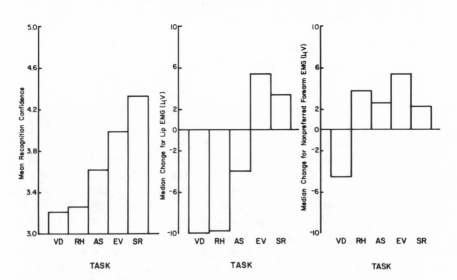

FIGURE 11.6. EMG activity over the perioral region as a function of volume discrimination (VD), rhyme (RH), association (AS), evaluation (EV), and self-reference (SR) tasks (from Cacioppo & Petty, 1981a).

these tasks, too, can be differentiated using psychophysiological measures); (b) cardiac activity and the mean amplitude of EMG activity over a nonoral muscle region (i.e., nonpreferred superficial forearm flexors region) did not vary as a function of the type of task performed; and (c) the association between task and perioral EMG activity was temporally specific, with task-discriminating EMG activity observed only while subjects analyzed the aurally presented trait adjectives and formulated their response.

Facial EMG Activity as a Function of Persuasive Appeals.   Given evidence that perioral EMG activity varies as a function of semantic processing and that EMG activity over selected facial muscle regions (e.g., corrugator supercilii, zygomatic major) can discriminate between positive and negative affective states, we reasoned that facial EMG measures might prove informative regarding elementary processes evoked by the anticipation and presentation of personally involving persuasive communications. Brock (1967) and Greenwald (1968), for instance, posited that recipients of persuasive communications "cognitively responded" to message arguments, generating new associations, links, and counterarguments in the process. Miller and Baron (1973), on the other hand, argued that recipients did *not* engage in extensive cognitive activity when confronted by a persuasive communication (see, also, Langer et al., 1978; Miller, Maruyama, Beaber, & Valone, 1976). Experimental results based on subjects' reported attitudes and the thoughts and ideas they listed in retrospective verbal protocols ("thought listings") provided support for the former position (Petty & Cacioppo, 1977; cf. Cialdini & Petty, 1981), but others have expressed concerns that these data reflect post hoc rationalizations produced in response to post-experimental questioning rather than processes evoked by the persuasive communication.

An initial study supported the applicability of psychophysiological principles and procedures to the particular communications paradigm of interest: Localized increases in perioral EMG activity were observed when individuals followed the experimental instruction to "collect their thoughts" about an impending counterattitudinal editorial (Cacioppo & Petty, 1979a, Experiment 1; see Fig. 11.7).

A follow-up study was conducted in which subjects anticipated and heard a proattitudinal, counterattitudinal, or neutral communication (Cacioppo & Petty, 1979a, Experiment 2). Students were recruited for what they believed was an experiment on "biosensory processes," and as in the previous research, they were unaware that somatic responses were being monitored. After subjects adapted to the laboratory, we obtained recordings of basal EMG activity, forewarned subjects that in 60 seconds they would be hearing an editorial with which they agreed, an editorial with which they disagreed, or an unspecified message, obtained another 60 seconds of physiological recording while subjects sat quietly, and obtained yet another 120 seconds of data while subjects listened to a proattitudinal appeal, counterattitudinal appeal, a newsstory about an archeologi-

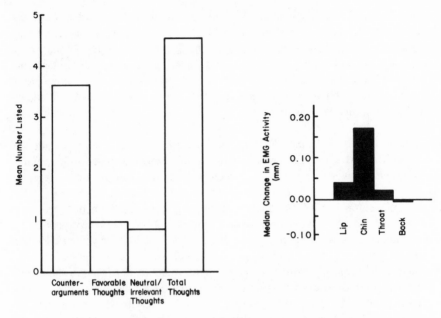

FIGURE 11.7.   Thought-listings and EMG activity over the perioral region as a function of a forewarning of an impending, personally involving counterattitudinal appeal (from Cacioppo & Petty, 1981a).

cal expedition. Subjects were not told to collect their thoughts in this study, but rather somatovisceral activity was simply monitored while subjects awaited and listened to the message presentation. This allowed us to assess the extent to which spontaneous thinking accompanied the anticipation of a persuasive communication.

As expected, subjects evaluated more positively and reported having more favorable thoughts and fewer counterarguments to the proattitudinal than to the counterattitudinal advocacy. Although unexpected, we also found that subjects reported enjoying the "neutral" message (which concerned an obscure archeological expedition) as much as they did the proattitudinal editorial. Analyses of perioral EMG indicated that perioral activity increased following the forewarning of an impending and personally involving counterattitudinal advocacy, and it increased for all conditions during the presentation of the message. This selective activation of perioral EMG activity during the postwarning–premessage period provided convergent evidence for the view that people engage in anticipatory cognitive activity to buttress their beliefs when they anticipate hearing a personally involving, counterattitudinal appeal. Moreover, as illustrated in Fig. 11.8 the pattern of subtle facial EMG activity was found to reflect the positive/negative nature of the persuasive appeal before and during the message. Presentation of the proattitudinal and "neutral" messages was accompanied by a pattern of facial EMG activity similar to that found to accompany pleasant

emotional imagery, whereas both the anticipation and presentation of the counterattitudinal message was associated with a pattern of EMG activity similar to
that found to accompany unpleasant emotional imagery.

*Facial EMG as a Function of the Direction and Intensity of Affective Reac-
tions.*   Finally, physiological measures have traditionally been viewed in communications and social psychology as useful only in assessing general arousal
and therefore incapable of distinguishing between positive and negative affective
states. The studies reviewed thus far, however, suggest facial EMG patterning is
influenced differentially by positive and negative affective states. In addition,
most of the studies have involved such mild affective states that autonomic
activation was not observed. Recent research has also suggested that these subtle, transient, and distinctive patterns of facial EMG activity vary in magnitude
with the intensity of the affective states (Cacioppo, Petty, Losch, & Kim, 1986).
Subjects were exposed to slides of moderately unpleasant, mildly unpleasant,
mildly pleasant, and moderately pleasant scenes. Subjects viewed each slide for
5 seconds and rated how much they liked the scene that was depicted, how
familiar the scene appeared, and how aroused it made them feel. Judgments of
the videorecordings of subjects' facial actions during the 5-second stimulus
presentations indicated that the scenes were sufficiently mild to avoid evoking
socially perceptible facial expressions. Nevertheless, analyses revealed that
EMG activity over the corrugator supercilii and orbicularis oculi muscle regions
differentiated the direction and intensity of people's affective reaction to the
scenes: The more subjects liked the scene, the lower the level of EMG activity

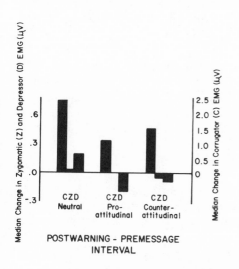 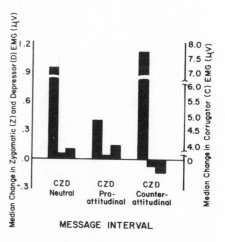

FIGURE 11.8.   Facial EMG activity as a function of a forewarning and
presentation of a proattitudinal, neutral, and counterattitudinal communication (from Cacioppo & Petty, 1981a).

TABLE 11.1
Mean Verbal Descriptions and Electromyographic Responses
as a Function of Affective Valence and Intensity

	Negative		Positive	
Measure	Moderately	Mildly	Mildly	Moderately
Verbal descriptions				
Liking	2.09_a	5.23_b	5.78_c	8.42_d
Arousal	6.64_a	5.27_b	4.94_b	5.08_b
Familiarity	3.16_a	4.82_b	5.50_c	5.74_c
Electromyographic responses*				
Corrugator supercilia	47.37_a	46.21_b	45.27_b	42.22_c
Zygomatic major	23.12_a	23.50_{ab}	24.04_b	24.16_b
Orbicularis oculi	28.39_a	28.56_a	28.83_a	30.32_b
Orbicularis oris	33.02_a	33.73_a	32.82_a	33.58_a
Medial frontalis	29.07_{ab}	29.35_b	28.65_a	28.82_{ab}
Superficial forearm flexor	23.50_a	23.56_a	23.25_a	23.57_a

Note. Means in a row with a similar subscript do not differ significantly by the Duncan multiple-range test ($p < .05$).

*Entries represent the mean amplitude of transformed scores for EMG activity.

over the corrugator supercilii region; moreover, EMG activity was higher over the orbicularis oculi region when moderately pleasant than mildly pleasant or unpleasant stimuli were presented. EMG activity over the zygomatic major region also tended to be greater for liked than disliked scenes, with EMG activity being significantly higher when liked than disliked scenes were presented (see Table 11.1). Importantly, neither EMG activity over the corrugator supercilii region nor EMG activity over the zygomatic major region covaried with reported arousal, nor did EMG activity over the perioral (orbicularis oris) region or a peripheral muscle region (superficial forearm flexors) vary as a function of stimulus likeability. These data, therefore, are more consistent with the view of response specificity in the facial actions accompanying cognition and affect than with the view that somatic activity increases generally as affective intensity increases (Cacioppo, Losch, Tassinary, & Petty, 1986; Cacioppo & Petty, 1981a).

INFERENTIAL CONTEXT: AFFIRMING
THE CONSEQUENT ERRORS AND REVERSE
ENGINEERING DESIGNS

It should be emphasized that the psychological processes in these studies (such as the extent and affectivity of covert information processing) are viewed as being *an* antecedent rather than *the* antecedent of the observed physiological reaction. What is known about the physiological system underlying the physiological endpoint and the context in which the measures are obtained, therefore, are considered in order to derive specific hypotheses with limited ranges of construct validity and application. For instance, Ekman (1972) and Friesen (1972) have demonstrated, facial actions are clearly controllable and serve deceptive as well as communicative and emotionally expressive functions. The EMG patterning observed in this research is subtle and is easily distorted, requiring optimal experimental conditions to obtain (cf. Cacioppo, Petty, & Marshall-Goodell, 1984; Fridlund & Cacioppo, 1986).

Moreover, psychophysiological assessments often are useful to social psychologists and communication researchers only to the extent that they can infer the presence or absence of a particular antecedent or process (e.g., negative affect) when a particular target physiological response (e.g., corrugator EMG activity) is observed. Yet, a point often not fully appreciated when one ceases to think of psychophysiology as a reductionistic search for invariants, is that *knowing that a given factor (e.g., silent language processing; general arousal) leads to a particular physiological response (e.g., perioral EMG activation; increased electrodermal activity) is a necessary but not sufficient reason for such an inference.* This is because research that establishes the cause-outcome relationship A leads to B does *not* imply that given B, A was the antecedent or that given not-B, A was absent. For example, increased electrodermal (EDA) is evoked by a variety of factors, ranging from stress to novelty to arousal to significant events. To infer that a person was physiologically aroused based simply on increased EDA, therefore, is to commit a logical error (i.e., affirming the consequent).

How can one avoid this logical error while also using physiological responses as markers of communication processes? One way is to also consider: (a) what is known about the likelihood of observing the target physiological response in the experimental context in the *absence* of the psychological antecedent of interest; and (b) the likelihood that the psychological antecedent leads to something other than the target physiological response in the experimental context when interpreting the physiological data. There are, in fact, two studies of this type that address the psychophysiological links we have suggested using what might be termed *reverse engineering* designs.

Facial EMG as a Marker of Affect.   The research reviewed previously, for instance, has linked EMG activity over the corrugator supercilii muscle region to negative emotional imagery and to negative affective reactions to auditory, visual, and social stimuli. The question addressed in a recent study (Cacioppo, Petty, & Martzke, 1987) is whether distinctive bursts of activity over the corrugator supercilii muscle region during a social interaction was associated with more negative thoughts and images than periods in which EMG activity over this region was quiescent. Pilot research suggested that the form of the EMG burst might provide additional information about the nature of emotional thoughts and images. To examine these issues, undergraduate women were recruited to participate in a study on self-disclosure. Following a recruitment meeting, during which time the procedures were described and a plausible cover story was presented, subjects were interviewed individually while unobtrusive videorecordings and recordings of facial EMG activity (integrated using a time-constant of .20 seconds) and verbalizations were obtained. Subjects were seated in a dimly illuminated room and were asked to close their eyes and relax throughout the interview. Following adaptation to the lab, subjects were asked to talk about themselves with the goal of disclosing their underlying nature. The interviewer, who was located in a separate room and was blind to experimental condition, sought descriptions ranging from the superficial (e.g., physical attributes, demographics) to the intimate (e.g., perceived strengths and inadequacies, traumatic experiences). Throughout the interview, two other experimenters blind to the experimental hypothesis identified exemplars of each of four types of EMG responses over the corrugator supercilii muscle region: (a) *control*—quiescent period at least 10 seconds in duration; (b) *mound*—smooth response no longer than 5 seconds characterized by a gradual onset and offset; (c) *cluster*—multimodal response from 1 to 5 seconds characterized by an abrupt onset and offset; and (d) *spike*—unimodal response with sharp onset and offset. To assure these periods were otherwise comparable, exemplars were selected only if the individual was speaking, and EMG activity over the corrugator region did not reflect a blink or generalized activation of the facial muscles.

Immediately following the interview, the interviewer conducted a videotape reconstruction with the subject. Subjects were shown the entire videorecording, which was paused at 20 separate segments (five randomly selected exemplars from each of the four response types just identified). At each pause, subjects were asked to report what thoughts and images "flashed through their minds" at that moment during the interview, and the entire videotape reconstruction was audiotaped. Subjects returned within a few days for a final session, at which time they rated each of the 20 reported recollections along the differential emotions scale and in terms of how self-disclosive and personally insightful was the recollection. The results are summarized in Fig. 11.9. Analyses revealed the ratings of the associations recalled during control and spike intervals were equivalently positive and nondisclosive; those recalled during EMG clusters and mounds were rated as being relatively negative and self-disclosive. It is possible that the EMG spikes over the corrugator region marked more transient negative affect that were so transient that subjects failed to recall or repressed the experience during videotape reconstruction. For instance, subjects were subsequently classified as sensitizer or repressor based on a median split of their scores on the Byrne repression/sensitization scale, and subjects' ratings of the thoughts and images that covaried with EMG spikes and control intervals were contrasted. Results revealed that repressors tended to rate the thoughts and images covarying with EMG spikes over the corrugator muscle region as less "insightful" than those that occurred during control intervals, whereas sensitizers revealed the opposite pattern.

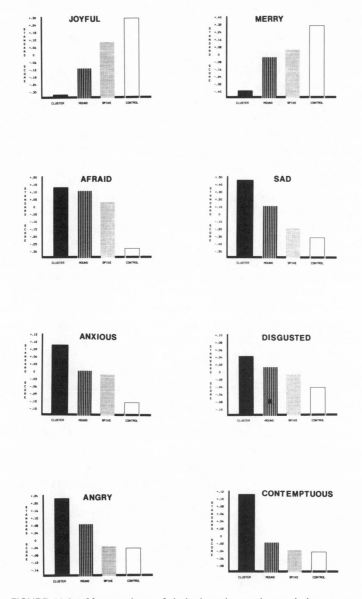

FIGURE 11.9. Mean ratings of their thoughts and associations as a function of the form of EMG discharge observed (from Cacioppo, Petty, & Martzke, 1986).

239

Perioral EMG as a Marker of Silent Language Processing.   Shimizu and Inoue (1986) reported a conceptually similar study regarding perioral EMG activity as a marker of silent language processing. Electroencephalographic (EEG), electrooculargraphic (EOG), perioral EMG, and nonoral EMG activity were recorded as subjects slept. Subjects were awakened during either rapid eye movement (REM) or State 2 sleep—as determined by inspection of the EEG and EOG recordings. When subjects reported dreaming, subjects were asked whether or not they had been speaking in their dreams. Dream recall during REM sleep occurred in approximately 80% of the awakenings, and it occured during State 2 sleep in approximately 28% of the awakenings. Awakenings without dream recall were excluded from further analyses, as were awakenings preceded by phasic discharges in the perioral musculature that were accompanied by any vocalization. Results revealed the following: (a) When phasic discharges over the perioral musculature were observed within the 30 seconds preceding the awakening, subjects reported having been speaking in their dreams in 88% of the awakenings from REM sleep and 71% of the awakenings during State 2 sleep; (b) when phasic discharges over the perioral musculature were not observed within the 30 seconds preceding the awakening, subjects reported having been speaking in their dreams in only 19% of the awakenings from REM sleep and in 0% of the awakening's during State 2 sleep; (c) when phasic discharges over the nonoral rather than perioral musculature were observed within the 30 seconds preceding the awakening, subjects reported having been speaking in their dreams in only 28% of the awakenings from REM sleep and in 0% of the awakenings during State 2 sleep; and (d) when phasic discharges were not observed over any region within the 30 seconds preceding the awakening, subjects reported having been speaking in their dreams in 62% of the awakenings from REM sleep and in 43% of the awakenings during State 2 sleep.

In summary, previous research had indicated that negative affective reactions influenced the EMG activity over the corrugator supercilii muscle region and that silent language and numeric processing influenced the EMG activity over the perioral muscle region. The research just reviewed further suggests that phasic EMG discharges over the corrugator supercilii and over the perioral muscle region can be used to mark episodes of negative affect and silent language processing, respectively. In addition, the results of both studies raise interesting questions about the sensitivity of these somatic markers, at least within these measurement contexts, too difficult to report affective and cognitive events.

CONCLUSION

The conceptualization of the psychophysiological enterprise as involving the identification of episodic markers of behaviorally relevant cognitive and affective processes is a fairly recent development in psychophysiology and is still sometimes misunderstood (cf. Cacioppo & Petty, 1985, 1986). At least part of this misunderstanding has a factual basis and a long history. For instance, Allport (1947) cited the following as being said by Carlston during a then-recent presidential address to the American Psychological Association:

> I believe that robotic thinking helps precision of psychological thought, and will continue to help it until psychophysiology is so far advanced that an image is nothing other than a neural event, and object constancy is obviously just something that happens in the brain. (p. 185)

Allport's criticisms of reductionism and of the search for psychophysiological invariants to explain social behavior, as well as his early defense of social cognition were cogent and influential. But rather than questioning the charge that the promise of psychophysiology was to generate a list of physiological invariants, Allport rejected the entire approach to the study of communication and behavior:

> In taking stock of the situation I observe how many of us seem so stupefied by admiration of physical science that we believe psychology in order to succeed need only imitate the models, postulates, methods and language of physical science. If someone points out the present inutility of mechanical models in predicting anything but the most peripheral forms of human behavior, we are inclined to reply: "Wait a thousand years." (p. 182)

Given recent developments in psychophysiology, perhaps it is time that we reconsider Allport's protests against the psychophysiological enterprise.

ACKNOWLEDGMENT

Preparation of this chapter was supported by National Science Foundation Grant Nos. BNS-8414853 and BNS-8444909 to JTC.

REFERENCES

Allport, G. W. (1947). Scientific models and human morals. *Psychological Review, 54,* 182–192.
Allport, G. W. (1969). The historical background of modern social psychology. In G. Lindzey & E. Aronson (Eds.), *The handbook of social psychology* (2nd ed., pp. 1–80). Reading, MA: Addison-Wesley.
Ax, A. F. (1964). Goals and methods of psychophysiology. *Psychophysiology, 1,* 8–25.
Bem, D. J. (1972). Self-perception theory. *Advances in Experimental Social Psychology, 6,* 1–61.
Bower, G. H., & Gilligan, S. G. (1979). Remembering information related to one's self. *Journal of Research in Personality, 13,* 420–432.

Baddeley, A. D. (1978). The trouble with levels: A reexamination of Craik and Lockhart's framework for memory research. *Psychological Review, 85,* 139–152.

Brock, T. C. (1967). Communication discrepancy and intent to persuade as determinants of counterargument production. *Journal of Experimental Social Psychology, 3,* 269–309.

Cacioppo, J. T., Losch, M. E., Tassinary, L. G., & Petty, R. E. (1986). Properties of affect and affect-laden information processing as viewed through the facial response system. In R. A. Peterson, W. D. Hoyer, & W. R. Wilson (Eds.), *The role of affect in consumer behavior: Emerging theories and applications* (pp. 87–118). Lexington, MA: D. C. Heath.

Cacioppo, J. T., & Petty, R. E. (1979a). Attitudes and cognitive response: An electrophysiological approach. *Journal of Personality and Social Psychology, 37,* 2181–2199.

Cacioppo, J. T., & Petty, R. E. (1979b). Lip and nonpreferred forearm EMG activity as a function of orienting task. *Biological Psychology, 9,* 103–113.

Cacioppo, J. T., & Petty, R. E. (1981a). Electromyograms as measures of extent and affectivity of information processing. *American Psychologist, 36.* 441–456.

Cacioppo, J. T., & Petty, R. E. (1981b). Electromyographic specificity during covert information processing. *Psychophysiology, 18,* 518–523.

Cacioppo, J. T., & Petty, R. E. (1985). Physiological responses and advertising effects: Is the cup half full or half empty? *Psychology and Marketing, 2*(2), 115–126.

Cacioppo, J. T., & Petty, R. E. (1986). Social processes. In M. G. H. Coles, E. Donchin, & S. Porges (Eds.), *Psychophysiology: Systems, processes, and applications* (pp. 646–679). New York: Guilford Press.

Cacioppo, J. T., & Petty. R. E. (in press). Stalking rudimentary processes of social influence: A psychophysiological approach. In M. P. Zanna, J. M. Olson, & C. P. Herman (Eds.), *Social influence: The Ontario symposium* (Vol. 5) Hillsdale, NJ: Lawrence Erlbaum Associates.

Cacioppo, J. T., Petty, R. E., Losch, M. E., & Kim, H. S. (1986). Attributions of responsibility for helping and harmdoing: Evidence for confusion of responsibility. *Journal of Personality and Social Psychology, 50.* 100–105.

Cacioppo, J. T., Petty, R. E., & Marshall-Goodell, B. (1984). Electromyographic specificity during simple physical and attitudinal tasks: Location and topographical features of integrated EMG responses. *Biological Psychology, 18,* 85–121.

Cacioppo, J. T., Petty, R. E., & Martzke, J. S. (1987). *Facial electromyographic responses index emotions during self-disclosures.* Manuscript submitted.

Cacioppo, J. T., Petty, R. E., & Morris, K. J. (1985). Semantic, evaluative, and self-referent processing: Memory, cognitive effort, and somatovisceral activity. *Psychophysiology, 22,* 371–384.

Cacioppo, J. T., & Sandman, C. A. (1981). Psychophysiological functioning, cognitive responding, and attitudes. In R. E. Petty, T. M. Ostrom, & T. C. Brook (Eds.), *Cognitive responses in persuasion* (pp. 81–104). Hillsdale, NJ: Lawrence Erlbaum Associates.

Cermak, L. S., & Craik, F. I. M. (Eds.). (1979). *Levels of processing in human memory.* Hillsdale, NJ: Lawrence Erlbaum Associates.

Chaiken, S. (in press). The heuristic model of persuasion. In M. P. Zanna, J. M. Olson, & C. P. Herman (Eds.), *Social influence: The Ontario Symposium (Vol. 5).* Hillsdale. NJ: Lawrence Erlbaum Associates.

Cialdini. R. B. (1984). Principles of automatic influence. In J. Jacoby & C. S. Craig (Eds.). *Personal selling: Theory, research, and practice* (pp. 1–28) Lexington, MA: D. C. Heath.

Cialdini, R. B., & Petty, R. E. (1981). Anticipatory opinion effects. In R. E. Petty, T. M. Ostrom, & T. C. Brock (Eds.), *Cognitive responses in persuasion.* (pp. 217–236). Hillsdale, NJ: Lawrence Erlbaum Associates.

Craik, F. I. M. (1979). Human memory. *Annual Review of Psychology, 30,* 63–102.

Craik, F. I. M., & Tulving, E. (1975). Depth of processing and the retention of words in episodic memory. *Journal of Experimental Psychology: General, 104,* 268–294.

Donchin, E. (1982). The relevance of dissociations and the irrelevance of dissociationism: A reply to Schwartz and Pritchard. *Psychophysiology, 19,* 457–463.

Edfeldt, A. W. (1960). *Silent speech and silent reading.* Chicago: University of Chicago Press.

Ekman, P. (1972). Universal and cultural differences in facial expressions of emotion. In J. Cole (Ed.), *Nebraska symposium on motivation, 1971* (Vol. 19). Cambridge: Cambridge University Press.

Ekman, P. (1982). Methods of measuring facial action. In K. R. Scherer & P. Ekman (Eds.), *Handbook of methods in nonverbal behavior research* (pp. 45–90). Cambridge: Cambridge University Press.

Ekman, P., & Friesen, W. V. (1975). *Unmasking the face.* Englewood Cliffs, NJ: Prentice-Hall.

Faaborg-Anderson, K., & Edfeldt, A. W. (1958). Electromyography of intrinsic and extrinsic laryngeal muscles during silent speech: Correlation with reading activity. *Acta Otolaryngologica, 49,* 478–482.

Ferguson, T. J., Rule, B. G., & Carlson, D. (1983). Memory for personally relevant information. *Journal of Personality and Social Psychology, 44,* 251–261.

Fishbein, M., & Ajzen, I. (1975). *Belief, attitude, intention, and behavior: An introduction to theory and research.* Reading, MA: Addison-Wesley.

Fowles, D. C. (1980). The three arousal model: Implications of Gray's two-factor learning theory for heart rate, electrodermal activity, and psychopathy. *Psychophysiology, 17,* 87–104.

Fridlund, A. J., & Cacioppo, J. T. (1986). Guidelines for human electromyographic research. *Psychophysiology, 23,* 567–589.

Fridlund, A. J., & Izard, C. E. (1983). Electromyographic studies of facial expressions of emotions and patterns of emotion. In J. T. Cacioppo & R. E. Petty (Eds.), *Social psychophysiology: A sourcebook* (pp. 243–286). New York: Guilford Press.

Friesen, W. V. (1972). *Cultural differences in facial expression in a social situation: An experimental test of the concept of display rules.* Unpublished doctoral dissertation, University of California, San Francisco.

Garrity, L. I. (1977). Electromyography: A review of the current status of subvocal speech research. *Memory and Cognition, 5,* 615–622.

Graham, J. L. (1980). A new system for measuring nonverbal responses to marketing appeals. *1980 AMA Educator's Conference Proceedings, 46.* 340–343.

Greenwald, A. G. (1968). Cognitive learning, cognitive response to persuasion, and attitude change. In A. Greenwald, T. Brock, & T. Ostrom (Eds.), *Psychological foundations of attitudes* (pp. 147–170). New York: Academic Press.

Hefferline, R. F., Keenan, B., & Harford, R. A. (1959). Escape and avoidance conditioning in human subjects without their observation of the response. *Science, 1,* 1338–1339.

Henneman, E. (1980). Organization of the motoneuron pool: The size principle. In V. B. Mountcastle (Ed.), *Medical physiology* (14th ed., Vol. 1, pp. 718–741). St. Louis: Mosby.

Izard, C. E. (1971). *The face of emotion.* New York: Appleton-Century-Crofts.

Izard, C. E. (1977). *Human emotions.* New York: Plenum.

Kaplan, H. B., & Bloom, S. W. (1960). The use of sociological and social-psychological concepts in physiological research: A review of selected experimental studies. *Journal of Nervous and Mental Disorders, 131,* 128–134.

Keenan, J. M., & Baillet, S. D. (1980). Memory for personally and socially significant events. In R. S. Nickerson (Ed.), *Attention and performance VIII.* Hillsdale, NJ: Lawrence Erlbaum Associates.

Kunst-Wilson, W. R., & Zajonc, R. B. (1980). Affective discrimination of stimuli that cannot be recognized. *Science, 207,* 557–558.

Langer, E., Blank, A., & Chanowitz, B. (1978). The mindlessness of ostensibly thoughtful action: The role of "placebic" information in interpersonal interaction. *Journal of Personality and Social Psychology, 36,* 635–642.

Love, R. E. (1972). *Unobtrusive measurement of cognitive reactions to persuasive communications*. Unpublished doctoral dissertation, Ohio State University.

Mayo, C., & LaFrance, M. (1977).*Evaluating research in social psychology*. Monterey, CA: Brooks/Cole.

McCaul, K. D., & Maki, R. H. (1984). Self-reference effects on memory: A reply to Ferguson, Rule, and Carlson. *Journal of Personality and Social Psychology, 47*, 953–955.

McGuigan, F. J. (1970). Covert oral behavior during silent performance of language tasks. *Psychological Bulletin, 74*, 309–326.

Mesulam, M., & Perry, J. (1972). The diagnosis of lovesickness: Experimental psychophysiology without the polygraph. *Psychophysiology, 9*, 546–551.

Miller, N., & Baron, R. S. (1973). On measuring counterarguing. *Journal for the Theory of Social Behavior, 3*, 101–118.

Miller, N., Maruyama, G., Baeber, R., & Valone, K. (1976). Speed of speech and persuasion. *Journal of Personality and Social Psychology, 34*, 615–625.

Morris, C. D., Bransford, J. D., & Franks, J. J. (1977). Levels of processing versus transfer appropriate processing. *Journal of Verbal Learning and Verbal Behavior, 16*, 519–533.

Petty, R. E., & Cacioppo, J. T. (1977). Forewarning, cognitive responding and resistance to persuasion. *Journal of Personality and Social Psychology, 35*, 645–655.

Petty, R. E., & Cacioppo, J. T. (1983). The role of bodily responses in attitude measurement and change. In J. T. Cacioppo & R. E. Petty (Eds.), *Social psychophysiology: A sourcebook* (pp. 51–101). New York: Guilford Press.

Porges, S. W., & Coles, M. G. H. (1976). *Psychophysiology: Benchmark papers in animal behavior* (Vol. 6). Stroudsburg, PA: Dowden, Hutchinson & Ross.

Rajecki, D. W. (1983). Animal aggression: Implications for human aggression. In R. G. Green & E. J. Donnerstein (Eds.). *Aggression: Theoretical and empirical reviews* (Vol. 1, pp. 189–211). New York: Academic Press.

Rankin, R. E., & Campbell, D. T. (1955). Galvanic skin response to Negro and white experimenters. *Journal of Abnormal and Social Psychology, 51*, 30–33.

Riddle, E. M. (1925). Aggressive behavior in a small social group. *Archives of Psychology*, No. 78.

Rinn, W. E. (1984). The neuropsychology of facial expression: A review of the neurological and psychological mechanisms for producing facial expression. *Psychological Bulletin, 95*, 52–77.

Rogers, T. B., Kuiper, N. A., & Kirker, W. S. (1977). Self-reference and the encoding of personal information. *Journal of Personality and Social Psychology, 35*, 677–688.

Scherer, K. R., & Ekman, P. (1982). *Handbook of methods in nonverbal behavior research*. Cambridge: Cambridge University Press.

Shapiro, D., & Schwartz, G. E. (1970). Psychophysiological contributions to social psychology. *Annual Review of Psychology, 21*, 87–112.

Shimizu, A., & Inoue, T. (1986). Dreamed speech and speech muscle activity. *Psychophysiology, 23*, pp. 210–214.

Smith, C. E. (1936). The autonomic excitation resulting from the interaction of individual opinion and group opinion. *Journal of Abnormal and Social Psychology, 30*, 138–164.

Steiner, J. E. (1979). Human facial expression in response to taste and smell stimulation. *Advances in Child Development and Behavior, 13*, 257–295.

Sternbach, R. A. (1966). *Principles of psychophysiology: An introductory text and readings*. New York: Academic Press.

Stewart, D. W. (1984). Physiological measurement of advertising effects. *Psychology and Marketing, 1*, 43–48.

Tognacci, L. N., & Cook, S. (1975). Conditioned autonomic responses as bidirectional indicators of racial attitude. *Journal of Personality and Social Psychology, 31*, 137–144.

Tomkins, S. S. (1962). *Affect, imagery, consciousness: Vol. 1. The positive affects*. New York: Springer.

Tulving, E. (1978). Relation between encoding specificity and levels of processing. In L. S. Cermak & F. I. M. Craik (Eds.), *Levels of processing in human memory* (pp. 19–92). New York: Guilford Press.

Valins, S. (1966). Cognitive effects of false heart rate feedback. *Journal of Personality and Social Psychology, 4,* 400–408.

AUTHOR INDEX

SUBJECT INDEX

58, 246